Scientific Karatedo

Scientific Karatedo

by Masayuki Kukan Hisataka

CHARLES E. TUTTLE COMPANY
Rutland, Vermont & Tokyo, Japan

Disclaimer
Please note that the author and publisher of this book are
NOT RESPONSIBLE in any manner whatsoever for any injury
that may result from practicing the techniques and/or following
the instructions given within. Since the physical activities
described herein may be too strenuous in nature for some
readers to engage in safely, *it is essential that a physician be
consulted prior to training.*

Published by the Charles E. Tuttle Company, Inc.
of Rutland, Vermont & Tokyo, Japan
with editorial offices at
2-6 Suido 1-chome, Bunkyo-ku, Tokyo 112

First Tuttle edition, 1995

LCC Card No. 95-60542
ISBN 0-8048-2019-8

Printed in Singapore

This book is respectfully dedicated
to Kaiso Kori Hisataka,
the founder of the classic and
scientific form of karatedo,
Shorinjiryu Kenkokan Karatedo.

Foreword

Born the 36th descendant of the 56th Emperor of Japan, Masayuki Hisataka received a very strict education; his training in the martial arts started when he was three. Bright minded and strong willed, he was always leading his fellows at school. He was trained in gymnastics and track and field under the guidance of Olympic stars. He was promoted to black belt at the age of 13. In junior high school he began assisting his father at the Kenkokan. He became *Shihan*, the rank of Master, while he was still a university student; his techniques were excellent and he already understood the spirit of karatedo.

He has thoroughly studied the history and theory of karatedo and other martial arts. They are presented in this book which also describes conditioning of the mind and body through the practice of karatedo.

Health is one of the most important things in life. In ancient Greece, it was thought that sickness was the result of the devil's action; that the giant Hercules was the model of all men; that Apollo was a demi-god to be idolized to prevent sickness; and that the only cure to illness was through the use of herbs. Scientific medicine was first developed in Germany on the basis of studies in anatomy and physiology. Then, by way of experimentation, modern medicine and therapeutics were developed.

Similarly, man at first pulled his own wagons, but then used oxen and, later, horses and steam engines to move them. Automobiles, airplanes, and jets were to follow, bringing down all cultural barriers.

In the sixteenth century, sabres had to be carried with two hands; later they became lighter and could be used with one hand. Then came firearms and missiles.

In much the same way, all around the world people have developed fighting arts according to their needs, physical characteristics, and historical context. Those arts that failed to evolve with the changes in times have become obsolete.

It is, in my opinion, the most scientifically advanced form of karatedo which is presented in this book. It has benefited from the study of all other martial arts and animal fighting techniques and from the application of modern sciences. It emphasizes circular and triangular motions to avoid clashing with the opponent in order to use his own action and to prevent injury. All the aspects of training and competition are explained in this book, as well as the historical meaning and philosophy of karatedo.

Shihan Masayuki Hisataka has devoted his life to karatedo and in this book, written with all his soul, he reveals the better part of his considerable knowledge, in a manner that is easy to understand for any reader.

I highly recommend this book to every student of karatedo, indeed, to any person interested in the history, techniques, and philosophy of modern karatedo.

Chofu Kuniba
Kensei (10th dan in karatedo)
Tokyo, Japan

Preface

As most of you are probably aware, karatedo has its origins in the Ryukyu Islands. From there it merged with Japan's ancient martial arts, giving rise to the numerous karatedo styles practiced today. One of these original styles is Shorinjiryu, which has spread from Japan to North and South America, Europe, Australia, New Zealand, Russia, Algeria, India, and a host of other countries over the past few decades.

I myself had the honor of studying Shorinjiryu Karatedo under the keen eye of Kaiso Masayoshi Kori Hisataka, founder of the Kenkokan school. In those days, however, the risk of incurring injuries during training and competition was ever-present. Even though Kaiso Hisataka made use of body protectors, it is only recently, after many years of intensive research and labor, that his son, the author of this book, Hanshi Masayuki Kukan Hisataka, perfected Supersafe protective equipment.

Seeking to make the fullest use of his achievement, Hanshi Hisataka then went on to create the Koshiki Karatedo competition system. This innovative system combines the use of Supersafe protective equipment with a new set of tournament rules, thus allowing martial artists from all styles, including kung fu and *kempo,* to compete against one another with almost no chance of injury. Participants in Koshiki Karatedo tournaments can truly test their techniques and clearly see the results of their actions, making it much easier to determine, with fairness and impartiality, who the true victor of the match is. Tournaments conducted under this system are an ideal mixture of realism and safety, and are also extremely exciting to watch.

This system's applications, however, are not limited to karatedo's sportive dimension. By integrating Koshiki Karatedo into training regimes, even noncompetitive karateka can get a taste of true combat. So it comes as no surprise to me that Koshiki Karatedo has rapidly gained popularity across the globe and that participation at Koshiki Karatedo tournaments has skyrocketed.

To help the reader gain a deeper understanding of Koshiki Karatedo, this updated version of *Scientific Karatedo* not only includes a copy of *Koshiki Karatedo Competition Rules* but also photos of Koshiki *kumite* (sparring) techniques using Supersafe protective equipment.

Koshiki Karatedo is, however, more than just a new fighting system; the ultimate goal of Koshiki Karatedo is to help foster the development of complete individuals capable of living in harmony with nature. It is an attempt to reestablish the bond between man and nature that has become seriously eroded in this modern age. This is why I sincerely hope that Koshiki Karatedo will find its way into educational systems the world over and gain further international recognition by eventually bringing karatedo into the Olympic Games.

TOKUICHIRO TAMAZAWA
State Minister, Director General of the Defense Agency
President, All Japan Koshiki Karatedo Federation

CONTENTS

Introduction

In the modern age, the progress of science has not yet fully contributed to the advancement of mankind. Our technologically oriented society has failed to free the individual to realize himself. Man is a prisoner of the machines that were designed to liberate him. Living conditions for most people have improved tremendously, but new evils have appeared. Obesity, heart disease, and nervous ailments are plaguing our societies, where many live at a frantic pace, alienated, in huge cities made of concrete and asphalt. We need to find a natural way to alleviate stress, to acquire a peaceful, relaxed mind, and develop a healthy and fit body.

Karatedo can fulfill all these needs at once. More than anything else, karatedo is a way of life. It is sometimes said, "Life is a heavy load that everyone has to carry to the top of the mountain." One has to prepare to reach this goal by building a strong body and mind. But if one is to overcome the difficulties of life, one must train hard and learn to fight. Karatedo teaches that to reach true peace of mind and harmony with nature, one must go beyond the rather narrow concept of winning and losing, and learn to win over oneself.

In the search for self-perfection, the student of karatedo will acquire the greatest virtues: patience, humility, respect for others, courage, and fortitude. It is hoped that this book can contribute to the fulfillment of some of the goals common to all mankind: health, happiness, and peace.

In the two decades that have passed since the first publication of this book, many changes have taken place in the world of karate generally and particularly for Shorinjiryu Karatedo. The development of Supersafe protective equipment has revolutionized karate training and competition as it allows practitioners to make solid contact with their strikes without the risk of serious injury to one another. This balance of realism and safety has been one of the biggest stumbling blocks in the development of karate both as a sport and as a method of self-defense. Furthermore the introduction of the Koshiki Karatedo competition system has broken the barriers that separated the different martial arts and is bringing competitors from a variety of styles together to compete and grow together through the tournament medium.

Koshiki has also brought together competitors from a variety of countries, and I hope that karate will continue to serve as a vehicle for the promotion of international exchange and friendship. It appears that at last karate will become an Olympic sport and through the efforts of Koshiki Karatedo competitors and supporters worldwide, I am sure that this is a goal we can achieve by the turn of the century.

As we enter the twenty-first century, it is with a sense of hope and excitement that I continue to promote and develop karatedo both as a sport and a way of life. I hope that by reading this and my other text, *Essential Shorinjiryu Karatedo* (also published by the Charles E. Tuttle Publishing Co.), that you may come to understand the many beneficial aspects of karate training and that in some way it may better your life and the lives of those around you.

chapter 1 Philosophy of Karatedo

1. Spiritual Development of the Individuality in Mind and Body

Spiritual development of the individuality in mind and body is the motto of Kenkokan Karatedo and expresses its philosophy. Karatedo, as initially developed, was a method of fighting to dispose of an adversary in the most efficient and acute way. It has evolved through the centuries and has been imbued with the Zen philosophy to become a way of life, where the goal is to further the development of the mind, the body and the spirit. From its origin, karatedo has kept the efficiency in techniques and the maximum concentration of physical and mental power that can only be possible when one's life is the issue of the fight. Zen has brought karatedo into the realm of religion. Man understood that his art, limited to destroying other men, could not liberate him from his most fundamental fear, the fear of death. The object of his fight changed from others to himself: if he could not surmount the fear of death by killing, he would do it, possibly, by living and applying the same methods against himself that he had used against others. Techniques would be a means of perfecting the body which would respond at once, and with determination. In the process of this absolute concentration of mental and physical activity, the mind would be freed from the material constraints created by the most fundamental issues of life and finally overcome the fear of death. The original goal of killing has become one of living.

In modern karatedo, where violence is tightly controlled, techniques are still to be executed as if it were a matter of life or death. The body is thus taught to react with all of its power at once under the complete control of the mind. In order to reach this stage of complete harmonious discipline of mind and body, techniques must be practiced thousands of times under all kinds of circumstances. The body will by then have gained an automatism which will free the mind of the task of controlling the execution of the technique. That is why it is said in karatedo that the *ki* should not be put entirely into one's technique because, absorbed with this, the mind will not see the opportunity for the attack. Neither should the *ki* be applied entirely to the opponent, because the technique will then be improperly executed. Instead the *ki* should be exercised everywhere, in oneself, in one's technique, against the opponent, in his technique, etc. This also means that the *ki* is nowhere in particular because the *ki* is 'being at one' and is located everywhere at the same time. This may appear as a contradiction to the dualistic logic of Cartesian thought, in which something is either here or not here, black or white, right or wrong. The oriental, however, reconciles this apparent contradiction with a more intuitive approach which says that a mind empty of thoughts is not necessarily in a state of nothingness. On the contrary, it is in a state of acute awareness but without goals. It can thus perceive everything at once but without concentrating on anything in particular; thus not being given the opportunity to be unaware of that which is seemingly less relevant. In this state of total awareness, the mind is at peace with itself and in harmony with its environment. Karatedo is one of the ways to reach the higher mental state described by most religions of the world; be it Buddhism, Islam, or Christianity, they all preach different methods for man to transcend into a superior state of grace. In the Nirvana or paradise, man is integrated with the universe or with god.

The road to this state of complete harmony with the universe is certainly a long one, but in this quest for the absolute, man can build a strong and healthy body; he can learn to know and control himself though the physical and mental exertion required by karatedo training; by confronting his will against others in *kumite* and *shiai* he will develop fortitude, humility, and respect for his fellowmen; he will not be afraid to stand for what is right. All these qualities will make him a better man and he will be able to transpose them into all aspects of everyday life, helping him to fulfill his commitments to himself and to society. The Kenkokan school of karatedo stresses the positive development of mind and body. The student must develop himself according to his own physical and mental characteristics. He must first possess a good technical knowledge of karatedo and learn to know himself, his weaknesses, and his strong points. Then he must improve himself, correcting his weaknesses but basing his development primarily on his strong points. There is no standard way of reaching the highest state of mental and physical development. Each individual must find his own way by himself after he has come to know himself and mastered the techniques of karatedo well enough. From this point on, his physical and mental strong points must spearhead his development. For example, in competition (and the same reasoning is applicable to every other aspect of life) the student must possess a set of favorite techniques or combinations of techniques in which he will have developed the highest skill. This skill will give him great confidence in himself and will allow his mind to be intense and at the same time calm. Furthermore, if he knows himself well, his strength in techniques can easily cover his weak points.

The individual can progress faster with this positive attitude than by conforming to a rigid norm not necessarily suited to his personality. In this way everyone can benefit from the practice of karatedo. A person not physically gifted can develop a strong spirit to compensate for his lack of speed or strength. This kind of attitude, transposed into everyday life, can induce the individual to search for fulfillment whatever his qualities or failings, by correcting the latter but relying on the former to achieve his goals.

The student of karatedo must always try to perfect himself. He should never become complacent, as there will always be something to improve. Whatever his rank, he should consider himself a novice who always has something else to learn. He must realize that hard training is the only way to better himself in every aspect of life, and that whatever the difficulties, he must never give up but fight to win over himself in an endless search for truth. *Shiai* and *kumite* provide the student with direct contact with others so that he can compare himself and improve. This is the true test of proficiency in karatedo. It does not necessarily mean that only the winners are understanding and progressing in the way of karatedo. The essential thing is to participate with dedication, always trying to better oneself, always trying to win. But winning should remain secondary because winning itself is not the goal, only an indication that the individual is on the right path toward reaching his goal. If winning were to become the goal, then the path would be lost for the losing student, who would get discouraged and stop his search for self-perfection. On the other hand, the one who wins would be content, having reached his goal, and again the true spirit of karatedo would be lost. To use a now famous Zen illustration, "One should not mistake the finger pointing to the moon for the moon itself." Winning is the finger pointing to the moon, and the moon is at the end of the long but supremely fascinating journey with oneself amidst the immensity of the universe.

2. The Secrets of Karatedo

The remarkable feats demonstrated by karatedo masters have led many people to believe that these masters posess some mysterious secrets, or some source of extraordinary power. This is not the case. There is no formula which, when properly utilized, allows someone to perform supernatural acts. The secret is karatedo itself. When a man has mastered the techniques to perfection, when his mind has reached a state of intense serenity and plenitude, and when his mind and body are united into a single entity, then he is able to perform things that an untrained person cannot do under ordinary circumstances. But, under the stress of an intense emotion, even an ordinary person can accomplish unthinkable exploits. A mother can lift up a truck forty times the weight that she can normally lift, if her baby is pinned under it. A father can jump in the lion's den and attack it with his bare hands to save his son. Examples of this sort only sometimes make the headlines of the newspapers but, in fact, they abound. How can someone perform such remarkable deeds? Where does this extraordinary force come from? In a split second an intense excitation suddenly unleashes the inner power of these individuals which in normal circumstances remains hidden and even unsuspected.

Karatedo strives to liberate these forces consciously at the price of constant and assiduous training. But there is no secret to it. The method is not reserved for a chosen few and anyone can reach this stage if, and only if, he is willing to strive to do it. All people have an equal chance; there is no age or sex barrier. Training with a strong will to always progress and perfect oneself is the only secret of karatedo. The secret behind the extraordinary power of techniques demonstrated in *tameshi wari*, some of the best expressions of technical proficiency performed with hard objects such as boards, tiles, stones, etc., rests in years of practice in karatedo. Again, there is no secret. It requires strong concentration, will power, and correct technical execution with speed and accuracy. It is only a means of testing the technique and mental concentration of the student, however astonishing some performances are. It is against the spirit of karatedo to present them as a show, because people will see in it only the destructive power of karatedo techniques. *Tameshi wari* is, on the contrary, a positive way for the individual to test his power and develop his confidence.

While in the old days *tameshi wari* was the only way to test the efficiency of the techniques, in modern karatedo the use of protective equipment allows students to truly test their techniques on moving targets. The closest thing to a secret in karatedo is undoubtably breathing. Breathing plays an essential part in the union of the mind and body and in producing the inner power; it frees the mind by bringing it peace and serenity. Breathing brings harmony between the mind and the universe. During the retention of each breath, the body is full of *ki* and the mind is clear, free, and full of nothingness (*mushin*) which is equated to *ku* or *kara*, the emptiness. In this state the mind is at one with the universe, located everywhere and nowhere at the same time. It is this third stage of the respiration process —retention—which is the most important in generating power and in realizing the union of mind and body, the ultimate goal of man.

chapter 2 What is Karatedo?

1. Principles and Aims of Karatedo

In essence, karatedo is a set of techniques and mental attitudes systematized and codified in a martial art which, through a rigorous and systematic training of the mind and the body, strive to achieve knowledge of oneself and others to ultimately create a state of complete harmony between oneself and the universe. It is a discipline which advocates the development of a strong body and the awakening of the mind by a constant search for self-perfection both physically and spiritually in order to fully realize oneself.

But karatedo is also one of the most efficient fighting arts. Initially it was developed as a training method for personal combat and war, where vanquishing the adversary was the only important goal. However, like the other martial arts of the *budo*, the need to win over oneself is inseparable from the goal of combat and has become an end in itself. Thus, karatedo is an all-encompassing way of life which, far from being a violent method of fighting, teaches humility with confidence and courage, and self-defense with respect for life and restraint. It contributes to giving man a placid mind by surmounting his fears and his pride. At peace with himself and others, and in possession of a strong mind and body, man can thus fulfill his commitments to himself and to society. To reach these goals, the mind and body are trained and developed through use of the punching, kicking, striking, throwing, strangling, and armlock techniques which constitute *karate-ho* (the empty-hand techniques), and through the use of long and short weapons as an extension of the hands to thrust, throw, sweep, and strike *buki-ho* (the weapon techniques). *Karate-ho* and *buki-ho* together constitute karatedo.

2. The Meaning of Karatedo

The word "karatedo" is composed of three ideograms: *kara* (唐) *te* (手) and *do* (道). *Kara* (in Japanese) refers to one of the most brilliant periods in Chinese history when the T'ang dynasty ruled China (A.D. 618–907) and has come to represent China itself for the Japanese. *Te* means "hand" or "technique". *Do* signifies "philosophical way" or "principle" with which to realize oneself.

Thus karatedo literally means "the way to self-perfection through the practice of techniques originating during the T'ang period."

The word "karate" was first introduced in Okinawa to designate "Chinese fighting techniques" which included both bare-hand and armed techniques (*karate-ho* and *buki-ho*). But, as is often the case in the Japanese use of Chinese ideograms, *kara* can also be written (空), pronounced *ku* or *sora*, meaning "empty", "free like the air", or "infinite like the sky."

Thus, another sense of karatedo is "the way to self-perfection through the practice of techniques of emptiness," emptiness being understood both physically (without weapons) and mentally (with an empty or free mind).

It is unfortunate that when karate was introduced to Japan, the rising nationalism and antagonism against China at the time of the Sino-Japanese War (1894–95) led some karate instructors to deny karate its first meaning, retaining only the sense of "empty-hand fighting." By doing so they excluded from karatedo one of its important components, *buki-ho*.

3. The Value of Karatedo

Karatedo is essentially a martial art (*budo*) and as such it is also a means of reaching the "way" (*do*) by the "practice of weapons" (*bu*). As in any other martial art, karatedo is, and requires, a solid discipline. The body must go through long and strenuous exercises for many years. This develops not only a strong body but also great strength of character. Control is required over not only one's techniques but also emotions such as fear, pain, and hate. As a fighting art, karatedo involves the confrontation of two wills, each determined to win. This develops such qualities as fortitude, but also humility and respect for oneself and others.

Karatedo is also a formidable means of self-defense which does not require any particular weapon. Weapons are always available when needed. A considerable advantage of karatedo for self-defense purposes is that the defense can be matched exactly with the aggression; if you use a firearm for self-defense, you can not do anything but shoot your opponent. With karatedo, you can completely dispose of your opponent without maiming or killing him. Self-defense attitudes help the individual avoid many natural diseases and accidents by developing a more careful approach to everyday life.

The physical value of karatedo is unique. It is an all-around activity which equally develops every part of the body without having to worry about some muscles being underdeveloped or overdeveloped. It can be practiced anywhere; there are no particular requirements as to the place of practice. It can be practiced alone without a partner; this being a definite advantage over most other sports. Anyone can practice karatedo and benefit from it. There is always the possibility of matching your training with your physical condition or goals. It has now become a very popular competitive sport and as such can satisfy the need of younger people to discover themselves.

4. The Origins of Karatedo

The origins of karatedo are lost in antiquity. In all times and places in the world, people have learned to defend themselves and fight with bare hands first, and then with weapons.

They first relied only on their strength, but then developed fighting techniques and weapons to give even weaker persons a chance to survive in a hostile environment. Perhaps the weakest of all creatures, man not only succeeded in surviving but also in establishing his supremacy over the animal kingdom. Methods of fighting came to be codified through the course of the centuries, reflecting the specific characteristics and needs of peoples and their environments. However, the first fighting techniques were mostly defensive. Their purpose was self-defense against animals and other men. The Sumerians, who had created a brilliant civilization with flourishing arts and philosophy some 3,700 years ago, practiced a form of combat reminiscent to our modern wrestling and boxing scenes of hand-to-hand fighting. Similar depictions are found on the base reliefs of Egyptian tombs 3,000 years old. Statues of Buddhas' guardians in fighting stances are found at the doors of Indian temples also several thousand years old.

Before the advent of Buddhism in India, medicine had already discovered and codified the vital points of the human body. It is said that their practical applications to fighting were made on live subjects by local fighters.

In ancient Greece, where courage and physical development were valued at their highest, it is said that around 800 B.C. every Greek male was adept in pankration, a very violent form of fighting which often ended with the death of one of the contestants. Pancration was then a basic training for war as well as a popular sport.

a. The Chinese Origins: *Kempo*

One of the most influential forms of fighting was begun in China more than three thousand years ago during the Shu period when the Yellow River district was unified. This fighting art, *ch'uan-fa*, or *kempo* in Japanese

(the way of the fist), is illustrated in the *Kansho*, an old Chinese book. Later, around 770 B.C., when nomadic Mongolian tribes invaded Northern China, they introduced a form of fighting which was to influence the development of both Chinese wrestling and boxing. This form, called *sumo*, was a test of strength between two contestants wearing ram heads, thus its first meaning, "evaluating the strength of the horns."

Sumo was then performed ritually as a preparation for war in a dance-like fashion, from which comes its second meaning of "bare hands dance." *Sumo* became very popular and its influence is still apparent in Chinese opera. Later still, during the Chi'in and Han periods, *sumo* came under the influence of *kemari*, a kicking game designed to develop the feet for war, and gave birth to another form of fighting called *shubaku*. Both *kemari* and *shubaku* are documented on scrolls from this period, rich in wars and upheavals, which also saw the development of the principles of war by a warlord named Sonshi. It is interesting to note that in China today, modern martial arts are still called *shubaku*.

During the enlightened T'ang dynasty (A.D. 618–970), *kempo* was restored to favor. Huge competitions were organized on the steps of the Imperial Palace and in every public square throughout the country. The winner, *Ruidai* champion, was the one who survived all of the fights held on the stage (ruidai). Champions were crowned inside the palace and became immensely popular.

About 1,400 years ago a monk named Bodhidharma (Daruma in Japanese) traveled from a kingdom in southern India, of which he was the third prince, and settled in the Shaolin temple (Shorin Ji in Japanese) in the Hao Shan mountains. He was also the 28th descendant of Shaka (or Shason), the founder of Buddhism. At the Shaolin temple he undertook the teaching, of Zen Buddhism, a form of contemplative religion aimed at creating a state of grace by sudden illumination (*satori*). Asceticism and meditation in sitting positions (*zazen*) are the two main forms of Zen practice and it is said that the monks were so weakened by the harshness of their training that many passed away. To enable them to recover their health, and to strengthen their bodies so that they could keep on with the practice of Zen, Bodhidharma developed a training method which encompassed both the spiritual and physical development of the monks. He asserted that mind and body are inseparable and have to be treated as a whole. Soon the physical condition of the monks improved and Zen was spreading throughout the country. This physical aspect of Zen, *I-chin-ching*, was further refined to include methods of self-defense, as the monks were often confronted with highwaymen who were ransacking a country shaken by civil war. As their religion prohibited the use of weapons, the monks had to rely on these methods of empty-hand fighting which were known as *shorinji kempo*. Scenes of monks practicing *kempo* are depicted in the wall paintings of the hakuiden room in the temple. The techniques are long and supple, and performed mainly with open hands. The movements are fluid and inspired by the Zen philosophy of non-violence and harmony and also by the fighting attitudes of animals such as the tiger, crane, monkey, snake, and dragon. *Shorinji kempo* also included methods of fighting with "natural weapons" such as the *bo*; a walking stick carried by monks in their peregrinations. *Kempo* was taught only to monks but its fame spread to the whole country when the monks were driven out of the temple and the temple was burned. During the Sung period (A.D. 960–1279), most revolutions were led by *kempo* Masters. In A.D. 1280's, 100,000 *kempo* practitioners rebelled against the ruling Mongolian Genghis Khan in an attempt to restore a purely Chinese dynasty.

Between 1840 and 1900 China, undermined by internal dissension, became the prey of foreign colonial powers (the Opium War with England in 1840–42, wars against France in 1884, Japan in 1894–95, etc.) This led to the Boxer Rebellion (the boxers were a sect of ultranationalist kempo practitioners) which was crushed by the Ch'ing dynasty in 1901. The boxers were executed in great numbers; *dojos* (training houses) were closed and *kempo* was completely eradicated. This truly Chinese fighting art was never to revive in China but before dying out *kempo* had spread to the Ryukyu Islands where it was to give birth to karate.

b. The Development of Karate in Okinawa

China had established a flourishing trade relationship with the Ryukyu Islands during the Sui dynasty around A.D. 607. In 1372 King Satsudo of Okinawa (the largest island of the archipelago) became the vassel of the Ming Emperor. An exchange of officials between the two countries resulted and in 1392 Chinese families emigrated to Okinawa, introducing *kempo* to the islands. In 1429 the Okinawan King Shohashi unified the islands under his rule and banned all weapons. This prohibition led the people into overt opposition and gave a tremendous impulse to the arts of empty-hand fighting. Moreover, in 1609 the Ryukyu Islands were conquered by the Japanese warlord Shimazu of the Satsuma clan. Because the Okinawans had refused to help Shimazu and the ruler of Japan, Toyotomi Hideyoshi, in their unsuccessful war of 1592–96 against the Chinese protectorate of Korea, Shimazu issued strict laws prohibiting all weapons and martial arts practice. Once again the Okinawans went undercover and developed the art of empty-hand fighting to a formidable degree of efficacy, developing a parallel practice of using farm implements as defensive weapons against the *samurai* swords. Hands and feet were turned into deadly weapons by assiduous practice on *makiwara*, a vertical board covered with straw. This fighting art became known as *Okinawa-te* (*te* means "hand" or "technique") and it was not until 1722 that Sakugawa, who had studied *kempo* and *bo* fighting in China, started to teach in Shuri what he called *karate-no-Sakugawa*. This is the first time the name karate was used; *kara* is a reference to the T'ang dynasty and for the Okinawans, as for the Japanese, had come to mean China itself. Karate thus meant "the Chinese techniques."

Later, around 1830, an Okinawan official, (Bucho) Sokon Matsumura, was sent to China where he mastered Shorinji kempo and after returning to Okinawa founded in Shuri the "*Shorinryu-gokoku-an-karate*", the original name of *Shorinryu karate*. One sidelight of this history is that he also introduced to Okinawa the Chinese form of checkers called 'go'. In 1848 Master Matsumura was named Chief Martial Arts Instructor for Okinawa. At that time Okinawan karate emphasized hard blocking techniques in reaction to an offensive action, and this often resulted in severe injuries when the attacker was armed. Master Anko Asato, a student of Master Matsumura, brilliantly demonstrated the superiority of dodging over blocking by defeating one of the greatest swordsman of that time, Toshiaki Kirino. A number of masters became famous during this period and were to greatly influence the development of karate in Japan. They were Master Chojun Kyamu, himself a student of Master Anko Asato and one of the instructors of *Shinan* Kori Hisataka, founder of Shorinjiryu Kenkokan Karatedo; Master Anko Itosu and Master Kanryu Higaona, foremost instructors respectively of *Shuri-te* and *Naha-te* (karate from Shuri and Naha, two of the biggest cities in Okinawa); Gichin Funakoshi, Chojun Miyagi, and Kenwa Mabuni, themselves students of Masters Asato,

Itosu, and Higaona, who were later to develop, respectively, the Shotokan, Gojuryu, and Shitoryu styles of karate in Japan.

c. The Development of Karate in Japan

Sumo was introduced from China around the year A.D. 200, at the end of the Han period, the same time as the origin of *chikara kurabe*, a brutal fighting method which already included kicking techniques as testified by the relation of the fight between Nomi No Sukune and Tagima No Kehaya, the oldest fighters recorded in Japanese history. Tagima was the champion of the Yamato region (now Nara) and his fame was such that it reached the Emperor who chose Nomi to challenge him. Tagima lost the fight for the Yamato region when his ribs were crushed and his hips broken by Nomi's kicks. These fights to the finish became extremely popular and were organized, like the *ruidai* in China, in almost every city. *Chikara kurabe* was also practiced as preparation for war and this explains the fact that there were no restrictions on the techniques used. As the centuries passed, *chikara kurabe* evolved and became codified under the name of *kumi uchi*. Some restrictions were introduced in the fights as human life became more highly respected. It was at this time that the tradition of burying all of the Emperor's court in his tomb at his death was abandoned and *hauiwas* (dummies) were substituted. At the end of the Nara period (A.D. 784) the advent of armor on the battlefield made the use of punches and kicks preposterous and *kumi uchi* was soon replaced by the more practical *jujitsu* which advocated throwing techniques, armlocks, and strangulations.

Kempo (*ch'uan-fa*) was introduced to Japan under the name of karate (the Chinese fighting art) or *kempo*, the way of the fist, around 1627 or 1644 by Chen Yuan Ping (or Gen Pin Chin), a well educated Chinese who, besides karate, introduced also the *sai*, which adopted and slightly modified by the police became the *jittesai* with only one branch. Gen Pin Chin was also a poet and an artist who has left his name in ceramics (the famous Gen Pin pottery).

The beginning of the Meiji era (1868) marked the end of Edo, the feudal age. The *samurai* had to lay down their arms and cut their *chon mage* (the tress, symbol of their status). The *kimono* was abandoned for western-style clothing. Japan opened itself to the foreigners while the popularity of *jujitsu* and *kendo* declined. Master Jigoro Kano introduced a new art, *judo*, which eventually superseded *jujitsu* after its decisive victory in a competition held in 1886 at the Tokyo Police Department. In 1879 the Ryukyu Islands became Japanese provinces and Okinawan karate went to Japan. In 1886 Master Anko Asato toured Japan, defeating every other martial artist, including Sakujiro Yokoyama, the strongest *judoka* of the Kodokan at that time.

In 1911 Admiral Dewa, commander of the 1st Fleet of the Japanese Navy on station in Okinawa, selected ten of his officers to learn karate. The first official karate demonstration outside of Okinawa* was held at the Kyoto Martial Art Center in 1916 by a number of Okinawan experts including Gichin Funakoshi. In 1921 the Crown Prince of Japan stopped in Okinawa en route to Europe and was given a demonstration by karate Masters which led to their invitation to give a demonstration the following year at the first National Athletic Exhibition in Tokyo under the auspices of the Ministry of Education.

In 1922 the first karate book was published by Gichin Funakoshi under the title "Ryukyu Kempo Karate." The following year Motobu went to Osaka to teach karate, followed in 1929 by Chojun Miyagi, founder of the Gojuryu style, and Kenwa Mabuni, who founded the Shitoryu style. The first university karate club was established by Keio University in 1924. The University of Tokyo was the first to introduce the use of protective equipment for competition in 1930.

Shinan Kori Hisataka introduced karatedo to Taiwan in 1929. In 1932 he reintroduced karatedo to China at the celebration of the creation of the Chinese Confederation of Manchuria, the first official recognition of Japanese karatedo by China. He then introduced karatedo to Thailand, Korea, Burma, Afganistan, Russia, and Mongolia.

Karate was introduced for the first time to the United States by Norimichi Yabe who had been invited to demonstrate it on the west coast in 1920; but it was not until shortly after World War II that karate became popular in the U.S. when Masutatsu Oyama gave a series of impressive demonstrations, fought against professional wrestlers and boxers, and confronted bulls with his bare hands.

In 1963 Shihan Masayuki Hisataka introduced Shorinjiryu Kenkokan Karatedo to the United States where he began to teach and demonstrate. In 1964, he officially represented Japan at the New York World's Fair, the first official presentation of karatedo at a world event. He again was asked to represent his country at Expo' 67 in Montreal, Canada, following which he instructed there for several years, thus introducing Kenkokan Karatedo throughout North America.

In ways such as these, karatedo soon spread throughout the world and is now practiced in almost every country.

5. Shorinjiryu Kenkokan Karatedo

Shorinjiryu Kenkokan Karatedo was founded by Shinan Kori Hisataka soon after World War II. Born in Shuri (in Naha City, Okinawa) on April 22, 1907,

---

*The first public demonstration of katate was given in Okinawa in 1906.

he is a descendant of Kyowa, the 56th Emperor of Japan. Shinan Kori Hisataka studied Okinawan karate including studying with Master Chojun Kyamu, and then returned to Kyushu Island, where he had spent his infant years, in order to study *jujitsu*. He then entered the army where he learned soldiery, bayonet handling, and was exposed to true fighting. He continued his training in the martial arts but could not satisfy himself with the *dojo* practice and was always looking for an opportunity to increase and test his knowledge with other Masters. In 1929 he toured Taiwan for almost a year with master Chojun Kyamu, never losing a fight to the local kempo practitioners. He returned to Japan where he sudied judo at the Kodokan with Master Sanpo Toku, attaining the rank of fourth dan in only one year. . . a truly remarkable achievement. He also studied kendo and traveled throughout Japan competing in every police department against local fighters without losing a single encounter. In one of his many demonstrations, he was challenged by a swordsman, in a test of strength. He defeated him by breaking a hardwood board that even the sword could not cut.

As a result, a duel between he and the swordsman evolved. He, weaponless, defeated the swordsman. Continuing his search for other martial arts, he returned to China to master Shorinjiryu kempo.

During World War II he worked as a Station Master in Manchuria, at the same time teaching karate. At the end of the war, when the Japanese were evacuating Manchuria under pressure from the Allied Forces, he saved the lives of countless civilians working in one of the two stations he was supervising. These station employees had been bombed and were in shock. A suspension bridge was thrown over a deep precipice but no one dared to venture on to it. Shinan Kori Hisataka helped them cross the bridge one by one, carrying some who had become almost hysterical with fear, after having knocked them down. He credited this act of composure and bravery to his years of training in karate which had given him complete control of himself, allowing him to keep this placid state of mind called "*heijoshin*" when others were overcome by fear and hysteria. This event was of immeasurable importance in displaying to him the virtues of karate. So much so that upon his return, to find his country demoralized and disheartened by the aftermath of war where people living in poor conditions of health and without food, he undertook to help them rebuild their lives and a better society.

With the systematic and scientific method of karatedo he had developed over the years, and by the disciplining of mind and body, he assumed that undertaking. He founded the Kenkokan School of Karatedo in Fukuoka Prefecture in Kyushu, naming his art Shorinjiryu Kenkokan Karatedo after his two main sources of inspiration: Shorinryu karate, and Shorinjiryu kempo,

placing the suffix "*do*" on karate to emphasize that it is a "way" of reaching the highest mental state.

In addition to this greater emphasis on the spiritual development of the individual, Shinan Kori Hisataka has introduced into karatedo a number of other innovations:

a) In basic techniques, he has placed a greater emphasis on the use of the feet, and in particular the heel, which is more solid than the toes. The whole body is put into action when executing a technique in a follow-through fashion.

b) This also led to the use of the vertical fist (*tate ken*) which is stronger, natural and also safer for the wrist.

c) Also, stress is placed on the practice of *yakusoku kumite*, where two or more karatedo practitioners execute a sequence of prearranged offensive and defensive techniques. This type of *kumite* is one of the best forms of training in karatedo, as it teaches the most effective techniques of attack and defense against actual opponents.

d) The use of protective equipment (*bogu*) which allows karatedo students to really test their techniques in a safe way and without having to hold back their blows.

e) The practice of weapons (*buki-ho*) is an integral part of Kenkokan Karatedo, along with *karate-ho*, the art of empty-hand fighting. These two facets are inseparable in Kenkokan Karatedo, weapons being an extension of the arm and their practice having the same virtues as the empty-hand practice, as well as helping to "bring to life" the karate techniques by displaying the actual clear-cut degree to which the limbs are true weapons.

All these points will be treated in more detail in subsequent chapters.

6. Prelude of Karatedo Training

a. Place of Practice and Epuipment

The *dojo* is the place of practice for karatedo. *Dojo* literally means "training" or "learning" place, (*jo*) means place, (*do*) the way. Its name comes from Buddhism where it designated a place of worship. Later it came to denote a place for the practice of martial arts. It is not necessarily a closed practice hall or gymnasium but any area where one trains one's mind and body in the way of karate. As such a *dojo* should be respected almost as a temple, and one should always observe a correct attitude and act with proper decorum. Anything which disturbs the concentration of karatedo should be avoided. Smoking should be prohibited and spectators should observe the silence. An atmosphere of mutual respect and of mutual aid between the students, who are in fact helping each other develop themselves, should reign in a *dojo*.

The front wall of the *dojo*, called *shomen*, is the place

of honor. In most *dojos* there is a picture of the founder of the school hanging on the wall. In Japan, where Shintoism is the main religion, the *shomen* is a kind of altar called a *Shinzen* "the place of god." The instructors sit on the *shomen's* left side, *joseki,* while the students sit on the opposite side in descending order of rank from the *shomen.*

The *karatedogi* is the training outfit for karatedo; it consists of a jacket *(uwagi)* and trousers *(zubon)* made of white canvas and a belt *(obi),* the color of which indicates the rank of the student. The lower ten ranks *(kyu)* of non-black-belt holders *(mudansha)* are divided into the following belt colors: white, ranks 10 and 9; yellow, 8 and 7; orange, 6 and 5; green, 4 and 3; and brown, 2 and 1. The upper ten ranks *(dan)* of black-belt holders *(yudansha)* all wear the black belt for ranks *(dan)* 10 to 1; though on special occasions, ranks 6, 7, and 8 wear a ceremonial red belt with white stripes, and ranks 9 and 10 wear a red belt, symbolizing their respective levels of achievement. Junior students (under age 14) are ranked in the same way but half of their belt remains white while the other half indicates their rank; on becoming seniors, they are reclassified.

On special occasions, advanced instructors may also wear the *hakama,* the black pleated traditional trousers worn by the samurai of old. The *hakama* is worn over the trousers of the *karatedogi* with the *obi* on top.

The *karatedogi* was originally the underwear worn by monks. Its white color was a symbol of purity. The belt ranking system has been derived from the monks' ranking system according to the surplice *(kesa)* worn around their necks.

How to wear the *karatedogi*

The *karatedogi* must be large enough to allow complete freedom of movement. The jacket must completely cover the hips and its sleeves must cover more than half of the forearms. The trousers must be long enough to cover more than half of the calf, and the belt long enough to be wound twice around the hips, tied with a square knot, and leave about one foot hanging down on each side of the knot. The trousers must be pulled on first with one end of the drawstring passed through the loop in front before tying them up at the waist.

The jacket is then put on with the left flap coming over the right flap (this enabled the samurai to draw their swords more easily). The strings on each side of the jacket must be tied. To put on the belt, hold the middle in front of your navel and wind it twice around your hips; tie it up with a square knot, after having pressed the loose end

under the first turn of the belt so as to avoid constricting the stomach when someone pulls on your belt.

In Shorinjiryu Kenkokan Karatedo as in the Koshiki Karatedo competition system, the preferred dogi is the authorized Supersafe *karatedogi,* which is plain white in color, with red and black stripes along the sleeves and down the legs of the trousers. Alternatively, a totally white *dogi* can be worn. The *dogi* should have no further designs, except that the mark of the training style can be worn on the left chest, and that of the World Koshiki Karatedo Federation can be worn on the right sleeve. Names can be written on the right flap of the jacket and on the upper left part of the trousers. Belts can be marked with the names of the person and the school.

To undress, take off the belt first, then the jacket and trousers. The *karatedogi* should then be folded in the following way: lay the jacket on he ground and put the trousers inside; fold in the sleeves of the jacket, and then fold in about one third of each side of the jacket. Fold the jacket and trousers once lengthwise and once again in the other direction. Hold the belt in its middle and tie it around the *karatedogi* with about one-third of it open so that you can pass your arm through to carry it.

In Shorinjiryu Kenkokan Karatedo and the Koshiki Karatedo competitive system, protective equipment is used for practice and in competition. Known as Supersafe *anzen bogu,* this gear was developed by Master Masayuki Kukan Hisataka at the request of the Technical Research Committee of the World Union of Karatedo Organizations in order to provide a greater level of safety and realism to karatedo training.

Supersafe gear consists of the *men,* or face guard, the

do, which protects the chest and stomach, and the *kin ate,* which protects the groin. The *men* is made of durable translucent material allowing for complete vision while offering protection for the face. The *do* is made of fiberglass with padding to stop skin abrasions. The equipment is light and flexible, affording maximum protection without hampering movement.

The equipment requires proper care so that it maintains maximum protection for its entire life span. After use, the equipment should be wiped clean and the *men* checked for scratches. It should be replaced when cracks appear or serious scratching has occurred. The equipment should not be struck by full contact, uncontrolled techniques, nor by weapons.

Makiwara

The *makiwara* is the most important piece of training equipment in karatedo. It typically consists of a wooden board covered with straw rope. It is used to develop the power, speed, stance, and form of every technique and at the same time condition natural weapons such as the fists, knuckles, elbows, knees, and feet. Practice with the *makiwara* toughens the skin, strengthens the joint's articulation, and generally strengthens the technique. It used to be the only way to practice delivering blows with full force and it was used to learn proper concentration of force and focusing of the whole mind and body on the target. In modern karatedo, protective equipment allows the student to work on a moving target. This has somewhat lessened the use of the *makiwara,* which, however, still remains essential, especially when training by oneself.

The *makiwara* should be approximately six feet high (the height of a man) and have just enough spring in it to absorb the shock of the impact without generating too great a reaction force. This reaction force is absorbed by the body and may damage the joints or be detrimental to the organs, particularly the heart, if absorbed in a straight line through the limbs. If the expression of force causes as much damage to the instrument generating the force as to

the target, the purpose is defeated. In earlier times, karate practitioners practicing on the *makiwara* over a long period of time sometimes sustained internal injuries (especially when the joints were locked and the body not fully twisted into techniques). Cyclists have discovered that using their limbs, particularly their arms (elbows and wrists), as shock absorbers to buffet and dissipate the jolts received from the ground, tires them immeasurably less than absorbing these shocks directly. Their consequent gain in stamina is obviously a sign of less body damage occurring, thus reducing the amount of energy needed to maintain the exercise, and allowing for the maximum gain with the minimum expenditure. This is a primary axiom of all athletic motion, and one of the reasons why in Kenkokan karatedo, the punching arm is slightly bent and shoulders are fully twisted so that they end up being perpendicular to the target. In this way the reaction force is better absorbed and dissipated by the arm and shoulders. For further explanation and evolution of these principles of dynamics, see Chapter 3, p. 29.

Makiwara can also be tailored for developing hand and foot techniques. After constant striking, *makiwara* can lose their resiliency and become slightly deformed. So it is preferable to have two separate *makiwara,* one for the hands and one for the feet.

Other equipment used in the practice of karatedo includes sandbags and speed bags to develop the power and speed of techniques, dumbbells and weights for general conditioning, and iron clogs or weights specially designed to strengthen kicking and punching.

b. Karatedo Etiquette

Karatedo practice begins and ends with courtesy. The politeness surrounding combative activities like *kumite* or *shiai* is certainly inherited from the origins of karatedo and is an essential element of the art because of the potential danger involved if both partners do

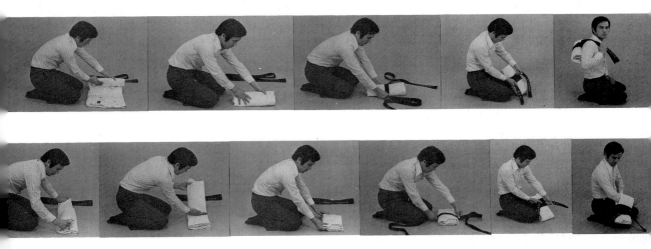

not display an attitude of restraint, respect for each other, and sportsmanship. In training, both partners are, in fact, trying to improve themselves and each other. They must therefore control themselves to avoid any risk or injury. This is true of any martial art (*budo*). *Budo* not only means "the way of weapons" but also "the way of non-violence." The true goal of karatedo is to win without hurting the opponent; that is the meaning of the bow which precedes and follows every act in karatedo. It is a gesture of respect for the opponent and a reminder to oneself of the spirit in which karatedo must be practiced. The bow is not merely a physical gesture but an expression of one's whole attitude.

There are three different forms of the bow:

a) *Keirei* is the ceremonial salutation used to bow to your instructor or to show your respect for others and the *dojo*. To perform *keirei*, adopt the *musubi dachi* stance with your hands falling naturally on each side of your body. Bend your head and shoulders 25° to 30° forward with your eyes looking downward and your hands in front of your knees. Keep this position for about two seconds then look up.

b) *Kenko ritsurei* is the fighting salutation used to bow to your opponent (or partner during practice). Standing in the *shizen hontai* stance a few feet from your opponent (3 yards in a shiai), look him straight in the eyes and bend the upper part of your body 10° to 15° forward without losing eye contact. Your arms should be extended in front of your thighs, hands closed. Hold this position for one second then straighten your body. As soon as you have bowed the fight is engaged.

c) *Zarei* is the sitting salutation (ceremonial and fighting bow). Standing in the *musubi dachi* stance, bend your left leg and put your left knee, then your right knee, on the ground (your knees should be the width of two fists apart). Put your hands on your thighs, keeping your body straight by pulling your shoulders backward. Look at your opponent; then bend the upper part of your body 45° forward, bringing your hands down in front of your knees. Hold this position for two to three seconds, then straighten your body and stand up on your right foot first in a *musubi dachi* stance. In the fighting form, *kenko zarei*, you sit down on the tip of your toes and bend your body 10° to 15° forward keeping eye contact with your opponent.

c. Hygiene, Diet, and Training Schedule

A proper diet, good hygiene, and careful planning of practice are essential in supporting efficient training regimen for karatedo. They help prevent sickness, abnormal tiredness, and injury.

The practice of karatedo should take place in a clean *dojo* to avoid breathing dust and dirt. For the same reasons, *karatedogi* must be kept unspoiled and protective equipment kept in good order to avoid any risk of injury. Before practice it is advisable to eat lightly, preferably high energy foods rich in glucose, which provide the muscles with adequate nutrition during practice. The bladder should be empty to avoid risk of rupture. Always practice with full dedication, putting all of your body and mind into it while exercising enough control and care to avoid accidents. Because the digestion process slows down after practice due to physical exhaustion, slowly ingest high calory foods containing vitamin B and glucose to help speed up the recovery process.

The lactic acid remaining in the muscular tissues must be evacuated by doing some light exercises accompanied by deep breathing, meditation, relaxation, massages, and rest. A good sleep is the best way to recover from practice as it relaxes all the body, facilitates blood circulation, and regenerates the nervous and cerebral activities.

A training schedule should be established by any student who wishes to attain proficiency in karatedo. Such a plan should reflect the student's goals in karatedo, his life habits (such as the time he can devote to karatedo both in and outside the *dojo*), and his physical condition. The student should consult his instructor in setting up his own schedule. As karatedo is practiced all year round, it may become monotonous and tedious without a schedule which defines the activities and goals to be realized on a daily, weekly, monthly, and yearly basis. The annual plan should reflect all of the major activities the student wants to undertake such as competitions and tournaments, training camps, and grading examinations, etc. Accordingly, a monthly plan can be derived and broken down into weekly and daily schedules. It has already been indicated that a schedule must be specifically designed for each and every student, however, examples of daily and weekly schedules are as follows:

Daily schedule
—In the morning: half an hour of running and *makiwara* practice or alternatively preparatory and complementary exercises and *kata* practice. Regular class which consists of:
—Salutation and *mokuso* (meditation): 5 to 10 minutes.
—Preparatory exercises: 5 to 10 minutes.
—Basic techniques and body movements: 5 to 15 minutes for advanced students and 15 to 30 minutes for beginners who have to devote more time to basic techniques.
—*Makiwara*, sandbag, and speed ball practice: 5 minutes for advanced students and 15 to 30 minutes for beginners (advanced students should practice more outside of regular classes).
—Basic *kumites*: single and multiple kumite techniques according to the technical level of the student: 15 to 30 minutes for advanced students and 30 to 60 minutes for beginners.
—*Yakusoku randori* kumite (prearranged sparring kumite): 15 to 60 minutes for advanced students and 30 to 60 minutes for beginners.
—*Jiyu randori kumite* (free sparring kumite): 30 to 60 minutes for advanced students and 15 to 30 minutes for beginners.

—Kata: 15 to 30 minutes for advanced students and 30 to 60 minutes for beginners.
—*Renshu shiai* (competition training): once a week or every two weeks or more often according to the circumstances (for advanced students only).
—Complementary exercises: as needed.
—Supplementary exercises: 3 to 10 minutes.
—Salutation and meditation: 5 to 10 minutes.

A regular class lasts between one hour and a half and two hours and a half. Some of the activities described have to be alternated from one class to the other; this schedule should not be repeated every day of the week. Kata, kumite and shiai should be practiced at each class but their relative emphasis should be varied. For example, if one attends three classes a week, his weekly schedule could be as follws:

Tuesday: —Morning: running and preparatory exercises
—Regular class: emphasis on kata* normal practice of kumite* some shiai* practice

Thursday: —Morning: running and complementary exercises
—Regular class: emphasis on kumite normal practice of shiai some kata practice

Saturday: —Morning: running and *makiwara* practice
—Regular class: emphasis on shiai normal practice of *kata* some kumite practice

Objectives of a monthly schedule could be to learn a kata or a kumite, devoting a full week for each of the following: form, technique, speed, power, and finally, perfection of execution. For the basic techniques it could be to increase their practice progressively.

After every schedule, a critical review of the student's training should be máde together with his instructor. In each practice one should prepare for the worst possible cases so that he will be able to handle any real-life situation.

Shinan Kori Hisataka

chapter **3** **Theory of Karatedo**

Throughout the centuries karatedo has been developed empirically as an art. However, in recent years the basic underlying principles of karatedo have been systematically and scientifically analyzed. This has led to the improvement of some techniques, particularly in Kenkokan Karatedo which has been responsible for a number of technical innovations now adopted by many other schools of karate.

A thorough understanding of the fundamental principles of karatedo should help the student progress faster in the practice of this art, leading to a better understanding and improving control of himself, thus making it possible to fully achieve the goals of karatedo and ultimately, self-realization.

1. Essential Principles

The amazing power of a karatedo technique is the result of a rational application of physical, physiological, and psychological principles that everyone, even a weak or aged person, can learn to utilize through assiduous practice. The principles have to be combined all at once in the execution of a technique and as such are somewhat difficult to dissociate. However, for clarity of explanation, they will be treated separately.

a. Physical Principles

Needless to say, the human body follows the physical laws of nature. For example, it is attracted to the ground with a force which is directly proportional to its weight; this is the gravity force. When you move, you generate a momentum which is the product ($M \times V$) of your weight (M) and velocity (V). If you hit the ground or a wall with a force F, it creates a reaction force R which is directly proportional to F and in the opposite direction. In general, for any action there is a corresponding reaction of proportional intensity. Also, the impact generated by a mass (or weight) M moving with a velocity (or speed) V is proportional to the square of the speed (kinetic energy $= \frac{1}{2}M \times V^2$). Finally, the last important force brought into play in karatedo is the muscular force resulting from the contraction and/or extension of some of the 400 muscles of the body. Certain muscles are very powerful but move slowly while others, less powerful, move much faster. One of the characteristics of muscular force is that it is cumulative. In other words, the effects can be added, two identical muscles producing twice as much force as one.

How can one apply these physical principles in karatedo?

Use of body dynamics
First, good balance is needed. Because of the law of reaction, a punch creates reaction in the opposite direction. Therefore, it would be completely ineffective if the body were to move back on impact. Thus gravity force is used to nullify the effect of the reaction force. The stability of the body is determined by three major factors: the weight, the base, and the position of the center of gravity. The weight is a constant factor: the base is determined by the position of the feet on the ground; and the center of gravity is located approximately one inch below the navel. As the surface of the base is increased, the mobility of the body decreases, the best compromise being when the feet are shoulder width apart. It can also be easily demonstrated that maximum stability is achieved when the center of gravity is located vertically over the center of the base. In this position, the weight is equally spread on both legs. The knees must be bent to insure a correct dispersion of weight on each foot and to be able to use the spring of the legs to move faster. The body should be kept erect so that its center of gravity continues to fall over the center of the base.

From this basic position of stability, the motion of the body can now be fully utilized. There are three kinds of motion possible: linear motion, which is a translation of the center of gravity; circular motion, which is a rotation around the center of gravity; and pendular motion, which is a swing of the center of gravity in a vertical plane. As the center of gravity is located between the hips, and as the hips and abdominal region account for about one-third of the weight of the body, it is clear that a considerable momentum can be generated by either moving the hips forward, rotating them, or swinging them. Thus, every action in karatedo must start from the hips. Another reason for this is that muscles of the waist and abdominal region are very powerful but because of their configuration can only be slowly brought into action and must therefore be contracted at the earliset stage of the movement.

A linear momentum is generated when the body is propelled forward by the rear leg. At first the hips are moved backward to shift the weight of the body on the rear leg. The spring of the leg (muscular action) and the reaction force created by the ground are then transmitted to the hips resulting in a forward motion. The center of gravity describes, in fact, a slightly curved trajectory because of the vertical component of the impulse force.

A circular momentum is generated when the body rotates around a vertical axis going through the center of gravity. The spring of the rear leg, the reaction force, and the force of the abdominal region are used to create a rotation of the hips, shoulders, and head in horizontal planes. The circular momentum is increased when the body is first twisted in the opposite direction, in a winding up motion, and by the antagonistic action of the hands (push-pull type of motion). These principles are used primarily in circular techniques.

A pendular momentum is generated when the hips swing backward and forward in a vertical plane going through the center of gravity. The pendular motion of the hips is used mainly in direct kicking techniques.

Concentration of force

The importance of the hips and abdominal region cannot be overemphasized. Because muscular force is of a cumulative nature, as many muscles as possible must be used in the motion (obviously these muscles have to be convergent and not antagonistic). Because of the reaction law, the long and flexible muscles of the extremities have to rest on the stronger and more stable muscles of the body to produce an effective result. Of all the profound muscles, the waist muscles are the strongest and therefore they must be contracted first to support the next closest muscles which in turn support adjacent long muscles and so on to the extremities of the body used for punching or kicking. The movement has to be executed fast to generate a high momentum. For the arm or foot to move quickly, muscles have to be strongly contracted. But if the muscular tension is kept throughout the motion, it will slow it down. Therefore the initial contraction of a muscle should be followed by a decontraction while the fist travels. At the time of impact, the muscles have to be tightened again to straighten the joints of the arm, insuring the maximum transmission of force. Otherwise, the reaction force will cancel out the force of the elbow. These periods of intense contraction and decontraction have to be well coordinated and it is only through intensive practice that one can develop a feeling for the right time at which the contraction or decontraction of the muscles should take place.

The relation between the force and the momentum is given by the equation: Momentum $= M \times V = F \times T$, T being the time during which the force F is applied to produce the momentum $M \times V$. In the execution of a punch, M would be the mass of the fist; if M and V are constant, it can be seen from this equation that the force will increase when T decreases ($F = \dfrac{M \times V}{T}$).

Thus the shorter the time, the greater the force generated. As a result, the force should be concentrated in as little time as possible. Therefore, speed being directly proportional to force, it is conceivable that a person of smaller physical structure (who is generally capable of greater speed than his counterpart of a larger structure) is able to create enough force to match and possibly supercede the force of a much larger man. Thus, it is said of a karate practitioner that size has no bearing on capability in the fighting art.

In modern karatedo, not only are the hips used in linear, circular, or pendular motions, but also the shoulders and head. This horizontal counterbalancing of the head and shoulders, added to (A) the horizontal pendular motions, (B) horizontal and vertical motions of the hips, and (C) circular motions of the feet, increases the momentum of the back counterbalance motion of the elbow. This supports and enhances the executions of the hand technique. This support counterbalance theory is particularly of importance in the Kenkokan system, where the motion is not stopped at the time of impact, but, in fact, followed through. With this, the acceleration of the striking mass is increased and thus creates a greater force ($F = \dfrac{M \times V}{T} = M \times A$, A being the acceleration). Other reasons for using follow-through motions will be given in the next paragraph.

The reaction force

The reaction force is that which results from the application of a force to a specific point and directly opposes the initial impact. If you kick on the ground with your foot, using your muscular force and gravity, it creates an upward force in your foot and body which can be reutilized in another direction. It is this reaction force which is used by high jumpers when they stamp on the ground before jumping. It is used in karatedo in much the same way. The ground is kicked just before punching or kicking and the reaction force is transmitted through the body to the fist or the foot, adding a momentum proportional to the force of the kick on the ground [when there is no loss of momentum. (If the ground is soft it may absorb part of the energy generated by the kick.)]

While the reaction force can be used positively, it can also have detrimental effects. When hitting a target, a reaction force results, which may lessen the force of your blow. This is why a strong stance is needed and explains the advantage of using follow through motions rather than stopping on impact, because the reaction force is completely nullified by the continuing momentum of the technique.

The law of reaction is applied in many different ways, as, for example in the use of antagonistic muscles. It is well known that the contraction of the biceps will produce an extension of the triceps (these muscles are called antagonistic muscles). This property can be turned to account in karatedo. Before kicking, the heel is raised backward, almost to the buttock, extending the fore-muscles of the thigh. When the heel is thrown forward, not only are these muscles strongly contracted, but the foot describes a longer trajectory and in doing so, gathers more momentum.

The reaction principle is also utilized in push-pull types of motion. If you are punching with your right fist, pull your left fist back to the side of your left hip. When kicking, pull your hands back to your waist or downward on each side of your body. In fact, a technique is not completed until after the blow has been pulled back. The punch or kick has to be executed and retracted at the same speed and in a single continuous motion to take full advantage of the action reaction principle.

Inner power

This is perhaps the most important single source of power of the human body and also the most difficult to generate because it requires the coordination of physical as well as physiological principles. Physically, the inner power is the result of the force of the abdominal muscles located below the diaphragm. They are the strongest muscles of the body and take a prominent part in the transmission of force as they link the upper and lower body. When the abdominal muscles are contracted, the whole body becomes one single mass concentrated around its center of gravity; thus, in momentum $M \times V$ transmitted to the striking extremity, M represents the total weight of the body. Abdominal muscles must thus be contracted right at the beginning of the motion to solidify the body into one mass, on which, step by step, other muscles are going to rest to transmit the striking force.

The force of the abdominal region is developed by correct breathing and use of the centripetal pressure of the abdominal muscles. The proper way to breathe is to inhale deeply from the nose, lifting the diaphragm and filling up the lower abdomen (*tanden*) with air. The breath should then be held in the *tanden* and the abdominal muscles should contract to create an antagonistic pressure called centripetal pressure. This is truly the source of inner power. The lower abdomen should always remain slightly tensed, filled with *ki*, in a position of equilibrium between the centrifugal force excited by the breathing and the centripetal pressure of the abdominal muscles. This kind of respiration provides a constant massage of the internal organs (liver, spleen, and stomach) and facilitates blood circulation by pushing back to the heart like a pump, the blood irrigating the lower part of the abdomen. The movement of the diaphragm relaxes the solar plexus which is an important nervous center, and as a result, the functions of the central nervous system are better controlled and the mind becomes more serene.

Another effect of abdominal respiration is the lowering of the center of gravity. In normal respiration, the chest is inflated and the shoulders are lifted, thus the center of gravity moves up. Breathing with the lower part of the diaphragm creates a centripetal pressure by which the internal organs are pushed downward and the center of gravity is lowered considerably, thereby increasing the stability of the body.

Distance, timing, and speed

These three factors are lightly correlated and are extremely important for the transmission of a maximum force to the point of impact.

Distance refers, in this paragraph, to the length of segment joining the striking part and the target. Your reach is important for this particular technique. If this distance is too long, the force of the blow will be wasted. You may lose your balance and the opponent will have a chance to counterattack. If the distance is too short, the striking part will not have attained its maximum speed. Therefore its momentum will be small and the blow will be ineffective. Furthermore, if you are too close, the opponent will have a chance to hit you before you strike. The reach is usually the full length of the arm or leg, and is developed by practice with the makiwara (a board used for punching, kicking, and striking practice).

But in karatedo, the two opponents usually do not stand within reach but rather just over one step out of reach. Therefore, to deliver a blow one has to close the gap and bring the opponent within his own reach. Body movement to close the gap provides additional momentum, usually a linear momentum. The feeling for the right distance is developed through assiduous practice of pre-arranged *kumite* and *shiai*. The proper distance, called *maai*, depends on a number of factors, such as your own stance, the technique used, physical characteristics (size and speed), and those of your opponent. If he is moving, the direction and speed of his move have to be taken into account. It is like shooting a bird; you do not actually shoot at the bird, but at some point ahead on its trajectory.

If the opponent stands too close for you to properly execute your technique, you can either push him backward or step back or sideways to create enough distance. You can also change your technique, using elbow or knee techniques more appropriate for close fighting.

Timing refers to the propitious moment for the execution of a technique. It is the moment when your concentration of force is at its maximum and the opponent presents an opening in his guard at the right distance. Timing is thus the precise coordination of your own action with the opponent's attitude. Such opportunities occur when:

a) your opponent is just about to attack: at this time he is usually too preoccupied by his own attack to think about his defense. It is the most favorable time because in this case you win without actually fighting.

b) your opponent has just finished his attack and is about to withdraw: his energy has reached its peak and he cannot mount any resistance to your action.

c) your opponent is moving backward after an attack or away from you; he cannot offer any resistance because your energy goes in the direction of his movement.

d) your opponent is blocking your first technique; he is then open to the following one.

e) your opponent stops his motion or loses his concentration; there is a disruption in the flow of his energy

f) your opponent is exhaling or has just finished exhaling; he is losing his *ki* and his energy is at its lowest point.

g) your opponent is off balance, or changing stances, or shielding his eyes; he is then open to an attack.

Proper timing can only be achieved by intensive training in kumite and shiai.

Speed is important not only in reducing the risk of a counter-attack by an opponent during the execution of a technique, but also because speed is transformed into power. The kinetic energy of a mass M moving with a velocity V is proportional to the product of this mass by the square of its velocity. Thus the kinetic energy of a mass moving at 10 meters per second is 100 times greater than the energy of the same mass moving at 1 meter per second. This clearly shows the advantage of executing a technique with speed.

Speed is produced by muscular action. The coordination of the proper muscles can be improved by repetition, eliminating the contraction of antagonistic and unnecessary muscles.

An example will help illustrate how these different physical principles are utilized in the execution of punching and kicking techniques.

For an offensive technique, the preparation phase will consist of a forward body motion (using *neko ashi* or *fumikomi ashi*), which generates a linear momentum used in the execution phase described below.

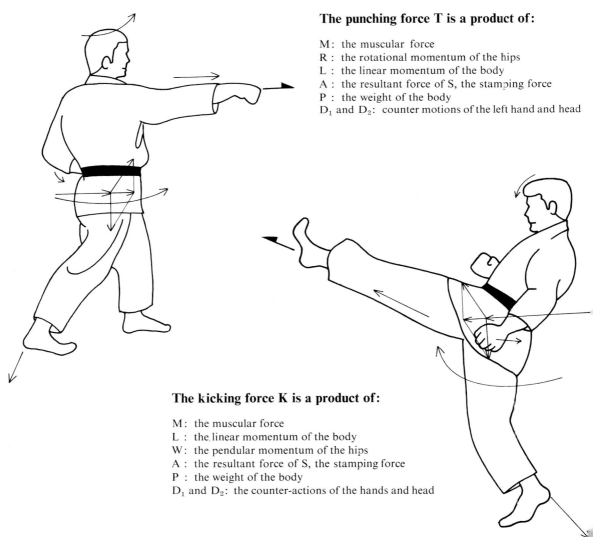

The punching force T is a product of:

M: the muscular force
R: the rotational momentum of the hips
L: the linear momentum of the body
A: the resultant force of S, the stamping force
P: the weight of the body
D_1 and D_2: counter motions of the left hand and head

The kicking force K is a product of:

M: the muscular force
L: the linear momentum of the body
W: the pendular momentum of the hips
A: the resultant force of S, the stamping force
P: the weight of the body
D_1 and D_2: the counter-actions of the hands and head

Hineri zuki: **Twist punch:** Standing in *hanmi*, 'half-face front' posture (body diagonal to the front), left foot forward, and breath held in the *tanden*:

1—Rotate your hips and shoulders 45° to your right in a winding up motion. Your right fist will travel a longer distance and attain a greater velocity.

2—Abruptly stop the winding up motion and, using the spring of your rear leg and the reaction force of the ground, rapidly rotate your hips, shoulders, head, and right leg 90° to your left,. This generates a circular momentum in which the mass is the mass of the whole body and the velocity is the circular speed of the hips. The reaction force and the spring of the leg add a linear momentum to this motion.

3—Throw your right fist forward, successively contracting the muscles of your arm and forearm. The muscular force of your arm is brought into play and develops a linear momentum.

4—Counter-balance the motion of your right arm by pulling your left fist to the side of your left hip. This increases the circular momentum generated by the rotation of your hips and cancels the reaction force created by the impact on the target.

5—Tighten your elbow and wrist articulations on impact to insure a maximum transmission of force and put your whole mind and body into your fist.

6—Immediately after impact, abruptly stop the motion of your hips, rotate them rapidly in the other direction, and pull back in this order: right shoulder, elbow, and fist. In this manner the kinetic energy generated by your punch will be propagated through the opponent's body in an exploding way and not just push him backwards.

These six phases are combined in single motion performed with complete determination and at maximum speed. The momentum of the punch delivered at impact is the sum of the momentum generated in every phase of the motion including the preparation phase.

Hineri geri: **Twist kick:** In a left foot forward stance or left cat stance:

1—Move your hips backward, lowering your body and extending your arms forward. This is a winding up motion to give more power to the hips.

2—Raise your right heel close to your buttock. This extends the muscles of the thigh and will allow the heel to travel a longer distance.

3—Swing your hips forward, to generate a pendular momentum, and use the reaction force of the ground by pushing on it with your front foot. Push your elbows backward to counter-balance the motion of the hips.

4—Press off the ground with your left leg to use its muscular force and the reaction force.

5—Throw your right foot forward on a 45° angle, successively contracting the thigh and calf. The muscular force is used to produce a linear momentum.

6—The knee and ankle should be tightened on impact to insure the maximum transmission of force.

7—Immediately after impact, first pull your hips back in a pendular motion, then the thigh and calf as rapidly as they were thrown forward.

In step 5, the leg is thrown with a 45° angle because this angle yields the largest resultant from the set of vertical and horizontal forces produced by the motion of the hips and legs.

b. Physiological and Psychological Principles

Considerations on breathing

Breathing is life itself. In the lungs, the inhaled oxygen is absorbed by the blood and carried to the cellular tissues where a number of chemical reactions take place. Among others, the combustion of glucose by oxygen provides muscular energy. The carbon dioxide resulting from the combustion is in turn carried by blood to the lungs and exhaled. Breathing also eliminates the lactic acid accumulating in the blood as a result of physical exercise. Lactic acid slows down the work of the muscles. The respiration process is thus a source of energy essential in insuring intense muscular activity and at the same time preventing the fatigue resulting from such activity.

The role played by abdominal breathing as a source of muscular power has been explained in the preceding section. Breathing is also the link between these physical and physiological considerations. It helps achieve the indispensable union of mind and body. When air is inhaled deeply and held in the *tanden* with correct centripetal pressure, the blood circulation is activated and the nervous system stimulated. As a result, the mind becomes more serene and mental concentration is increased. Perception becomes more acute and can detect any of the opponent's actions. The body can mobilize its resources to react in a split second.

In order to achieve these goals, respiration must become a conscious function which can be utilized at will. Breathing exercises should be practiced, inhaling deeply from the nose and lifting the diaphragm. The breath is then held in the *tanden*, the region around the navel, and a slightly downward centripetal pressure must be exerted by the abdominal muscles. It is at this time that the body can develop its maximum physical strength. The breath should not be held for too long, otherwise the blood becomes saturated with carbon dioxide and the muscles are slowed down. Expiration is done through the mouth. The rhythm of breathing must vary according to the circumstances of the fight. Your rhythm should always be concealed from your opponent who could otherwise attack when you are out of breath or inhaling. Inhalation should take place before the execution of any technique or move and the breath will usually be held until it is completed. In combination techniques, the breath may sometimes be held for more than one technique.

Kiai

Kiai is the materialization of the *ki*, the inner power resulting from the concentration of the mind and body by proper breathing. It is the expression of this power liberated all at once in a fraction of a second. In karatedo, techniques must always be executed with *kiai*. That is to say, they must literally explode from the body under the utmost internal pressure.

Kiai is often confused with the shrill sound caused by the rapid expulsion of a small amount of air which sometimes accompanies the execution of a technique. It is also some times thought that an ordinary scream which supposedly surprises the opponent and breaks his concentration, is *kiai*. But *kiai* is, rather, an unconscious expression of the *ki* and, as such, any attempt to consciously imitate it would only result in a waste of *kiai*.

Self-control

In karatedo the mind and body must be able to act at once and with determination. This requires a complete control over emotional disturbances which could affect the functioning of the mind. The mind should be clear, like water, to reflect the opponent's attitude. If the surface of the water is troubled, then the opponent's image will be distorted and his attack may surprise or confuse you.

The mind should exercise full control over the body. It is well known that all of our actions are commanded and controlled from the brain. Thus, if the mind is clear, then the body will execute whatever is required without the slightest hesitation. Likewise, a perfectly controlled body will execute a technique exactly as required.

Thus, self-control starts with the control of the mind and achieves the control of the body and of the techniques. How can control of the mind be realized? By mastering the techniques. When one has mastered the techniques, he is in full possession of his body, and his mind is liberated from emotional disturbances.

At peace with oneself, one will always win and ultimately fulfill oneself.

2. Conditioning of the Body and Mind

a. *Junbi Undo*: Preparatory Exercises

Preparatory exercises are necessary before practicing any sport. In karatedo, where the mind and body must respond at once with great speed and power, they are indispensable.

These exercises have a twofold objective:

▶Physical preparation. Every part of the body has to be prepared in order to eliminate the risk of injury resulting from harsh training. Preparatory exercises increase the intake of oxygen and stimulate the blood circulation. The muscular tissues are better irrigated and the combustion of glucose is more complete. This results in better elimination of the lactic acid resulting from the combustion of glucose and other carbon hydrates by oxygen. The muscles including the heart gain more strength and do not tire as easily. As the temperature of the body is increased, the muscles slip more easily into one another. This results in a gain of speed. The motor nerves of the body are also stimulated by better irrigation and chronaxy time is reduced, making reflexes more rapid.

As the joints are flexed, more oil is produced, reducing the risk of sprains. Every part of the body becomes better irrigated, stimulated, and more fit for training.

▶Mental preparation. The preparatory exercises relieve the tension preceding an effort and help the mind concentrate progressively on the training.

Preparatory exercises consist of general warming-up and loosening-up exercises as well as exercises more specific to karatedo. They may be performed either alone or with a partner. They should be neither too strenuous, to avoid any useless fatigue, nor too lax, in which case they are worthless. They should range from 5 to 10 minutes for an hour of karatedo practice and from 10 to 15 minutes for a two-hour practice.

All the preparatory exercises fall into one of the following categories: jumping, stretching, bending, twisting, and circling. They should be performed in a sequence starting with the extremities of the body and proceeding gradually towards the heart. Thus one should start with exercises for the legs (toes, ankles, and knees), then hips, trunk, shoulders, arms (elbows, wrists, and fingers), and finally the neck.

1. Deep breathing and body stretching exercises

2. Jumping exercises

a. Jumping and down   b. 'Jumping Jack'

3. Chest, shoulder, and arm stretching exercises

c. 'Squat jump'

4. Neck exercises

a. Twist head left and right   b. Bend neck forward and backward

c. Bend neck side to side

d. Rotate head in wide circle motion

b. Body bends side to side

c. Body twist left and right

d. Arm swing upward left and right

7. Hip rotation exercise

5. Swing arms in a wide circle motion
6. Trunk exercises

a. Body bends forward and backward

e. Body rotation

8. Knee exercises

a. Knee rotation

9. Leg stretching exercise

b. Knee bend and knee stretch

b. Body bend and leg stretc
forward

c. Leg spread and body bend
forward

c. Leg spread and body bend
left and right

11. Stomach and leg exercises

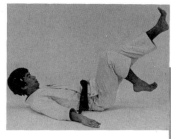

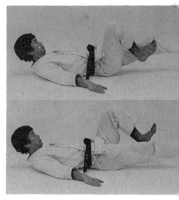

a. Kick up with ball of foot

b. Kick forward with heel of foot

10. Sitting position exercises

a. Loosen: leg, knee, angle, toe, arm, elbow, wrist and finger

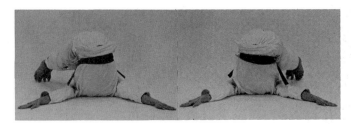

b. Body bend and leg stretch
   backward: left, right and center

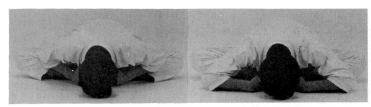

d. Body bend from lotus position with feet facing each other

c. Leg spread and body bend
   left and right with twist

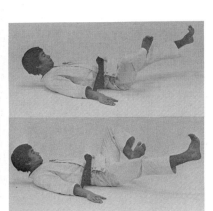

d. Lift both legs to 45°, then open, close and cross

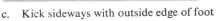

c. Kick sideways with outside edge of foot

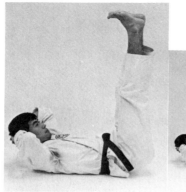

e.   Leg raise to 90° and down

12.   Push ups (hand spread)

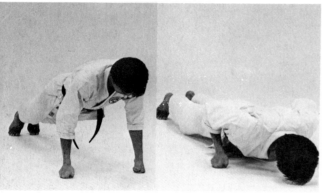

b.   Row boat push ups (rotating push up)
     on finger tips

a.   Push ups (hand spread)
     on fists

15.   Kicking exercises

16.   Deep breathing exercises

a.   Forward

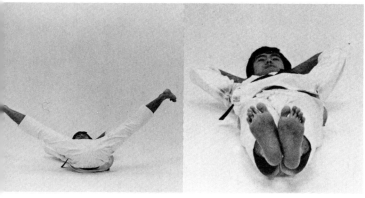

f.   Circle outward and inward

g.   'Jack knife'

b.   Row boat push ups (rotating push up)
     on palms

13.   Calves exercise
14.   Knee bends: 'squat'

b.   Feet together

a.   Feet apart

b.   Backward

c.   Sideways
d.   Leg raise to the side (spread up)

b. *Seiri Undo*: Supplementary Exercises

These exercises are to be completed after every practice. They are intended to relax the body and mind and to steady the breathing and heartbeat. They help the body to return to a normal state and to recover gradually from the weariness of the training. Incomplete combustion of glucose remains in the muscles, slowing then down and giving a feeling of heaviness. The supplementary exercises are intended to burn lactic acid by stimulating the blood circulation and carrying more oxygen to the muscles. Thus, these exercises are to be done slowly with a particular emphasis on breathing. They are also followed by a period of meditation to relax the mind and gradually bring it back to its normal state.

Supplementary exercises should take from 3 to 5 minutes for an hour of training and from 5 to 10 minutes for a two-hour practice. They can be performed alone but are more beneficial when performed with a partner.

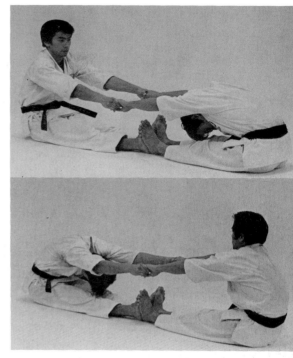

c. *Hojo Undo*: Complementary Exercises

These exercises serve to develop a good overall conditioning of the body, essential in karatedo, and to strengthen the specific muscles used in karatedo techniques. They also serve the purposes of improving less-utilized muscles and gaining endurance. Thus, some of the complementary exercises are of a general nature aimed at improving the performance of every muscle, while others are more specifically related to karatedo training. These exercises may be done with or without equipment almost anywhere and anytime. They must be practiced regularly and a program should be established, preferably with one's instructor or coach, to reflect the needs and goals of the individual. Other sports such as skiing, tennis, soccer, and so forth can also be practiced as complementary exercises.

In this section only the most necessary exercises will be described.

1—Running. This is the basic exercise of all sports and the best way to develop endurance, determination, and breathing. It gives speed and a sense of rhythm. It corrects the posture of the body, develops the muscles of the legs, increases mental concentration, and provides an excellent massage of the internal organs. Running should last from 30 to 60 minutes each session in the following sequence.

First jog a steady pace. Then run a succession of short dashes and slow to an ordinary run for a while. Then while still running, do some shadow boxing exercises and body motions such as *neko ashi, okuri ashi* and *yoko tobi*.

2—Rope skipping. This exercise, widely used for boxing, develops the legs and strong internal muscles. It is practiced alternately on each leg and then on both.

3—Duck walk. This is another exercise for developing the legs. Walk on your toes with heels up, body straight, and hands behind your back, alternately forward, backward, and zig zag.

4—Squats. This is a leg exercise. Squat on both feet or alternately on each foot, keeping the other one stretched in front of your body. Feet should be kept shoulder width apart. This exercise can also be performed with a partner on your back or with weights respectively.

5—Sit ups. They develop abdominal muscles. Laying down on the ground, feet together and hands behind your head, bend to touch your knees with your forehead keeping your legs stretched, then return to your starting position. It is best to have your feet held on the ground by your partner.

6—Push ups. They develop the chest, arms, and shoulders. They should be practiced alternately on two arms then on one, and on your fists, fingers, and palms. Hands are usually shoulder width apart before going down.

7—Rub-outs (row boats). These are similar to push ups but are performed with a motion from back to front (or front to back) when going down, "rubbing" the ground with your forehead and chest.

A number of other complementary exercises should also be performed. These include weight lifting to develop strength and gain weight; opening and closing the hands several hundred times, with or without a rubber ball, to develop the grip and the forearms; and also the use of equipment such as the *makiwara*, sand bags, speed balls, and iron clogs, which are described in the next chapter.

All these exercises should be practiced ten times at first, increasing their number progressively. Deep breathing should accompany every exercise. Relax your body shortly before and after hard exercise. While performing the exercises, understand which part of the body is being used and for what purpose. Finally, do not overexercise; harmonize the condition of your body with your program of training in karatedo.

d. *Mokuso*: Meditation

Meditation is to the mind what the physical exercises are to the body. It develops a strong mental attitude by bringing peace and serenity to the mind, allowing it to harmonize itself with the surrounding universe. Meditation is a reflection on oneself, in order to perceive oneself and the outside world intuitively by completely emptying the mind of any thought. In a state of total relaxation and utmost concentration, the mind can suddenly free itself from physical disturbances such as fear, hate, and pain, and can become an enormous force liberated at will. There are many examples of the manifestation of this force even in daily life. The materialization of this force is seldom achieved consciously. In karatedo the purpose of practice is to consciously liberate this mental force.

Meditation has beneficial effects on the whole organism. It has been scientifically demonstrated that meditation reduces the level of stress, as indicated by the decrease in oxygen consumption. The blood lactate diminishes substantially and blood pressure is decreased, resulting in a reduction of the work load of the heart, and the nervous system shows a greater stability.

Meditation is always thought of as a passive act. *Zazen*, the sitting meditation, and *ritsuzen*, the standing meditation, are both performed in a state of complete immobility. But the practice of kata, kumite, or shiai is also a meditation, an advanced form called active Zen. Meditation should at first be performed in its passive form. Later, as the student progresses, he will discover the meaning of active Zen.

To meditate in *zazen*, sit down in the *anza* position, legs open and crossed in front of you. Straighten your back and put your shoulders down, pushing your stomach forward with correct centripetal pressure. Put your hands on your knees, arms stretched and fingers lightly closed (you may also clasp your hands together). Keep your eyes and mouth closed but without force. Concentrate your breathing in the *tanden*, inhaling from the nose and fully lifting your diaphragm at each inhalation, while slightly tensing your abdominal muscles. Exhale from a slightly open mouth. The rhythm of respiration should be natural and there should always be a retention of breath after the inhalation process. This is an important phase of the respiration cycle, as the organism is full of fresh air and oxygen is carried to the muscular tissue. The mind should be fully concentrated on breathing and especially at this point when the fusion of the mind and body should be total.

Do not attempt to drive out the thoughts coming across your mind, as it would only distract you even more, but concentrate on your respiration, seeing yourself whole, without concentrating on any one part. Meditation precedes and follows every regular karatedo practice, but for a limited period of time. One should meditate by oneself everyday for half an hour, preferably in the early morning when the air is fresh.

chapter **4** **Practice of Karatedo**

Some knowledge of human anatomy is necessary to properly understand how the muscles, bones, and nerves of the body are all brought into play in the execution of karatedo techniques and how they determine the vulnerable points of the body at which these techniques are aimed. The human body has more than 200 bones connected by ligaments covered by muscles. Bones support the body and protect most of the internal organs, while muscles set the body and protect most of the internal organs, while muscles set the bones into motion very schematically. When a stimulus is received, it is transmitted by sensory nerves to the cerebrum which in turn excites the proper muscles through motor nerves. The contraction and or extension of the muscles create the relative displacement of the bones. The power, flexibility, and endurance of the muscles used in karatedo techniques should be developed to increase their efficacy.

1. *Kyusho:* Striking Points

The *kyusho* are the weak points of the human body which, when struck with a powerful enough blow, will either result in acute pain, loss of consciousness, or even death. The distinction between vital points, those which can actually cause death, and non-vital points is not an easy one. Blows to some points can lead to death if the person is not reanimated within a certain amount of time. In this section only the points for which no reanimation techniques (*katsu*) can be successful have been classified as vital points.

Vulnerable and vital points are points usually left unprotected by the bone structure, nerves emerging from the edge of the muscles, or the point of articulation of two bones. The main *kyusho* will be described together with the most common natural weapons used to attack them and the resulting effects.

Front side of the body

1. *Tento* (top of the head): located at the suture of the frontal and parietal bones.
    —Causes extreme pain and loss of consciousness or death by damage to the sensory and motor nerves and concussion of the cerebrum.
    —Attacked mainly by *shuto* and *kentsui*.
2. *Miken* (pineal gland): located at the juncture of the brow ridges and frontal bone.
    —Causes trauma to the cerebrum and furthermore, severe damage to the cranial nerves and motor reflexes, loss of eyesight, loss of consciousness, and possibly death.
    —Attacked mainly by *shuto* and *naka daka ken*.
3. *Bito* (bridge of the nose).
    —Causes damage to the cranial nerves, extreme pain, abundant tears and bleeding, and loss of consciousness.
    —Attacked mainly by *seiken, shotei, kentsui, nekoze ken, hirate,* and *haishu*.
4. *Bisen* (base of the nose): located at the base of the nose between the eyes.
    —Causes severe trauma to the cerebrum leading to cranial nerve damage. Also causes loss of eyesight, disruption of sensory and motor functions, and loss of consciousness.
    —Attacked mainly by *shuto* and *naka daka ken*.
5. *Kasumi* (temples): located at the suture of the temporal and frontal bones.
    —Causes disruption of the nervous system, concussion of the cerebrum accompanied by loss of nervous coordination (loss of balance), loss of eyesight, and loss of consciousness.
    —Attacked mainly by *seiken, shuto, kentsui, nekoze ken,* and *koken*.
6. *Gankyu* (eyeballs):
    a) eye socket (upper and lower circum or vital region):
    —Causes loss of eyesight and trauma to the nervous system, and loss of consciousness resulting from loss of nervous control.
    b) eyeballs:
    —Causes loss of eyesight and loss of consciousness produced by severe trauma to the cerebrum, resulting in disruption of the cranial nerves and loss of the sensory and motor functions.
    —Attacked mainly by *ippon ken, nihon nukite,* and *naka daka ken*.
7. *Jinchu* (upper lip): located at the juncture of the jaw bones.
    —Causes damage to the cranial nerves, damage to the teeth along with abundant bleeding, and occasionally loss of consciousness due to concussion.
    —Attacked mainly by *seiken, shuto, kentsui, nekoze ken,* and *koken*.
8. *Kagaku* (lower part of the jaw): located at the point of the chin.
9. *Mikazuki* (mandible, base of the lower jaw): located at the edge of the jaw, below and in front of the ears.
    —Damages to both areas causes dislocation or fracture of the jaw, loss of nervous coordination, and frequently,

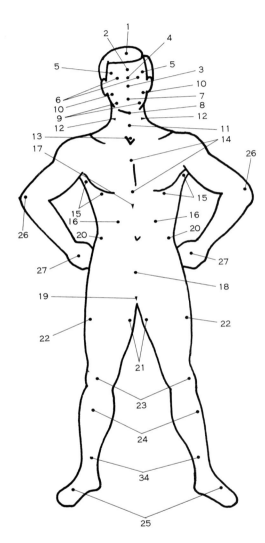

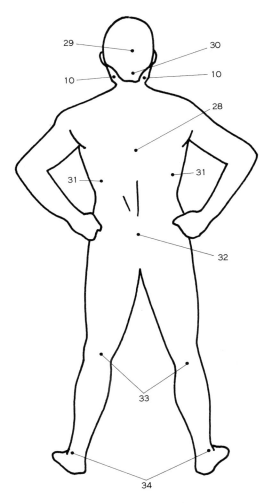

loss of sensory and motor functions. Also causes loss of consciousness due to disruptive trauma of the cranial nerves, or more seriously, due to concussion.

—Attacked by *seiken, kentsui, nekoze ken,* and *keri.*

10. *Ryo jikou kabotoke* (mastoid): cavity below the ears.
   —Causes damage to the eardrum and sometimes loss of hearing. Also causes damage to the motor function and loss of nervous coordination (loss of balance and direction).
   —Attacked mainly by *nukite, shuto,* and *ippon ken.*

11. *Nodo botoke* (Adam's apple)
   —Causes damage to the windpipe, disruption of the respiratory function, and occasionally, loss of consciousness and/or death due to suffocation.
   —Attacked mainly by *shuto, handa ken, nukite, nekoze ken,* and *koken.*

12. *Keido myakubu* or *matsukaze* (jugular vein area or carotid artery): located on both sides of the neck.
   —Causes trauma to the vagus nerve and loss of sensory and motor functions leading to shock. Frequently causes loss of consciousness and death due to severe trauma of the blood circulation of the brain. It is one of the most vital points of the human body.
   —Attacked mainly by *shuto, nekoze ken, koken,* and *sokuto.*

13. *Hichu* (neck's notch): located at the base of the neck, above the sternum.
   —Causes damage to the windpipe and trauma to the carotid artery leading to loss of consciousness and eventually death by suffocation.
   —Attacked mainly by *nukite* and *ippon ken.*

14. *Kyokotsu* (sternum) includes *kyosen* (xiphoid process) and *tanchu* (sternal angle):
   —Shock to the chest musculature causes collapse, contraction (cramping), and loss of consciousness due to trauma of the lungs (bronchus). Damage to the pulmonary artery and the heart laed to respiratory system malfunction and shock.
   —Attacked mainly by *seiken, shuto, shotei, kentsui,* and *keri.*

15. *Ganka* (rib cage region below the nipples) including *kyoei* (just below the armpit cavities): located between the 5th and 6th ribs on each side of the chest.
   —Causes severe disruption of the respiratory function. Damage to internal organs, lungs, and associated nerves may result from broken ribs and on the left side can lead to death by concussion of the heart.
   —Attacked mainly by *seiken, kentsui, shuto, shotei, empi* and *keri.*

16. *Rokkotsu* or *denko* (rib cage area): located between the 7th and 8th ribs.
   —Causes internal injury to the lungs, and trauma to the liver resulting in a loss of the nervous function between the liver and lungs on the right side, and to the spleen and stomach on the left with effects on the lungs and heart possibly caused by loss of the nervous functions associated with these organs. Direct damage by broken

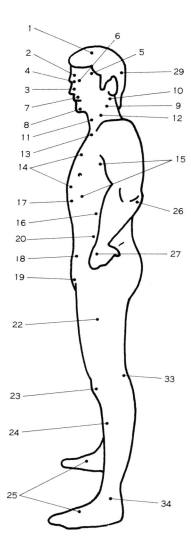

ribs may also result.

—Attacked mainly by *seiken, kentsui, shuto empi,* and *keri.*

17. *Mizo ochi* or *suigetsu* (solar plexus): concavity located just below the sternum.

—Primarily causes loss of the respiratory function, disruption of all nervous function, and trauma both to the liver and stomach. Severe damage will lead to death.

—It is commonly attacked by most hand and foot techniques.

18. *Kafuku bu* (lower abdomen, *tanden*): located just below the navel.

—Causes trauma to the small intestine and bladder which in turn affects the stomach artery blood vessels, and nerves in the abdomen leading to loss of the motor function and shock, thus, inability to maintain body strength.

—Attacked mainly by *tsuki, keri,* and *uchi waza.*

19. *Kinteki* (testicles)

—Causes trauma to the nerves and arteries in the groin resulting in the loss of sensory and motor functions. The testicles are pushed up and disruption of the respiratory function occurs, leading to unconsciousness and sometimes death.

—Attacked mainly by keri, *nekoze ken, shuto,* and *kentsui.*

20. *Inazuma* (side of the stomach): located between the 11th and 12th floating ribs.

—Causes damage to internal organs (spleen on the left side and liver on the right side) and disruption of the respiratory function, leading to loss of consciousness. Effects are similar to those when a blow is thrown to the *rokkotsu* or *denko* area.

—Attacked mainly by *keri, tsuki, uchi,* and *ate.*

21. *Yako* (inguinal region): located between the thigh and the lower abdomen including the inner region of the upper thigh and part of the musculature of the pubic bone.

—Causes trauma to the motor nerves of the leg along with numbness of the leg accompanied by unusual pain in the abdomen and back. May also cause severance of the femoral artery.

—Attacked mainly by *keri, tsuki, uchi,* and *ate.*

22. *Fushito* (outside thigh): located halfway up the external side of the thigh.

—Causes trauma to the muscles and motor nerves of the leg and thus acute lasting pain spreading to the abdomen with a possibility of loss of consciousness.

—Attacked mainly by *keri.*

23. *Shitsu to* (knee cap): located on the front part of the knee.

—Causes damage to the knee cap and knee joint and trauma to the motor nerves of the leg. The usual result is disorder to the motion of the knee joint.

—Attacked mainly by *keri, sokuto,* and *ka sokutei.*

24. *Keikotsu* or *kokei* (tibia): located on the edge of the leg bone.

—Causes acute trauma and pain to leg nerves along with loss of strength in the leg. Damage is sometimes severe enough to cause hemorrhaging from the nose with possible shock, leading to loss of consciousness.

—Attacked mainly by *keri*.
5. *Sokko* (instep): the medial portion of the top of the foot.
   —Causes trauma to the nerves of the leg which is transmitted through the entire nervous system causing unusual pain in the leg, hip, and abdomen. Also causes loss of the motor function.
   —Attacked mainly by *keri, empi*, and *seiken*.
6. *Hijitsume* (elbow):
   —Causes trauma to the motor nerves of the arm leading to acute pain, numbness of the arm, and sometimes loss of consciousness.
   —Attacked mainly by *seiken, shuto, empi*, and *nekoze ken*.
7. *Haisu* (back of the hand): located on the the back of the hand between the forefinger and the middle finger.
   —Causes trauma to the motor nerves of the hand followed by a momentary paralysis of the hand.
   —Attacked mainly by *uraken, nekoze ken, kentsui*, and *naka daka ken*.

Back side of the body

8. *Kassatsu* (spine): located between the 5th and 6th vertebrae.
   —Causes rupture of the spine, also disruption of the respiratory function and concussion to the entire spinal cord leading to cerebral trauma, loss of the motor and sensory functions, and death.
   —Attacked mainly by *seiken, shuto, kentsui, nekoze ken, empi*, and *keri*.
9. *Kotobu* (back of the head): located at the suture of the cranial bones.
   —Causes acute cerebral trauma, loss of memory, tears, nose hemorrhage, and numbness of the entire body sometimes causing severe brain damage and paralysis or death.
   —Attacked mainly by *seiken, hirate, uraken, shuto, kentsui*, and *nekoze ken*.

30. *Keichu* (back of the neck): located between the 3rd and 4th vertebrae.
    —Causes trauma to the cerebrum and cranial nerves and concussion to the spinal cord sometimes producing paralysis of the upper part of the body and then loss of consciousness. If the spinal column is ruptured, death is imminent.
    —Attacked mainly by *shuto, seiken, kentsui, empi*, and *keri*.
31. *Ushiro rokkotsu* or *ushiro denko* (kidneys): located below the floating ribs (lumbar region of the back).
    —Causes concussion of the kidneys and in turn trauma to associated nerves and blood vessels leading to disruption of the respiratory function, shock, loss of the motor function, and unconsciousness.
    —Attacked mainly by *seiken, shuto, empi*, and *keri*.
32. *Kibi* (spine tip): located at the lower extremity of the spine.
    —Causes acute pain, loss of consciousness due to concussion of the entire spinal column and thus trauma to the cerebrum, and loss of the sensory and motor functions.
    —Attacked mainly by *keri* and *empi*.
33. *Hiza kubomi* (back side of the knee).
    —Causes acute trauma to the sensory and motor nerves of the leg, usually accompanied by a collapse of the knee joint. In cases of severe concussion, damage to the joint and the tibial artery may result.
    —Attacked mainly by *nekoze ken* and *keri*.
34. *Kuru bushi* (ankle): located below the ankle bone on the inside and outside of the foot.
    —Causes acute trauma to the tibial artery leading to a numbness of the leg and, in some cases, a peculiar type of pain in the hip as far reaching as to be felt in the head and possibly leading to a loss of the motor function (loss of consciousness).
    —Attacked mainly by *seiken, shuto*, and *keri*.

2. Natural Weapons

In karatedo, almost every part of the body can be turned into a weapon, differing in this respect with most other martial or fighting arts. Usually, the edge of the bones, which are the most resistant, are systematically strengthened to be used both as offensive and defensive weapons. There are about forty natural weapons in the human body, classified into three broad categories:

Arm weapons:
—Hands: fingers, knuckles, palm, wrist, (backside, inside and outside edges).
—Forearms: inside and outside edges (cubitus and radius).
—Elbows.
Leg weapons:
—Feet: toes, ball of the foot, heel, sole, instep, and outside edge.
—Knees.
Head weapons:
—Forehead (frontal bone).
—Side of the parietal bone.
—Chin.

Hips and shoulders are also sometimes used (hip bone and acromion). The teeth, nails, facial expressions, yelling, and spitting can also, to a certain extent, be considered weapons. For parts of the body to be used as effective weapons not only should the skin be hardened, but also the corresponding joints should be strengthened and used with a proper body movement and mental attitude.

Natural weapons will be described with some of the corresponding striking points.

Arm weapons:

Seiken (or *Genko*): Closed Hands

To form the fist, fold the second and third phalanx of your four fingers either together or one by one, starting from the index finger. Then clench them into your palm, locking them firmly with your thumb* on the second phalanx of your index and second fingers. Squeeze them in to tighten your wrist putting your power in the tips of your fingers. On impact, clench your fist with all your strength, putting all your body and mind into it.

*Until Master Jigoro Kano visited Okinawa in 1927 at the Shodokan Martial Art Exhibition, judo and jujitsu members used to tuck their thumb under the fingers (to protect it in close fighting), but this technique of forming the fist has since been abandoned, giving much more power to the punch.

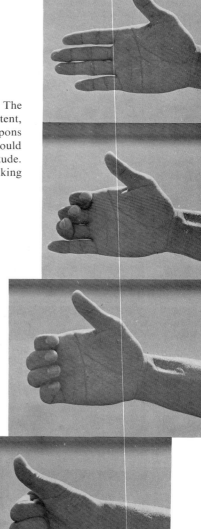

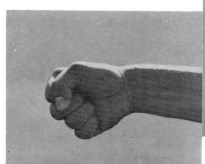

Tate ken: Vertical fist

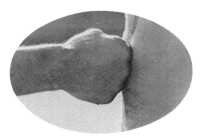

This is the fundamental fist form used in karatedo. It is a natural position for both the wrist and the elbow joint, and thus allows the use of more power without damage to the joints.

When the fist is thrown horizontally, as in *gyaku ken* and *yoko ken*, the arm joint is locked** and is far less resistant to shock. The reach of the arm is also reduced. In *tate ken*, the fist is perpendicualr to the ground, thumb up with the wrist, elbow, and shoulder in a straight line to transmit all of the power originating from the body. Contact is made on three points: the first and second knuckles of the forefinger, and the first knuckle of the second finger.

Tate ken is used mainly to attack the face, temples, solar plexus, and ribs in any direction, but mostly in frontal attacks.

**In the execution of an armlock, for example, the arm must be twisted to weaken it before applying pressure to the joint; in this position the arm cannot resist the pressure.

Gyaku ken: Reverse fist

In *gyaku ken*, the fingers are facing up and the elbow is bent. This is similar to the position of the fist in an uppercut. The contact area is the same as that for *tate ken*. *Gyaku ken* is used in close fighting to attack mainly the solar plexus, ribs, and chin in an upward motion.

Yoko ken: Horizontal fist

Yoko ken used to be the main fist utilized in karate. However, in this position with the fingers facing down, the wrist is more vulnerable to damage and thus it is used only in snapping motions to attack mainly the face, ribs, and solar plexus in frontal and circular attacks. The contact area is the same as that for *tate ken*.

Ura ken: **Back fist**

Contact is made with the back side of the fist, using the knuckles of the forefinger and second finger.

Ura ken is used for close fighting, with a snapping motion of the arm, to laterally attack the temples and nose.

Kentsui: **Hammer fist**

Contact is made with the inside edge of the fist only, and not with the little finger. It is used for sideways and circular attacks to the top of the head, the temples, face, solar plexus, ribs, groin, and the joints.

Soto kentsui: **Outside hammer fist**

Contact is made with the outside edge of the fist. Same uses as for *kentsui.*

Handa ken: **Four-finger knuckles**

Bend the first and second phalanx (joints) of your four fingers. Contact is made with the knuckles of the third phalanx. The thumb must be tightened against the forefinger; keep your wrist straight.

Handa ken is used in direct attacks to the temples, eyes, nose, throat, solar plexus, ribs, and kidneys.

Ippon ken: Forefinger knuckle

Bend the first and second phalanx of your forefinger, thumb tightened against it with the other fingers clenched. *Ippon ken* is used in snapping motions to attack the solar plexus, eyes, jaw, and the neck's notch.

Naka daka ken: Middle finger knuckle

Bend the first and second phalanx of your middle finger, the other fingers being clenched as in *tate ken*. It is used to attack, in snapping motions, the face (pineal gland and eyes), neck, and back side of the hand.

Nekoze ken: Back of the wrist (Cat-back)

Bend the wrist downward, hand loose; join the tips of your fingers together. Contact is made on the upper part of the wrist. *Nekoze ken* is used in almost any direction to attack the temples, face, throat, jugular vein, solar plexus, groin, ribs, and spine, etc. It is also used for blocking.

Kaishu (or *Kaite*): **Opend Hand**

Shuto (or *tegatana*): **Knife hand (Karate chop)**

Straighten your fingers and bend your thumb, pressing it on the outside edge of the hand. Contact is made with the inside edge of the hand only and not the little finger. At the moment of impact the little finger, third finger, and middle finger can be slightly bent to tighten the external muscle. The hand must hit the target with approximately a 30° angle. *Shuto* is one of the most basic natural weapons, and is used in any direction to attack almost any point, as well as being used to block and deflect.

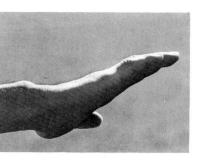

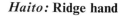

Haito: **Ridge hand**

Contact is made with the outside edge of the hand by bending the thumb and pressing it against the index finger. The little finger, third finger, and middle finger are slightly bent as in *shuto*. *Haite* is used in straight and circular attacks mainly to the nose, throat, jugular vein, or temple.

Nukite: Spear hand

In *yonhon nukite*, the tips of the forefinger, middle finger, and third finger are used. These fingers must be straightened but the middle finger is usually slightly bent. The hand is either vertical, or horizontal with the palm down. In *nihon nukite*, only the forefinger and middle finger are used.

The thumb is bent and pressed against the outside edge of the hand. *Nukite* is used in direct frontal attacks, mainly to the throat, eyes, solar plexus, and ribs.

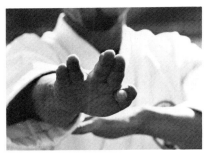

Shotei: Heel of the palm

The first and the second phalanx of the fingers must be bent. Contact is made with the heel of the palm, wrist bent upward. *Shotei* is used in direct frontal attacks to the nose, chin, solar plexus, ribs, and also to block.

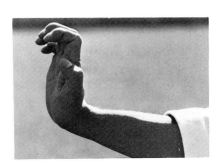

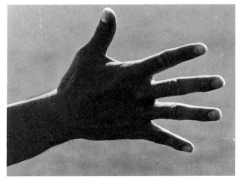

Haishu: **Back of the hand**

The back side of the hand is used with the fingers stretched, joined together, or open in circular motions to attack the nose, ears, or temples.

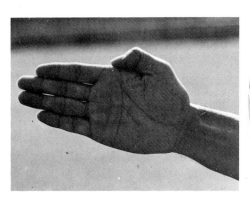

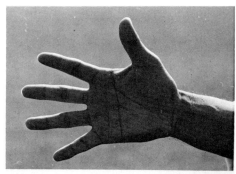

Hirate: **Open hand**

In *hirate*, the frontside of the hand is used in much the same way as *haishu* and also for sweeping blocks.

Other Arm Weapons

Empi: Elbow (Monkey elbow)

The head or the edge of the radius is used either in hitting or striking techniques in three directions: downward, upward, and sideways. The elbow must be bent and the fist closed tightly and kept close to the body. Attacks are directed mainly at the solar plexus, ribs, heart, kidneys, chin, and limbs. *Empi* is also used for blocking.

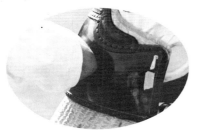

Kote: Forearm

The inside and outside edge of the forearm (cubitus and radius) are sometimes used to attack the neck, arms, and legs, but mainly in blocking, deflecting, and sweeping techniques.

Leg Weapons

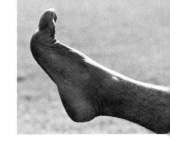

Jo sokutei: Ball of the foot

Bend the toes upward to use the ball of the foot in direct or circular attacks to the solar plexus, ribs, groin, shins, kidneys, and face.

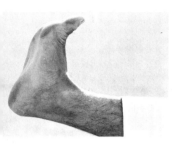

Ka sokutei: Heel of the foot

Bend the ankle upward to use the heel in direct attacks either forward or backward, or in circular attacks to the solar plexus, groin, kidneys, shins, and instep of the foot; also to the face (chin).

Ushiro kakato: Back side of the heel

The back side of the heel is used in direct attacks either backward in circular attacks to the throat, jugular vein, solar plexus, groin, shins, ribs, and kidneys. The ankle must be bent upward.

Sokuto: Edge of the foot

The lower part of the outside edge of the foot is used, bending the ankle forward. The foot must also be bent sideways to form a 30° angle with the target as in *shuto. Sokuto* is used in frontal or lateral attacks, both forward and backward, to the throat, face, ribs, solar plexus, kidneys, knees and shins.

Sokko: Instep of the foot

The toes and ankle must be kept straight and tightened. Contact is made with the instep. Attacks are either direct or circular to the groin, ribs, solar plexus, kidneys, back of the knee, and face.

60 · PRACTICE OF KARATEDO

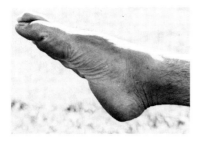

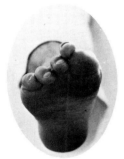

Head Weapon

Hitai: **Forehead**

The frontal bone between hair and eyebrows is used to attack mainly the nose or solar plexus. The neck must be tightened, the chin tucked into the neck and teeth firmly clenched together.

Ryokado: **Back side of the head**

Contact is made with the parietal bones or any side of the head. The neck must be tightened with the mouth half open. Attacks are directed to the nose, temples, and jaws.

Ago: **Chin**

The lower part of the chin is used in close fighting situations for snapping attacks to the jugular vein, solar plexus, stomach, and ribs. The neck must be tightened with the teeth clenched together.

Tsuma saki: **Spear-foot**

The extremity of the first toe is used with the ankle stretched; thrusts are delivered to the solar plexus, ribs, shins, throat, and face.

Sokutei: **Sole of the foot**

The toes are tightened upward with the ankle stretched. Contact is made with the sole of the foot in sweeping motions aimed at the ankles, knees, elbows, wrists, solar plexus, kidneys, and face.

Hiza: **Knee**

Contact is made either with the knee cap, the upper part of the knee, or the inside of the knee. Direct or circular attacks are aimed at the groin, solar plexus, ribs, kidneys, thighs, and insteps; also to the face and jaw.

Other Weapons

Kata: **Shoulder**

The outside edge of the shoulder is used in close fighting to attack the chest, jaw, or solar plexus. The neck must be tightened with the elbow pressed against the body, tightening the armpit in.

Koshi: **Hip**

The back side of the hips is used in snapping motions to attack the groin. The crestiliac bone is also sometimes used (*Ryoyoko*).

3. *Tachi Kata* and *Kamae:* Postures and Stances

Tachi kata

Body and foot positions are of prime importance in karatedo to build correct and effective basic techniques. The legs support the body and participate in the execution of any technique. The body must be at the same time steady and able to move quickly and at once, thus the spreading of the feet should insure an adequate distribution of weight on each leg to allow for a quick shifting of the center of gravity by using the spring of the toes, ankles, knees, and the rotation of the hips.

The body must be kept straight with the spine in a vertical position between the head and hips. The head and center of gravity should also be on a vertical line falling in the center of the parallelogram formed by the feet.

The chest should be open with the shoulders pulled backward and falling naturally to liberate the diaphragm and facilitate the breathing.

The stomach should be kept centered between the hips, with the abdominal muscles slightly tensed and pushing downward to lower the center of gravity. Breathing should originate from the stomach and should be held there during the execution of a technique to transmit the power of the hips to the arms or legs.

The face should be relaxed, with the eyes open naturally and the mouth closed but not contracted. The tongue should touch the upper palate to facilitate the secretion of saliva and keep the throat from drying. The muscles of the neck should be relaxed. The inner energy, *ki*, should be located mainly in the center of gravity about one inch below the navel but also in the top of the head and in the diaphragm. Breathing, the source of *ki*, should be deep, smooth, and come from the stomach and diaphragm, not the upper part of the chest.

Musubi dachi: Attention stance

This stance is used mainly before any action, usually before and after the salutation. The body is in 'full face front' posture (body straight forward or parallel to the front), heels together, toes pointing 45° to the outside, hands extended on the thighs, and the chest out. The *tanden* must be tensed with *ki*.

Heisoku dachi: **Feet-together stance**

This is a variation of *musubi dachi* but the feet are parallel.

Shizen hontai dachi: **Natural stance**

This is a very basic and flexible stance used in many situations. The body faces forward, and the feet are parallel at one shoulder width with the knees slightly bent, the weight resting on the balls of the feet and the heels raised slightly off the ground.

Heiko dachi: **Parallel-foot stance**

A variation of *shizen hontai* but usually lateral standing sideways with the feet parallel.

Uchimata jigo hontai dachi: **Defensive closed-leg stance (feet and knees inward)**

This is a very strong and steady position and is one of the most fundamental fighting stances. The feet are spread apart at shoulder width, the weight resting equally on both feet. The knees are bent at approximately 45°. The toes and knees are tightened inward and the heels are raised slightly off the ground.

Sanchin dachi: Defensive closed-leg stance

This is a variation of *uchimata jigo hontai dachi* but in 'half-face front' posture (body diagonal to the front).

Naihanchin dachi: Horseman stance

This stance is used in sideways fighting only. The body faces sideways with the feet apart at a little more than one shoulder width. The knees and toes can be pointing either inward, outward, or be parallel. When parallel, the stance is similar to *kiba dachi* used in many other styles of karate.

Zenkutsu dachi: Forward stance

In this stance, the feet are spread apart at one-and-a-half shoulder's width longitudinally and at one shoulder width transversally. About 60% of the weight rests on the front leg which is largely bent forward while 40% rests on the back leg which is extended, and sometimes slightly bent. The knees and toes of both legs are pointing inward. The shoulders and hips should be parallel, in 'full face front' posture.

Sotobiraki jigo hontai dachi: **Defensive open-leg stance (feet and knees outward)**

This stance is very defensive and is used mainly for sideways fighting. The feet are spread apart one shoulder width, with the knees bent at about 30° and turned outward. The toes are pointing largely outside with the weight resting equally on each leg, with the feet are flat on the ground.

Kokutsu dachi: **Backward stance**

In this stance 60% of the weight rests on the back leg which is bent at 45° with the toes pointing outward. The front leg supports 40% of the weight and is extended with the knee slightly bent. The toes of this foot are pointed inward. The shoulders and hips are in 'full face front' posture. The distance between the feet is the same as in *zenkutsu dachi*.

Neko ashi dachi: **Cat stance**

This is the most fundamental stance in Kenkokan Karatedo as it allows great mobility and good balance. About 70% of the weight of the body rests on the back leg which is slightly bent with toes pointed 45° outward. The other 30% of the weight is on the ball of the front foot as the heel is raised off the ground. The shoulders and hips are in 'half face front' posture, body diagonal to the front. The distance between the feet is one shoulder width, both longitudinally and transversally, and the hips are pulled backward.

Ushiro neko ashi dachi: **Backward cat stance**

This is a unique stance used to complement *neko ashi dachi*. The body weight is 70% on the front leg which is slightly bent, foot flat on the ground, while 30% rests on the ball of the back foot, the heel being raised off the ground.

Kosa dachi: **Crossed-leg stance**

This stance is used only for short periods of time (to execute *yoko geri* or to move sideways) because it is not very steady. The legs are crossed and the feet spread at shoulder width with the knees one into the other. The weight is equally distributed on both legs.

Shiko dachi: **Sumo stance**

This stance is very steady, but does not allow good mobility. The feet are spread at one-and-a-half shoulder's width, with the toes and knees pointed largely outward. The hips are pulled backward but the body is kept straight.

Kata hiza dachi: **One-knee stance**

This stance is similar to the *zenkutsu* stance but the knee of the back leg rests on the ground. It is used mainly for ground fighting or to recover after having lost one's balance.

Sagi ashi dachi: **One-leg stance**

This stance is used to 'fake' the opponent or to wait for his attack. The supporting leg should be bent and the instep of the other foot placed behind the knee of the supporting leg. A variation consists of placing the sole of the foot on the other knee.

Stances can be held either in 'full-face front' (facing directly forward to the front [*shomen*]), in half-face front' (body diagonal to the front [*hanmi*]). Posture with shoulders and hips at a 45° angle to the front or side way with shoulders and hips perpendicular to the front.

The opponents can engage each other in frontal encounters *seitai*; in 'half-face front' (or diagonal encounters) of opposite stance (opposite foot forward) *kaitai*; or 'half-face front' in the same stance *dotai*.

Kamae

Kamae is really the fighting stance (posture) which encompasses the physical stance (*yuko no kamae*), to be presented here, and as well the mental attitude and preparation for fighting (*muko no kamae*), to be described in Chapter 6.

While *tachi kata* is mainly concerned with the general posture of the body, *kamae kata* includes the position of the hands, or guard. The various guards described below can be used with any of the stances described above, however, the most usual ones are noted. All of the guards can also be performed with open or closed hands or with a combination of both.

Jodan kamae: Upper level guard

The front hand should be in front of your face, pointed at your opponent's eyes, looking deep into them, and dissimulating your own eyes. The back hand should be in front of your solar plexus or on your hips. Both armpits should be closed tightly. This guard is used to protect your face, especially against taller opponents, mainly in conjunction with *shizen hontai dachi, neko ashi dachi,* or *sagi ashi dachi.*

Chudan kamae: Middle level guard

The front hand is at shoulder level pointed at the opponent's throat. The back hand is in front of the solar plexus or on the hips. This is the most common guard and is used in conjunction with *neko ashi dachi,* and *uchimata* and *sotobiraki jigotai dachi.*

Gedan kamae: Lower level guard

The front hand is stretched downward in front of the groin with the back hand in front of the solar plexus. This is a very aggressive guard used mainly in conjunction with *zenkutsu* and *kokutsu dachi.*

Hasso kamae: Versatile guard

The front hand is bent horizontally in front of the stomach with the back hand behind the head. This is a versatile guard which is most often used when switching guards.

4. *Tai Sabaki* and *Ashi Sabaki:* Body and Foot Movements

Body and foot movements are the necessary links between the stances and the techniques. From a stance which by definition is static, to the technique which is extended dynamically, *tai sabaki* and *ashi sabaki* serve the purpose of moving safely and quickly close enough to the target and of acquiring some supplementary momentum to execute the technique. *Tai sabaki* and *ashi sabaki* are also used to withdraw after completion of the technique or in avoiding a technique. There are eight main directions of movement: north (front), south (back), east (right), west (left), northeast (right front corner), northwest (left front corner), southeast (right back corner), and southwest (left back corner).

Basic stances and guards are also suggested for proper execution of the motions.

Hoko: Walking

Natural walking is often used in karatedo but differs from usual walking in that the weight of the body is shifted from one foot to the other as smoothly as possible, sliding the ball of the foot on the ground and rhythmically swinging the hands, keeping the body straight.

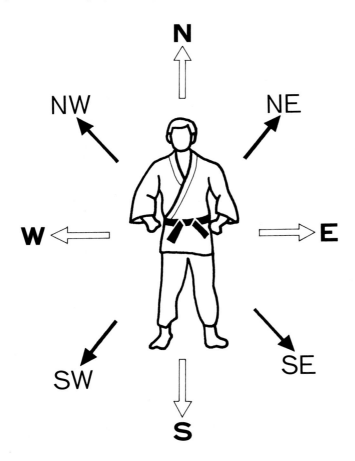

Sanchin hoko: **Crescent step**

This is a basic fighting body movement.
Basic stance: left *uchimata jigotai dachi*
Basic guard: *seiken chudan kamae*
Execution: 1—Twist both feet outward in the *soto biraki jigotai* stance.
 2—Slide your right foot close to the left and then forward in a continuous motion, finishing in a right *soto biraki jigotai* stance.
 3—Twist both feet inward in the *uchimata jigotai* stance.
Remarks: —Steps should be one shoulder width.
 —Keep knees in to protect your groin in step 2.
 —When moving forward execute *soto uke* simultaneously with the front hand (outward block).
 —When moving backward execute *uchi uke* simultaneously with the front hand (inward block).
 —Practice this movement in sand or in a swimming pool.

*See Section 5 on defensive arm techniques.

Hangetsu hoko: **Half-moon step**

This movement is similar to *sanchin hoko* except that the steps are wider and the distance between the feet is one-and-a-half shoulder's width.

Neko ashi hoko: Cat step

This is the most versatile body and foot movement. It is performed either forward, backward, in a zigzag motion, or in close succession.

Zenshin (neko ashi): Forward step
Basic stance: right *neko ashi*
Basic guard: *shuto chudan kamae*

Execution: 1—Lower your body and push your hips backward, pointing your toes upward.
 2—Spring off of your right leg, throwing your left foot and hips forward.
 3—Stand on the balls of your feet, the distance between them being one shoulder width, in the left *ushiro neko ashi dachi* stance (with your weight on the right leg).

Zigzag step
Perform as in the forward and backward step but diagonally, always keeping the same stance, right or left.

Close succession
This is used to close the gap with the opponent and at the same time gather additional momentum to execute a technique. Execute first a short *neko ashi* followed by a longer one in the same stance. This can be performed either forward, backward, or in a zigzag motion.

Remarks: To fully use the spring of the ankles and knees, the body should be lowered and then thrown forward, thus the center of gravity describes a curved trajectory which should remain as low as possible.

Kotai: Backward step
Basic stance: right *ushiro neko ashi dachi*
Basic guard: *shuto chudan kamae*
Execution: 1—Push hips forward.
 2—Spring backward with your right foot, throwing your left foot and hips backward and swinging your left hand in the direction of the move.
 3—Stand on the balls of your feet in the left *neko ashi dachi* stance.

Mawari ashi: Turning step

Mawari ashi can be performed in five different ways:
—*migi mae mawari ashi:* moving to the right, in front of the supporting leg.
—*hidari mae mawari ashi:* moving to the left, in front of the supporting leg.
—*migi ushiro mawari ashi:* moving to the right, behind the supporting leg.
—*hidari ushiro mawari ashi:* moving to the left, behind the supporting leg.
—*sonoba mawari ashi:* switching direction without moving the feet.

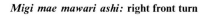

Migi mae mawari ashi: right front turn

Basic stance: *uchimata jigo hontai*
Basic guard: left *seiken chudan kamae*
Execution: 1—Slide your left leg to the right in front of your right leg, bending your knees with your body straight.
2—Put your left foot on the ground, the distance between your feet being one shoulder width, your body still in 'full face front' posture.
3—Rotate 180° to your right on the balls of your feet while executing *morote chudan soto uke.*
Remarks: —After completion you must be facing south (back).
—The rotation can also be executed on the heels of the feet but does not provide as much control of body balance as on the balls of the feet.

Sonoba mawari ashi

Basic stance: left *neko ashi dachi*
Basic guard: *shuto chudan kamae*
Execution: Rotate 180° to your right on the balls of your feet. After completion you are facing south in the right *neko ashi dachi.*

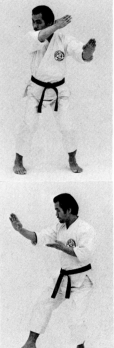

Migi ushiro mawari ashi: right back turn

Differs from *migi mae mawari ashi* in that the left leg slides behind the right leg and the rotation is to the left instead of the right. Execute *morote gedan soto uke* during the rotation.

Hidari ushiro mawari ashi: left back turn
Same as above, but your right foot slides behind the left and the rotation is 180° to your right. Execute *morote gedan soto uke* also.

Hidari mae mawari ashi: left front turn
Same as above, but move to the left with your right foot and rotate 180° to your left.

Okuri ashi: Sliding step

Okuri ashi is performed in a straight line to move either forward or backward.
Basic stance: left *soto biraki jigotai*
Basic guard: *seiken gedan kamae*
Execution (forward): Slide your right foot in a straight line until it reaches the left foot. At this moment, quickly slide your left foot forward, again in a straight line.
Remarks: The distance between the feet after completion must be one shoulder width. *Okuri ashi* is used to get close to an opponent by dissimulating the move of the back leg, and then suddenly jumping forward to deliver a technique.
Execution (backward): Pull your left foot back until it almost touches the right. Then quickly slide your right foot backward.
Remarks: There is some danger of being attacked when the feet are close together. Therefore, *okuri ashi* must be executed rapidly.

Fumikomi ashi: Stamping step

While in *okuri ashi* the body is propelled by the rear leg (back leg moves forward and front leg moves backward), in *fumikomi ashi* it is the front leg which is used to pull the body forward and the rear leg which is used to move backward.
Basic stance: left *kokutsu dachi*
Basic guard: *hasso kamae*
Execution (forward): 1—Bend your knees with your body straight and hips pulled backward.
2—Jump forward with your left foot, stamping the ground and bringing your right foot one shoulder width behind the left.
Execution (backward): 1—Bend your knees with your body straight and hips pushed forward.
2—Jump backward with your right foot stamping on the ground, bringing your left foot one shoulder width in front of the right.
Remarks: —The stamping foot must be flat on the ground. The steps taken with *okuri ashi* are narrower than with *neko ashi*.

Oi ashi: Lunging step (rear leg stepping in forward)

Basic stance: left *zenkutsu dachi*
Basic guard: *seiken jodan kamae*
Execution (forward): 1—Bend your knees slightly and push your hips backward.
    2—Step forward with the right leg, sliding it on the ground and keeping your knees in as you close your legs.
    3—Finish the motion in the right *zenkutsu dachi*.
Execution (backward): 1—Bend your knees slightly and bring your hips forward.
    2—Step backward with your right leg, sliding it on the ground and keeping your knees in as you close your legs.
    3—Finish the motion as you are in the left *zenkutsu dachi*.
Remarks: —The foot must slide on the ground but not exactly in a straight line, as it must be brought close enough to the supporting leg to protect your groin as you step.
    —In some cases the knee of the sliding foot can be raised to hips level as you step in.

Kosa ashi: Crossed-leg step

Basic stance: left *shiko dachi*
Basic guard: *chudan juji kamae* (middle cross-arm position)
Execution (forward): 1—Cross your right leg behind the left, bending your knees, but keeping them together. The feet should be apart one shoulder width.
    2—Bring your left foot forward in the left *shiko dachi*.
Execution (backward): 1–Cross your left leg in front of the right, bending your knees but keeping them together. The distance between the feet should be one shoulder width.
    2—Bring your right foot backward in the left *shiko dachi*.

Hiraki ashi: Open-leg step

Basic stance: left *heiko dachi*
Basic guard: *shuto jodan kamae* (upper knife hand position)
Execution (forward): 1—Step in to the NE corner (right front
corner) with your right foot.

2—Bring your left foot behind the right in the right
heiko dachi, pivoting on the ball of your right
foot.

Execution (backward): 1—Step back to the SW corner (left
back corner) with your left foot.

2—Bring your right foot behind the left in the left
heiko dachi, pivoting on the ball of your left foot.

Da ashi: Snake-crawling step

Basic stance: *uchimata* (or *sotobiraki*) *jigotai*
Basic guard: *shuto chudan kamae* (middle knife hand position)
Execution: 1—Pivot on the ball of the foot and then on the
heel, either one foot at a time, or sometimes
on both feet.
Remarks: —*Da ashi* is used to adjust your distance in close
fighting without upsetting your balance.
—Swing your hips as you pivot on your feet.
—Usually, motion starts from the rear leg, then
the forward leg.

5. *Joshi Waza:* Arm Techniques

All basic arm techniques can be classified as follows:

Kogeki waza: Offensive techniques

a) *Tsuki waza:* Punching techniques
1—*Shomen zuki:* Front punch
2—*Okuri zuki:* Straight punch
3—*Hineri zuki:* Twist punch
4—*Oi zuki:* Lunge punch
5—*Sokumen zuki:* Side punch
6—*Mawashi zuki:* Roundhouse punch
7—*Kagi zuki:* Hook punch
8—*Age zuki*: Uppercut punch
9—*Morote zuki:* Two-fisted punch

b) *Uchi waza:* Striking techniques
1—*Shuto uchi:* Knife-hand strike
2—*Uraken uchi:* Back-fist strike
3—*Kentsui uchi:* Hammer-fist strike
4—*Haito-uchi:* Ridge-hand strike
5—*Nekozeken uchi:* Cat-back strike (back hand wrist strike)
6—*Hirate uchi:* Open-hand strike
7—*Haishu uchi:* Back-hand strike
8—*Shotei uchi:* Palm-heel strike
9—*Empi uchi:* Elbow strike

c) *Ate waza:* Hitting technique
Empi ate: Elbow hit

d) *Sashi waza:* Stabbing technique
Nukite: Spear-hand thrust

Bogyo waza: Defensive techniques

a) *Uke waza:* Blocking techniques (deflection)
1—*Ude uke:* Forearm block
2—*Shuto uke:* Knife-hand block
3—*Nekozeken uke:* Cat-back block
4—*Morote uke:* Two-handed block
5—*Empi uke:* Elbow block

b) *Harai waza:* Sweeping techniques
1—*Gedan barai:* Leg sweep (downward block)
2—*Nagashi uke:* Sweeping block
3—*Sukui uke:* Scooping block

c) *Tome waza:* Stopping techniques
1—*Shotei uke:* Palm-heel stop
2—*Juji uke:* Cross block
3—*Seiken uke:* Punching block

d) *Tori waza:* Holding techniques
1—*Ude tori:* Elbow hook
2—*Tekubi tori:* Wrist hold
3—*Ashi tori:* Leg hold
4—*Eri tori:* Collar grappling
5—*Sode tori:* Sleeve grappling
6—*Morote tori:* Two-handed grappling

Tsuki waza are the techniques in which the fist, *seiken* (vertical fist), is used as a weapon in direct attacks to either *jodan, chudan,* or *gedan.* Other weapons such as *ippon ken, naka daka ken, handa ken, gyaku ken,* and *yoko ken* can also be used in the same way as *seiken.*

In *uchi waza,* the *shuto, shotei, kentsui, uraken, hirate, haishu, nekoze ken,* and *empi* are used to strike with circular motions of the arm. Strikes are also directed at the *jodan, chudan,* or *gedan* levels of the opponent.

In *ate waza,* the *empi* is used to hit with a direct motion of the elbow, using the body momentum. Attacks are mainly directed to *chudan* or *gedan.*

In *sashi waza,* the *nukite* is used to stab in direct attacks to *jodan* and *chudan.* The use of the body differs slightly, however, from *tsuki waza.*

Uke waza are the techniques where direct and hard contact is made to block an opponent's attack, mainly with *ude* (inside and outside edges of the forearm), *shuto,* and *nekoze ken,* but also with *seiken* and *empi.*

In *harai waza,* the attack is deflected with a sweeping motion, rather than blocked, using *ude, shuto,* or *hirate.*

In *tome waza,* the attack is stopped, preferably at the moment it is launched, using *shotei, shuto, hirate, haito,* or *nekoze ken.*

Tori waza are the holding or grappling techniques usually used after a blocking technique.

Stances, guards, and motions used in the description of the techniques are the most appropriate for their executions. This should not, however, preclude the utilization of other postures or moves.

Tsuki waza: Punching techniques

Shomen zuki: Front punch

Only the most basic form of *shomen zuki* will be described:

Basic stance: *uchimata jigo hontai dachi* (defensive closed-leg stance; knees, feet inward)

Basic guard: fists on the sides of the chest, fingers upward.

Execution: —Inhale deeply through the nose and hold your breath in the *tanden* (abdomen).

—Throw the right fist in a vertical position on a straight line from the shoulder, closing your armpits.

—At the same time, rotate your body 90° to the left on the ball of your right foot (the right ankle, hips, shoulders, and head must all twist together), pulling your left fist to your left hip and bending your right knee 45°.

—Pull your right fist back and return to your starting position, pivoting your body 90° to the right.

—Exhale from the mouth.

—Assume *zanshin*, the state of readiness that follows the execution of every technique.

Remarks: —In executing the punch, the whole body is used. The right ankle, hips, shoulders, and head must all rotate to the left in a single motion.

—The rotation of the body also serves the purpose of protecting the three most vital points of the body: the groin is protected by the right leg; the solar plexus by the rotation of the body; and the jugular vein by the right arm.

—The right arm and shoulders should be on a straight line, perpendicular to the target.

—The withdrawal of the fist and the body should be executed as fast as the punch itself.

Okuri zuki: **Straight punch**

Basic stance: left *sotobiraki jigo tai dachi* (defensive open leg stance; feet, knees outward)

Basic guard: *seiken chudan kamae*

Execution: —Inhale through the nose and hold your breath in the *tanden.*

—Move forward with a left *okuri ashi*, pulling your left fist to the side of your left hip and extending your right hand forward in a winding up motion.

—Throw your left fist forward in a straight motion, twisting hips and shoulders 90° to your right and bending your left knee inward. At the same time, pull your right fist back to the side of your right hip.

—Bring your left fist back and return to your starting position with a left backward *okuri ashi.*

—Exhale from the mouth and assume *zanshin.*

Remarks: —The left arm and shoulders should be on a straight line perpendicular to the target.

Hineri zuki: **Twist punch**

Basic stance: either left *uchimata jigotai dachi* (left defensive closed-leg stance) or left *kokutsu dachi* (left backward stance)

Basic guard: *shuto chudan kamae*

Execution:
—Inhale through the nose and hold your breath in the *tanden*.
—Step forward with your left foot using *fumikomi ashi*.
—Bring your right fist to the hip.
—Then throw it in a straight line, twisting your right foot, hips, shoulders, and head 90° to your left and pulling your left hand to your left hip.
—Pull your right fist back and return to your starting position with *fumikomi ashi*.
—Exhale from the mouth and assume *zanshin*.

Remarks:
—Beginners should keep the heel of their right foot on the ground. For more advanced students, the heel can be raised and stamped on the ground for more power at the time of impact.
—The right arm and shoulders should be on a straight line, perpendicular to the target.

Oi zuki: **Lunge punch**

Basic stance: left *zenkutsu dachi*
Basic guard: *seiken jodan kamae*
Execution: —Inhale through the nose and hold your breath in the *tanden*.
  —Move forward with *oi ashi*.
  —At the same time the right foot stamps on the ground, throw your right fist in a straight line, twisting your hips and shoulders 90° to the left and pulling your left fist to your hip, in the right *zenkutsu dachi*.
  —Bring your right fist back and return to your starting position with a backward *oi ashi*.
  —Exhale from the mouth and assume *zanshin*.
Remarks: —The punch is executed in the right *zenkutsu dachi*.
  —The right arm and shoulders should be on a straight line perpendicular to the target.

Sokumen zuki: **Side punch**

Basic stance: left *neko ashi dachi*
Basic guard: *seiken chudan kamae*
Execution: —Inhale through the nose and hold your breath in
              the *tanden.*
            —Move forward with a left *neko ashi.*
            —Throw your left fist in a straight line, twisting
              your left foot, hips, shoulders, and head 90°
              to your right while pulling back your right arm.
            —Pull your left fist back and return to your start-
              ing position with a left backward *neko ashi.*
            —Exhale from the mouth and assume *zanshin.*
Remarks: —The left arm and shoulders should be on a
            straight line perpendicular to the target.

Mawashi zuki: **Roundhouse punch**

Basic stance: left *heiko dachi*
Basic guard: *seiken chudan kamae*
Execution: —Inhale through the nose and hold your breath in the *tanden.*
—Move to the SE corner (right back corner) with the right foot and bring your left foot behind with *hiraki ashi.*
—Immediately execute a right *sokumen zuki.*
—Bring your right fist back, exhale from the mouth, and assume *zanshin.*
Remarks: —*Hiraki ashi* and *sokumen zuki* must be executed in a single flowing motion without interruption.

Kagi zuki: **Hook punch**

Basic stance: left *uchimata jigotai dachi*
Basic guard: both fists on hips
Execution: —Inhale through the nose and hold your breath in
              the *tanden.*
              —Move your right foot forward with *sanchin hoko.*
              —Rotate your hips, shoulders, and left foot 45° to
              your right and deliver a punch with your left
              arm, elbow bent at 90° and kept 'tight' close
              to the body.
              —Twist your body back, pulling back your fist.
              —Exhale from the mouth and assume *zanshin.*
Remarks: —This punch can be delivered either with the left
              fist, as described, or with the right fist by twist-
              ing hips, shoulders, and right foot 45° to the left.

Age zuki: **Uppercut punch**

Basic stance: left *uchimata jigo tai dachi*
Basic guard: *seiken jodan kamae*
Execution: —Inhale through the nose and hold your breath in
the *tanden.*
 —Step forward with your left foot, using *fumikomi
ashi*, and bring your right fist to the hips.
 —Then throw it upward, elbow bent at 90°, pulling
your left fist to your hips and twisting your
body to the left.
 —Bring your right fist back and return to your
starting position with *fumikomi ashi*.
 —Exhale from the mouth and assume *zanshin*.
Remarks: —After *fumikomi ashi*, a left uppercut punch could
also be used. In this case the body should be
twisted to the right and the right fist pulled to
the hips.

Morote zuki: **Two-fisted punch**

Basic stance: left *neko ashi dachi*
Basic guard: both fists on hips
Execution: —Inhale through the nose and hold your breath in the *tanden.*
  —Move forward with a left *neko ashi.*
  —Shift your position to a left *zenkustu dachi* and punch with both fists in a vertical position.
  —Pull your fists back and return to your starting position with *neko ashi.*
  —Exhale from the mouth assume *zanshin.*
Remarks: —In *morote awase zuki,* both fists are side by side while in *morote nidan zuki,* the left fist is aimed at the upper level and the right fist at the middle or lower level.

In all punching techniques, as in all basic techniques, the whole body should be used in large and powerful motions. The momentum gathered should then be concentrated at the moment of impact on the target.

All the mental and physical power should be transferred to the fist and particularly to the tips of the forefinger, middle finger, and thumb. After completion of the technique, the fist should then be pulled back with the same speed and energy as it was thrown. The five following points are of the utmost importance in the execution of a punching technique:

1—Before execution, inhale deeply through the nose, then hold your breath in the *tanden* and exhale from the mouth after completion.

2—Use the whole body; the feet, hips, shoulders, and head should rotate all at once.

3—Always protect your three most vital points, the groin, solar plexus, and jugular vein, by the rotation of your body, your arms, and your feet.

4—Keep the arm used for punching near your body, tightly closing both armpits.

5—Keep your fist straight, tightening your wrist and putting power in the tips of the forefinger, middle finger, and thumb when punching, and in the tips of the fourth finger, little finger, and thumb when pulling back.

Uchi waza: Striking techniques

Shuto uchi (or tegatana): Knife-hand strike

Basic stance : left *neko ashi dachi*
Basic guard : hands open on hips, palms upward

a. *Yoko mawashi uchi*: Side roundhouse strike

Execution: —Inhale through the nose and hold your breath in the *tanden*.

—Move forward with a left *neko ashi*, at same time bringing your open right hand to your right ear, twisting your shoulders to the left, and extending your left hand, palm down, in front of your body.

—Then twist your right foot, hips, shoulders, and head 90° to your left, your right hand describing a circular motion on a horizontal plane to strike the target in front of your left foot. At the same time pull your left hand to your left hip and bend your knees to protect your three main vital points.

—Pull your right hand back, twisting your body to the right and return to your starting position with *neko ashi*.

—Exhale from the mouth and assume *zanshin*.

b. *Gyaku uchi:* **Reverse strike**

Execution: —Inhale through the nose and hold your breath in the *tanden*. From a left cat stance with your hands on your hips, palms upward:

—Cross your right leg behind the left simultaneously pulling your open left hand to your right ear, palm down, in a winding up motion.

—Step forward with your left foot into a left *zenkutsu* stance, simultaneously rotating your right foot, hips, and shoulders 90° outward and pulling your right hand to your hip. Strike with your left hand in a horizontal plane from your right ear to a forward focal point.

—Pull your left hand back and return to your starting position.

—Exhale from the mouth and assume *zanshin*.

c. *Uchi oroshi:* **Downward strike**

Execution: —Inhale through the nose and hold your breath in the *tanden.*

—Step forward with your right foot, using *oi ashi.* At the same time, wind up your right hand above and behind your head.

—Execute a strike with your right hand from the upper right to the lower left, ending the motion in a right *zenkutsu dachi.*

—Exhale from the mouth and assume zanshin.

d. *Morote uchi:* **Two-fisted strike**

Execution: —The motion is the same as in *gyaku uchi.* The right hand simultaneously executes *yoko mawashi uchi.*

Remarks: —In *morote awase uchi* both hands are joined together while in *morote nidan uchi* the left hand strikes at *jodan* and the right hand at *chudan.*
—In *morote hasami uchi* both hands simultaneously execute *yoko mawashi uchi.*

Uraken uchi: **Back-fist strike**

Uraken uchi is used with the same motion as *shuto uchi*. The wrist should be used with a snapping motion of the whole arm.

Kentsui uchi: **Hammer-fist strike**
(also called *tettsui uchi*)

The motion is the same as in *shuto uchi*. In *uchi kentsui uchi*, the
inside edge of the fist is used with the power being concentrated
in the little finger, third finger, and thumb. In *soto kentsui uchi*,
the outside edge of the fist is used with the power concentrated
in the forefinger, middle finger, and thumb.

Haito uchi: Ridge-hand strike

The motion is the same as in *gyaku uchi*. The snapping motion of the arm is used, tightening the hand on impact. *Haito uchi* can also be used as *yoko mawashi uchi*.

Nekozeken uchi: Cat-back strike

The motion is the same as in *shuto uchi*. The arm must be snapped, tightening the wrist on impact. *Nekozeken uchi* is used in almost any direction. For origin, see blocking techniques.

Hirate uchi: Open-hand strike

The motion is the same as in *gyaku uchi* or *yoko mawashi uchi*.
It is used mainly for attacks to the upper part of the body.

Haishu uchi: Backhand strike

The motion is the same as in *gyaku uchi*.

Shotei uchi: **Heel of the palm strike**

The motion is similar to *tsuki waza*, the heel of the palm being used as the fist.

Empi uchi: **Elbow strike**

The elbow is used either in circular, upward, or downward motions. The fist must be tightened and kept close to the body. The motion is otherwise similar to *shuto uchi*.

a. *Yoko mawashi uchi:* **Side roundhouse strike**
The elbow describes an inward circular motion, the forearm being parallel to the ground.

b. *Uchi age* : **Upward strike**
The elbow is raised with the fist close to the ear.

c. *Uchi oroshi:* **Downward strike**
The back of the hand should face forward.

Ate waza: Hitting techniques

Empi ate: Elbow hit

This technique is similar to *empi uchi*. The elbow is tightened before impact and the body momentum is transmitted by a direct hit of the elbow on the target, either sideways (*yoko empi ate*), or downward (*ushiro ate*). Power should be concentrated in the little finger, third finger, and thumb.

Sashi waza: Stabbing techniques

Nukite: Spear-hand thrust

The fingers and wrist must be tightened and kept straight, power being concentrated in the tips of the forefinger, middle finger, and third finger. It is used with a motion similar to *tsuki waza*, particularly *okuri zuki*, *hineri zuki*, *oi zuki*, and *morote zuki*. The hand is either vertical, or horizontal with the palm down.

Bogyo waza: Defensive techniques

Defensive techniques consist of blocking, sweeping, stopping, and holding techniques. It should be kept in mind that defensive techniques do not allow one to win. Therefore they should be used only in certain circumstances and must always be followed by a counter-technique. The general principle underlying the application of defensive techniques is to make use of the opponent's attack, turning it against himself. Hard and soft techniques must be used alternately. For example, a hard attack should be answered by a soft blocking technique, preferably a sweeping technique to absorb or deflect the momentum generated by the attack, and followed with a hard counter-technique.

In the execution of defensive techniques, the opponent's arms and legs should be considered dangerous weapons which cannot be touched. Therefore hard contact should be avoided as much as possible. Escaping, dodging with body motions, sweeping, or stopping techniques should be used rather than blocking.

Defensive techniques are best executed in *uchimata jigotai dachi* or *neko ashi dachi* because of the stability and mobility of these stances. Defensive techniques will be described with *shizen hontai* as initial stances.

a. *Uke waza:* Blocking techniques

Blocking techniques should be used only in certain circumstances when there is not enough time or space to avoid the attack or sometimes against a much stronger opponent. However, preventing the opponent's attack and hitting him before he attacks should be the ultimate goal in the practice of karatedo.

Ude uke (or *kote uke*)*:* Forearm block

Blocks are executed at the upper or middle level (*jodan* or *chudan*).

Soto ude uke: Outward forearm block
Execution: —Inhale through the nose and hold your breath in the *tanden.*
  —Execute a left backward *neko ashi* to the SE corner (right back corner), bringing your left fist to your right ear (or under the right armpit) in a winding up motion, and assume a left *uchimata jigotai dachi.*
  —Throw your left fist in the NW direction with outward motion, twisting your body, right foot, hips, and shoulder in this direction and pulling your right fist to your right hip. Your knees should be tightened inward. Block with the edge of the radius, tightening your fist and wrist and concentrating your power in the forefinger, middle finger, and thumb.
  —Assume *zanshin,* ready to counterattack, then exhale from the mouth.

Uchi ude uke: **Inward forearm block**

Execution: —Inhale through the nose and hold your breath in the *tanden*.

—Move your right foot to the SW corner with *hiraki ashi* and adopt a left *sotobiraki jigotai* stance. At the same time, bring your left fist to your left ear, elbow up at shoulder level, in a winding up motion.

—Throw your left fist with an inward motion in the NE direction. Block with the edge of the ulna, concentrating your power in the little finger, third finger, and thumb. Your body should be twisted in this direction, both knees tightened inward.

—Assume *zanshin*, ready to counterattack, then exhale from the mouth.

Remarks: —In *soto uke* and *uchi uke*, the fist of the arm used for blocking should be one shoulder width from the body either at shoulder level (*chudan*), or at eye level (*jodan*).

Age uke: **Upward block**

Execution: —Inhale through the nose and hold your breath in the *tanden*.

—Step forward with your left foot in a left *zenkutsu dachi.*

—At the same time, raise your left fist about 7 inches above and in front of your forehead, twisting your forearm, thumb down, to block with the inside of the forearm (palm or muscle).

—Pull your right fist to your right hip. The shoulders should be parallel to the line of attack and

the elbow must be tightened and pushed outward. Power should be concentrated in the little finger and third finger of the left fist.

—Step backward with a left *neko ashi*, assume *zanshin*, ready to counterattack, then exhale from the mouth.

Remarks: —*Age uke* can also be executed stepping backward to the SE corner. In this case, the angle between the arm and forearm should be wider to deflect the attack.

Shuto uke: **Knife-hand block**

Soto shuto uke: **Outward knife-hand block**

Execution: —Inhale through the nose and hold your breath in
                   the *tanden*.
                —Execute a left backward *neko ashi* to the SE
                   corner and adopt a left *neko ashi dachi*, bringing
                   your left hand to your right ear.
                —Execute a 45° downward strike to block with a
                   shuto above your left foot, pulling your right
                   hand back under your right armpit.
                —Pull your left hand back and assume *zanshin*,
                   ready to counterattack, then exhale from the
                   mouth.

Uchi shuto uke: **Inward knife-hand block**

The execution of this technique is similar to *uchi ude uke*, using
the inside edge of the hand instead of the forearm. It is best
performed with *neko ashi* rather than *hiraki ashi*.

Morote uke: **Two-fisted block**

Morote awase uke: **Clasped-hands block**

Execution: —Inhale through the nose and hold your breath in
                   the *tanden*.
                —Step forward with your left foot in a *zenkutsu
                   dachi*.
                —Execute *uchi ude uke* with your left arm, sup-
                   porting it with your right arm, your right fist
                   pressing on the middle of your left forearm.
                —Step backward with *oi ashi* and assume *zanshin*,
                   ready to counterattack, then exhale from the
                   mouth.

Remarks: —This technique can also be executed by pressing
                   your right fist and wrist against your left fist
                   and wrist (*morote soe uke*).

Nidan uke: **Two-level block**

Execution: —Inhale through the nose and hold your breath in
                   the *tanden*.
                —Move your right leg to the SE corner using
                   sanchin hoko, and adopt a left *uchimata jigotai
                   dachi*.
                —Execute *jodan soto uke* with your left arm and
                   soto gedan barai with the right.
                —Assume *zanshin* then exhale from the mouth.

Nekozeken uke: Cat-back block
(back hand wrist block)

Nekozeken uke is a technique unique to Kenkokan Karatedo. It was developed by Master Anko Asato and tested against sword attacks. It is performed with the same motion as *shuto uke*, contact being made with the back of the wrist.

Haishu uke: **back hand block**

Empi uke: Elbow block

Empi soto uke: Outward elbow block

Execution: —Inhale through the nose and hold your breath in the *tanden*.
—Execute a left backward *neko ashi* to the SE corner and adopt a left *neko ashi dachi*, bringing your left fist to your right ear.
—Execute a block with your left elbow, hitting in the NW direction with the elbow bent, and pulling your right fist under your right armpit.
—Assume *zanshin*, ready to counterattack, then exhale from the mouth.

Empi uchi uke: Inward elbow block

Execution: —Inhale through the nose and hold your breath in the *tanden*.
—Bring your right leg to the SW corner using *hiraki ashi*, and adopt a left *uchimata jigotai dachi*.
—With your left fist on the side of the left hip, twist your body rapidly to the right, blocking with your left elbow and pulling your right fist backward.
—Assume *zanshin*, ready to counterattack, then exhale from the mouth.

b. *Harai waza:* Sweeping techniques

Because a kick is perhaps three times as powerful as a punch, it is better to use sweeping techniques instead of blocking techniques against a leg attack. In effect, a block is the deflection of a force whereas a sweep is the moving with the force to re-direct it. It also has the advantage of upsetting the opponent's balance.

Gedan barai: Downward sweep (Leg sweep)

Soto gedan barai: Outside downward sweep

Note: Proper breathing in the execution of every technique has been emphasized a great deal. The reader is reminded of the fundamental importance of breathing and its constant consideration.

Execution: —Inhale through the nose and hold your breath in the *tanden.*

—Move your right foot to the SE corner using *hangetsu hoko,* and adopt a left *zenkutsu dachi* (or *hangetsu dachi*), bringing your left fist to your right ear in a winding up motion.

—Sweep with your left arm in a 45° downward motion, twisting your body to the left and pulling your right fist to your right hip.

—Contact is made with the inside of the hand or the forearm (ulna) in front of and above your left knee.

Uchi gedan barai: Inside downward sweep

Execution: —Move your right leg to the SW corner with *hiraki ashi.*

—Sweep with your left arm in a 45° downward motion in *zenkutsu dachi* (or *sotobiraki dachi*), twisting your body to the right and pulling your right fist to your right hip.

—Contact is made with the forearm (radius) or with the outside edge of the hand in front of and above your left knee.

—Assume *zanshin,* ready to counterattack then exhale from the mouth.

Nagashi uke: Sweeping block

Nagashi uke is usually performed at the upper level (*jodan*).

Execution: —Inhale through the nose and hold your breath in the *tanden.*

—Move your right foot to the SW corner using *hiraki ashi.*

—In the left *zenkutsu dachi,* sweep with your left hand in front of your face from the left side to your right ear, twisting your body to the right and pulling your right hand to your right hip.

—Contact is made with *hirate,* and sometimes *shuto* or *ude.*

—Assume *zanshin,* ready to counterattack then exhale from the mouth.

Sukui uke: Scooping block

Sukui uke is similar to *uchi gedan barai* but contact is made with *hirate* or the palmar muscles of the left arm, the palm facing up. In this case the left arm first describes an inward circular motion going 45° downward and then moves upward to sweep the opponent's leg.

Soto sukui uke is used less than *soto gedan barai*. The two motions are similar, but here again the left arm is pulled up after contact has been made with the inside of the forearm, palm facing down.

c. *Tome waza:* Stopping techniques

Shotei uke: Palm-heel stop

Shotei otoshi uke: Downward palm stop
Execution: —Inhale through the nose and hold your breath in the *tanden*.
  —Move your right leg to the SW corner with *hiraki ashi*, bringing your left hand to your left ear.
  —In the *soto biraki jigotai dachi*, bring your left hand down with an downward motion to stop the opponent's leg with the heel of the palm (*shotei*), twisting your body to the right and tightening your knees inward.
  —The right hand must be pulled to the right hip.
  —Assume *zanshin*, ready to counterattack, and then exhale from the mouth.

Shotei age uke: Upward palm stop
Execution: —Inhale through the nose and hold your breath in the *tanden*.
  —Move your right leg to the SW corner using *hiraki ashi*, and extend your left arm 45° sideways.
  —Adopting a left *neko ashi dachi*, bring your left hand in an upward circular motion in front of your shoulders or face, using *shotei* to stop the attack with a snapping motion of the wrist.

Shotei uchi uke: Inward palm stop
Execution: —Inhale through the nose and hold your breath in the *tanden*.
  —Step forward with your left foot using *oi ashi*.
  —Use your palm in an inward circular motion to stop the attack with a snap of the wrist.
  —Assume *zanshin* and exhale from the mouth.

Shotei morote uke: Two palm stop
Execution: —Inhale through the nose and hold your breath in the *tanden*.
  —Step backward with your right leg, using *neko ashi* or *hiraki ashi*, and bring your hands in front of your shoulders, elbows out.
  —In a left *neko ashi dachi*, bring both hands down in an outward circular motion stopping the attack with the heel of the palm. Put your hands together below your groin, keeping your arms, shoulders, and elbows in.

Juji uke: Cross block

Juji age uke: Upward cross block

Execution: —Inhale through the nose and hold your breath in the *tanden*.

—Move your right foot to the SE corner using *hangetsu hoko*.

—In a left *zenkutsu dachi*, cross your right hand behind the left 45° above and in front of your forehead, tightening your wrist and forearms, with the elbow bent slightly outward to absorb the shock of the attack. The hands can be opened or closed. (Contact is made with the forearms.)

—Then bring both hands 45° down on your right or left side, or each side respectively depending upon the opponent's, stance by doing so redirecting the line of attack, throwing his balance off, and preparing for a counterattacking position.

—Assume *zanshin* and exhale from the mouth.

Juji otoshi uke: **Downward cross block**

Execution:
—Inhale through the nose and hold your breath in the *tanden*.

—Move backward with a left *neko ashi* and bring your open hands to the sides of your chest.

—Close your hands and cross them in a 45° downward motion in front of your groin (left arm above the right), twisting your fists inward and concentrating your power in the little fingers, third fingers, and thumbs. Contact is made with the forearms.

—Then bring your fists to either side of your body as done in the follow-through to the upward cross block, for the same reasons.

—Assume *zanshin* and exhale from the mouth.

Seiken uke: **Punching block**

Morote seiken juji uke: **Punching cross block**

This motion is mimilar to *juji otoshi uke* but while the left forearm executes a block, the right fist comes over it to deliver a punch to the shin of the attacking leg.

Morote seiken awase otoshi uke: **Two-fist punching downward block**

Execution:
—Inhale through the nose and hold your breath in the *tanden*.

—Move your right foot to the SW corner using *hiraki ashi*, bringing both fists in front of your face.

—In the *soto biraki jigotai dachi*, punch downward with both fists.

—Assume *zanshin* and exhale from the mouth.

Tori waza: Holding techniques

These techniques are only illustrated.

6. *Kashi Waza:* Leg Techniques

The reader is reminded from the chapter relating to the history of karatedo how, from sumo, and this original form of unarmed combat (stressing the use of the arms and upper body) evolved *chikara kurabe* which included kicking techniques of a rather high order, as testified to by one of the earliest recorded fights in the history of Japan; that of *Nomi no Sukune* and *Tagima no Kehaya* where the former succeeded in killing his opponent by utilizing the great power of his leg techniques.

In premodern times, as trends shifted towards the use of weapons and their efficiency increased, legs became used less as instruments of combat. And, as weaponry improved, so developed armor which further restricted this aspect of fighting. As well, the traditional samurai ankle-length costume and wooden footwear, were in keeping with the attitudes of chivalry which stated that the use of the legs as fighting weapons was not honorable. Therefore his very garb did not permit him efficient use of the legs even in the most serious of situations.

Leg techniques are of prime importance in modern karatedo, particularly stressed in Kenkokan Karatedo, and it is said; "To master arm techniques takes perhaps three years, and to master leg techniques, more than six years."

The reason why leg techniques are highly stressed in Kenkokan Karatedo are fundamentally as follows: firstly, because of the great power advantage of the legs, three times that of the arms; secondly, in the development of the legs the entire body is used, which greatly improves the general condition of the body externally and internally, therefore not only improving the over-all technique, but also developing the 'athletic make-up' of the individual together with his health to a far higher degree than in the singular concentrated development of the upper body.

One can summarize by saying that in the growing of a complete tree, it is necessary to first develop a strong 'root' structure so as to ascertain the permanently strong growth of the entire tree.

Leg techniques can be classified in the same way as arm techniques, as follows:

Kogeki waza: **Offensive techniques**

a) *Keri waza:* Kicking techniques
b) *Harai waza:* Sweeping techniques
c) *Kari waza:* Reaping techniques
d) *Fumi waza:* Stamping techniques

Bogyo waza: **Defensive techniques**

a) *Uke waza:* Blocking techniques
b) *Harai waza:* Sweeping techniques
c) *Tome waza:* Stopping techniques
d) *Kawashi waza:* Withdrawing techniques

Most of the basic leg techniques are *keri waza*, kicking techniques where the foot is used in direct or circular attacks. In general, *jodan* is attacked with snap kicks (*keage*), *chudan* with thrust kicks (*kekomi*), and *gedan* with downward kicks (*keoroshi*).

In *harai waza*, the leg is used in a sweeping motion to attack not only the vital points of the body, but also the ankles, calves, knees, elbows, and wrists.

In *kari waza*, the leg is used in a small circular motion, as in a hook, to reap the opponent's leg behind the calf and throw him to the ground.

Fumi waza are the techniques in which downward kicks are used to attack the opponent's toes, insteps, or knees.

In *uke waza*, the leg is used to block the opponent's attack mainly with the knees, calf, or soles of the feet, while in *harai waza* the attack is not blocked but deflected with the leg.

In *tome waza*, the outside edge of the foot (*sokuto*) is used to stop the opponents' leg at the moment it is thrown. Contact is usually made on the opponent's shin.

Kawashi waza are the techniques of withdrawing a leg as it is attacked.

Once again, it should be noted that the stances and guards used in the description of the techniques are the most appropriate for correct execution.

Keri waza: Kicking techniques

Shomen geri: Front kick

Basic stance: left *uchimata jigotai dachi*
Basic guard: both fists on hips
Execution: —Inhale through the nose and hold your breath in
the *tanden*.
—Lower your position, pushing your hips backward and extending your arms in front of your
body in a winding up motion.
—Bring your right foot close to the left, tightening
your knees inward, then raise your right heel.
—Throw your right foot forward, pushing with
your hips and using the snap of the knee, your
heel at hip level. The chin must be tucked into
the neck and both arms pulled to the hips or
extended 45° downward, on the side of your
body. Contact is made either with the ball of
the foot (*jo sokutei*), the heel (*ka sokutei*), or
the tips of the toes (*tsuma saki*).
—Pull your right foot back to the knee of the supporting leg, toes pointed downward using the
snap of the ankle. The withdrawing motion of
the leg should be executed as fast as the kicking
motion.
—Put the ball of your right foot down on the
ground close to the left, then slide it backward in
a left *uchimata jigotai dachi*.
—Assume *zanshin*, then exhale from the mouth.

Important points in the execution:
—Breathing: Proper breathing is essential in the
execution of any karatedo technique.
—At the time of impact, the ankle must be tightened.
—In direct kicking techniques, the kicking leg
should be kept close to the supporting leg.
—The whole body should be used; the hips should
be pushed forward while the head and arms must
counterbalance the motion of the leg. However,
the head should not be thrown backward, but
rather tucked into the neck, on a vertical line
with the supporting foot. This foot should be
kept flat on the ground at first, but the advanced
student can raise the heel from the ground,
adding the spring of the ankle to the kick.
—Pull the kicking leg back with the toes first and
as fast as possible. The whole motion, kicking
and withdrawing, should be executed at the same
speed.
—Use the reaction of the ground by stamping
strongly before kicking and use the spring of
both knees and ankles to kick.
—Protect your main weak points (groin, solar
plexus, and jugular vein) by proper posture of
the body; advanced students can also use their
hands.

Okuri geri: Straight kick

Basic stance: left *sotobiraki jigotai dachi*
Basic guard: *seiken chudan kamae*
Execution: —Move forward with a left *okuri ashi*, pushing your hips backward and bending your knees 45°.
—Raise your left heel, then kick forward with your left foot, pushing with your hips and counterbalancing with your left hand extended on the side of your body, right hand in front of your solar plexus, and your head on a vertical line above your left foot, chin tucked into the neck. Contact is made either with the ball of the foot, the heel, or the tips of the toes.
—Pull your left foot back to the knee of your right leg, toes downward. Put it down on the ground in front of your right foot.
—Move backward with a left *okuri ashi*.

Hineri geri: Twist kick

Basic stance: left *uchimata jigotai dachi*
Basic guard: *shuto chudan kamae*
Execution: —Move forward with *fumikomi ashi* and pivot 90° to the left on the ball of your left foot, extending your right hand forward in a winding up motion.
—Raise your right heel and kick forward with your right foot, toes bent, ankle tightened with the ball of the foot or heel and pulling your right hand back to the right hip, the left hand in front of the solar plexus.

Oi geri: Lunge kick

Basic stance: left *zenkutsu dachi*
Basic guard: *seiken jodan kamae*
Execution: —Step forward with your right foot, using *oi ashi*.
—Raise your left heel backward, pushing your hips backward.
—Kick with your left foot up and forward 45°, pulling your left hand to the left hip, or to the left side of your body, to counterbalance your leg motion. The hips must be used to push the leg forward, also using the snap of the knee. Contact is made either with the ball of the foot, or the heel.
—Pull your hips back and bring your left foot to your right knee, toes first, and pointed downward. Put your left foot on the ground, close to the right one.
—Move backward with *oi ashi*.

Yoko geri: Side kick

Basic stance: left *naihanchin dachi*
Basic guard: *shuto jodan kamae*
Execution: —Cross your right leg behind the left, using *kosa ashi,* bending your knees, and pulling your hips backward.
—Raise your left leg to your right knee, straightening your ankle.
—Kick sideways at 45°, your left foot pushing forward with your hips. The sole of the right foot should remain flat on the ground, however, advanced students may pivot to the left on the ball of the foot to fully use the movement of the hips. The head should be on a vertical line above the supporting foot. Again, advanced students can throw their upper body in the opposite direction of the kick in order to generate more power.
—Pull your left foot back to your right knee, toes first with a whipping motion of the ankle. Your hips should be also pulled back. Adopt a *naihanchin dachi* with a *shuto jodan kamae*.
Remarks: — *Yoko geri* can also be executed by crossing your right leg in front of the left (instead of behind), or by using *okuri ashi*.

Mawashi geri: **Roundhouse kick**

Hineri mawashi geri: **Back leg roundhouse kick**

Basic stance: left *neko ashi dachi*

Basic guard: *shuto chudan kamae*

Execution: —Move forward with a left *neko ashi*. Then twist your left foot to the left, bringing your right hand in front of your face to protect it, and pulling your left hand to your left hip. Wind up by twisting your hips and shoulders to the right.

—Raise your right heel and throw your right foot in a circular motion across the front of your body to the left, rotating your hips, shoulders, head, and left foot in the same direction. The right foot should be kicking upward at 45° with the toes and ankle tightened. The head should be on a vertical line with the supporting foot. Contact is made with the ball of the foot and sometimes the heel or the instep of the foot. The rotation of the body is either 360° for *zen kaiten* (full turn) or 180° for *han kaiten* (half turn).

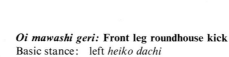

Oi mawashi geri: **Front leg roundhouse kick**

Basic stance: left *heiko dachi*

Basic guard: *shuto jodan kamae*

—Inhale through the nose and hold your breath in the *tanden*.

Execution: —Move forward with *kosa ashi*, crossing your right leg either behind or in front of the left. Wind up by twisting your hips and shoulders to the left and bring your right hand in front of your face to protect it.

—Raise your left heel and throw your left leg in a circular motion to the right, rotating your hips, shoulders, head, and right foot in the same direction and counterbalancing by pulling both hands to your left hip. The left foot should be kicking upward at 45°. Contact is made with the ball, or instep, of the foot. Bring your left foot back to your right knee, or rotate 180° on the ball of your right foot to end up in either a left or right stance.

—Assume *zanshin*, then exhale from the mouth.

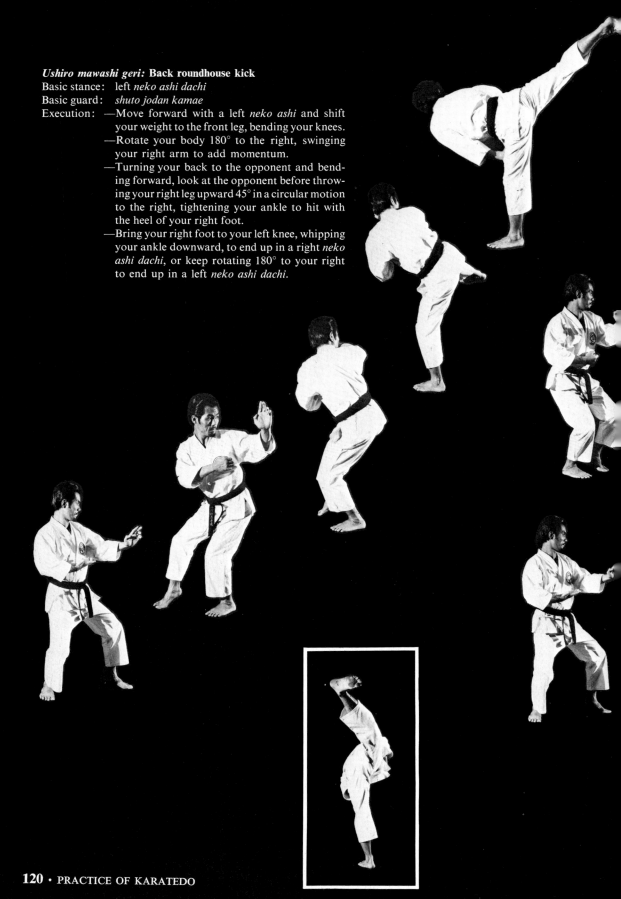

Ushiro mawashi geri: **Back roundhouse kick**

Basic stance: left *neko ashi dachi*

Basic guard: *shuto jodan kamae*

Execution: —Move forward with a left *neko ashi* and shift your weight to the front leg, bending your knees.

—Rotate your body 180° to the right, swinging your right arm to add momentum.

—Turning your back to the opponent and bending forward, look at the opponent before throwing your right leg upward 45° in a circular motion to the right, tightening your ankle to hit with the heel of your right foot.

—Bring your right foot to your left knee, whipping your ankle downward, to end up in a right *neko ashi dachi*, or keep rotating 180° to your right to end up in a left *neko ashi dachi*.

Gyaku mawashi geri: Reverse roundhouse kick

Basic stance: left _neko ashi dachi_

Basic guard: _shuto jodan kamae_

Execution: —Bring your right leg behind the left using _kosa ashi._

          —Twist your body to the right, bending low on your knees in a winding up motion.

          —Bring your left leg back to your right knee and move backward with either _kosa ashi_ or _neko ashi._

Remarks: —The head is on a vertical line above the supporting foot. Advanced students can lean backward to augment the reach and height of their kicking.

          —_Kagi geri_ can also be performed backward (_ushiro kagi geri_) in much the same way as _ushiro mawashi geri._

          —The snap of the leg should be used when hooking.

The other leg techniques mentioned at the beginning of this section can be considered variations of the basic techniques presented above and will not be described further.

Ushiro geri: Back kick

Basic stance: left *neko ashi dachi*
Basic guard: *shuto jodan kamae*

Hineri ushiro geri: Rear leg back kick

Execution: —Move forward with *neko ashi* and shift your
weight to the left leg.
—Pivot your body 180° to the right, turning from
your opponent, and look at him from under
your right armpit.
—Raise your right heel and kick backward with
your right leg in a straight upward line at 45°.
Tighten your ankle and hit with your right heel,
counter balancing your leg by bending your
body and raising your left elbow.
—Bring your right foot back to your left knee and
put it down close to the left foot. Then move
forward to the south with a left *neko ashi*, or
rotate your body 180° to your right before
moving backward with a right *neko ashi*.

Ushiro oi geri: Front leg back kick

Execution: —Without moving your feet, rotate your body
180° to your right, facing south.
—Step backward with your right foot, using *ushiro
oi ashi*, and bend your body forward.
—Look at your opponent from under your left
armpit and raise your left heel before kicking
backward at 45° with the same left heel. Counterbalance by extending your right elbow in the
opposite direction.
—Pull your left leg back, bending the knee of
your supporting leg, and put it down close to the
right.
—Rotate your body 180° to your right and step
backward with a right *neko ashi*.

Tobi geri: Jump kick

Basic stance: left *neko ashi dachi*
Basic guard: *shuto chudan kamae*

Shomen hineri tobi geri: Front jump kick with rear leg
Execution: —Step forward with a left *neko ashi*.
  —Jump up, raising your left knee, and while in the air, kick with a right *hineri geri*.

Shomen oi tobi geri: Front jump kick with front leg
Execution: —Step forward with a left *neko ashi*.
  —Jump up, raising your right knee, and execute a left *oi geri*.

Shomen nidan tobi geri: Double front jump kick
Execution: —Step forward with a left *neko ashi*.
  —Jump up and execute a right *hineri geri* and a left *oi geri*.
Remarks: —The first kick is usually not fully executed but serves mainly as an entrance technique to fake the opponent.
  —The second kick can also be a *yoko geri*.
  —The order of execution can sometimes be inverted (right *oi geri* and left *hineri geri*).

Hiza geri: Knee kick

Basic stance: left *shiko dachi*
Basic guard: *seiken chudan kamae*

Hiza ke age: Upward knee kick
Execution: —Move forward with *fumikomi ashi*.
  —Grab your opponent and pull him towards you.
  —Hit him with the upper part of your right knee in a 45° upward motion.
  —Bring your hips forward to add power to the kick, bending your supporting leg. The right ankle should be bent forward to tighten the muscles of the leg and joints.
  —Then push your opponent and move backward with *neko ashi*.

Hiza yoko mawashi geri: Roundhouse knee kick
Execution: —Move your right leg backward to the SW corner using *hiraki ashi*.
  —Grab your opponent, stamp on the ground to add momentum, and throw your right knee in a circular upward motion to your left. Your hips must also rotate to your left, counterbalancing their rotation by twisting your shoulders to your right, pulling your opponent to your right side. Your right ankle should be bent forward.
  —After hitting the opponent with your knee in the NW corner, bring your right foot back to its starting position.

Yoko tobi geri: Side jump kick

Execution: —Move forward with *oi ashi.*
               —Jump up and, while in the air, execute a left *yoko tobi.*
Remarks: —Before jumping up, bend low on your knees to use their spring to the maximum. After the kick, land on your toes and again bend low on your knees to recover your balance.

Hiza otoshi ate: Downward knee hit

Execution: —Move forward with *fumikomi ashi* and as your right foot slides on the ground behind the left, bend down while keeping your body straight.
               —Hit with the right knee, using the kneecap and pushing your body backward to put more power in the knee. The attack is directed at the instep or at a fallen opponent.
               —Regain your stance using *shiko dachi.*

b. *Harai waza:* **Sweeping techniques**

Mikazuki geri: **Crescent kick**

Basic stance: left *naihanchin dachi*
Basic guard: *seiken gedan kamae*
Execution: —Move forward with a left *okuri ashi.*
               —Sweep your right leg in a circular motion to the left, using the sole of the foot at hip level and toes pointed up or forward. Pivot 90° to the left on your supporting foot.
               —Pull your right foot back to your left knee and put it down close to your left foot.
               —Move backward with *okuri ashi.*

Kaiten geri: **Wheel kick**

Basic stance: left *uchimata jigotai dachi*
Basic guard: *seiken jodan kamae*
Execution: —Move forward with *fumikomi ashi*, twisting
your body to your left with your knees bent.
—Throw your right leg forward in a circular
motion to the left, tightening the ankle and hit-
ting with the back of the heel (*ushiro kakato*).
—Continue this hooking motion either describ-
ing a full turn or a half turn.
—Return to your starting position with *neko ashi*.

c. *Kari waza:* **Reaping techniques**

Kagi geri: **Hook kick**

Basic stance: left *neko ashi dachi*
Basic guard: *shuto jodan kamae*
Execution: —Move forward with a left *neko ashi* or *fumikomi
ashi.*
—Cross your right leg behind the left, using *kosa
ashi* and bending your knees. Wind up by
twisting your hips, shoulders, and arms to your
right.
—Throw your hips forward and rotate them to
swing your left foot 45° upward to the left,
bending your left knee and ankle to hit with the
back of the heel in the NW direction.

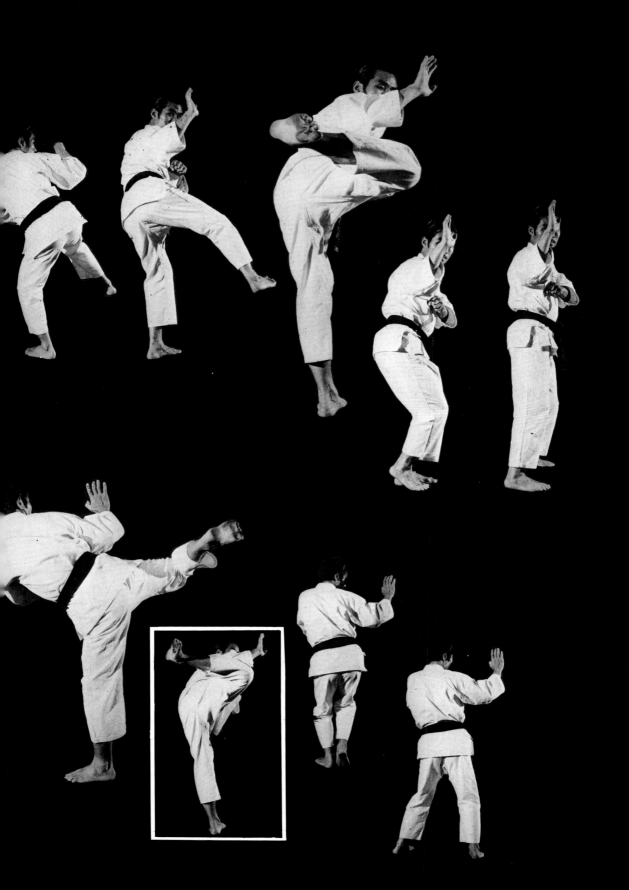

7. *Kawashi waza:* Dodging techniques

Kawashi waza are the techniques used to elude an attack, either because it is preferable to a block, there is no time or possibility to block, because one is caught off balance and seeks to recover by rolling on the ground, or even sometimes to attack. In *kawashi waza*, the whole body is involved in the motion and not only an arm or leg. Only the most important dodging techniques will be described in this paragraph along with their typical executions.

Mae sori mi: Leaning backward

Assuming you are standing in a basic stance, for instance *zenkutsu dachi*, and are attacked by a punching technique, shift your weight to your rear leg in *kokutsu dachi* with your shoulders leaning backward, and keep your head straight.

Mae kaga mi: Leaning forward

Assuming you are in a basic stance, for instance *kokutsu dachi*, and are attacked by *mawashi geri* to the face, shift your weight to the front leg and bend your body forward on this leg.

Yoko furimi: Leaning sideways

Assuming you are in a left basic stance, for instance left *neko ashi dachi*, and are attacked by a punching technique to the left side of your face, shift your weight to your right leg, bending on your knee.

Hineri hanmi: Rotation of the trunk

Assuming you are standing in a left basic stance, for instance left *neko ashi dachi*, and are attacked on the right side of your body, shift your weight to your left foot and twist your body to your right with your hips and shoulders parallel to the direction of the attack.

Hiraki mi: Open-legs rotation

Pivot your body 90° around your right or left foot moving either forward or backward with *hiraki ashi*.

Mawari mi: **Crossed-legs rotation**

Pivot your body 180° on the balls of both feet using *mawashi ashi.*

Otoshi mi: **Knee-bending**

Bend your knees deeply, keeping your trunk straight and looking at your opponent's eyes. Your arms are extended in front of
your body, in the direction of your toes, to keep your balance.

Fuse mi: **Forward fall**

Keeping your body straight, fall forward on your hands with
your elbows bent, fingers pointed inward, and one knee bent
but not touching the ground. Your body is twisted on this side,
while the other leg is extended.

Tobi mi: **Jumping**

Leap up in the air, bringing your knees up with heels close to the
buttocks.

Uke mi: Break-fall

Mae uke mi: Front break-fall

Fall forward, breaking the fall by hitting the ground with both hands, fingers pointed inward and elbows bent. Twist your head to either side. The legs are stretched out.

Ushiro uke mi: Rear break-fall

Fall backward and break the fall by hitting the ground with both hands, arms extended 45° to the sides of your body. Tighten your neck and tuck in your chin, looking at your stomach. Your hands should be flat on the ground with the wrists, elbows, and shoulder joints tightened. Your legs should be together, extended upward at 45°, and should not hit the ground.

Yoko uke mi: **Side break-fall**

For a side break-fall to the left, fall on your left side and break the fall by hitting the ground with your left hand, left arm extended at 45° to the side of the body. Your neck must be tightened and your chin tucked in, looking at your stomach. Your legs should be extended, the outside edge of the left foot and the sole of the right foot on the ground one shoulder width apart (be careful not to cross your legs).

Note: In all *ukemi*, at the time of impact the breath should be held in the *tanden* and the whole body must be tensed.

Zempo kaiten uke mi: **Forward rolling break-fall**

Standing in a left *neko ashi dachi*, shift your weight to the front leg in a *zenkutsu dachi*. Bend forward on your left knee and put your left hand on the ground, fingers pointed towards yourself. Put your right hand behind the left, fingers pointed towards the left hand. Both hands should be mid-way between your feet. Throw your body forward and roll on your left hand, elbow, shoulder, and across your back to your right hip. Then hit the ground with your right hand at 45°. Bend your right knee and put your left foot flat on the ground. Then, in a continuous motion push on the ground with your right hand and stand up in a left *neko ashi dachi*.

Note that the body should roll on the left arm, left shoulder, back, and right hip like a wheel or ball in a smooth motion. Do not remain on the ground but stand up immediately after the roll.

Koho kaiten uke mi: **Backward rolling break-fall**

Standing in a left cat stance, shift your weight to your rear leg in *kokutsu dachi*. Bend on your right knee, sitting on your right ankle. Put your right hand on the ground, fingers pointed forward and roll on your right hand, elbow and shoulder, across your back to your left shoulder. Hit the ground with your left hand at 45°. Bend your left knee and land on the sole of your right foot. Stand up immediately, pushing on your left hand, to a left *neko ashi dachi.*

This break-fall is unique to Kenkokan Karatedo.

Kaiten mi: **Rolling forms**

These techniques are sometimes used to prepare for an attack or to elude an opponent. They are also practiced to develop in students a sense of balance and enable them to cope with any situation that may arise in a real fight. As such, they should be preceded or followed by some other offensive techniques.

Zempo kaiten: **Forward roll**
Bend your body forward and touch the ground with your hands. Looking at your stomach, roll smoothly overhead on your back and finish standing on your feet.

Koho kaiten: **Backward roll**
Put your feet together. Sit down on your heels and roll on your buttocks, back, shoulders, and head, then push on your hands to stand up.

Zempo daisharin: **Forward cartwheel**
Standing in a left *neko ashi dachi* with *shuto jodan kamae*, move forward with *fumikomi ashi*. Put your left hand on the ground in front of your body and throw your right leg up in the air. Put your right hand in front of the left and throw your left leg up. Keep your arms straight. Land on your right leg and then bring your left foot down in a left *neko ashi dachi*.

Koho daisharin: **Backward cartwheel**
Standing in a left *neko ashi dachi* with *shuto jodan kamae*, move backward with *fumikomi ashi*. Put your right hand on the ground behind your right leg and throw your left leg up in the air. Then put your left hand behind the right and throw your right leg. Land on your left leg first and then bring the right foot down in a left *neko ashi dachi*.

8. *Nage Waza:* Throwing Techniques

a. *Te waza:* Hand techniques

1. *Sukui waza:* **Scooping techniques**
    Ashi sukui age: Upward leg scooping
    Hiza sukui hineri: Twisting knee scooping
2. *Otoshi waza:* **Dropping techniques**
    Ushiro hiki otoshi: Backward drop
    Tai otoshi: Body drop
    Osoto otoshi: Major outer drop
    Tani otoshi: Valley drop
3. *Tori waza:* **Holding techniques**
    Ryo ashi tori: Tackle throw
    Kata ashi tori: One leg tackle throw

b. *Ashi waza:* Foot techniques

1. *Ashi barai:* **Foot sweep**
    De ashi barai: Front foot sweep
    Okuri ashi barai: Sliding foot sweep
    Sokko hiza barai: Instep-foot-knee sweep
2. *Kari waza:* **Foot reaping**
    Kaiten gari: Leg wheel reap
    Osoto gari: Major outer reap
    Kosoto gari: Minor outer reap
    Ouchi gari: Major inner reap
    Kouchi gari: Minor inner reap
3. *Hasami waza:* **Scissors techniques**
    Do basami: Body scissors
    Hiza basami: Leg scissors

Ashi sukui age: Upward leg scooping

Ashi sukui age: Upward leg scooping

Ushiro hiki otoshi: Backward drop

Hiza sukui hineri: Twisting knee scooping

137

Tai otoshi: Body drop

Tani otoshi: Valley drop

Osoto gari: Major outer reap

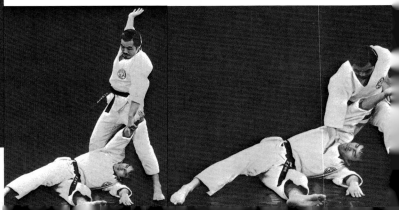

Tani otoshi: Valley drop

Ryo ashi tori: Tackle throw

Ryo ashi tori: Tackle throw

Kata ashi tori: One leg tackle throw

De ashi barai: Front foot sweep
Okuri ashi barai: Sliding foot sweep

Sokko hiza barai: Instep-foot-knee sweep

Kaiten gari: Leg wheel reap

Osoto otoshi: Major outer drop

Kosoto gari: Minor outer reap

Ouchi gari: Major inner reap

Kouchi gari: Minor inner reap

Do basami: Body scissors

Hiza basami: Leg scissors

9. *Gyaku Waza:* Armlock Techniques

Kote gaeshi. Outward wristlock

Waki gatame: Armpit armlock

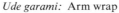
Ude garami: Arm wrap

Ude gaeshi: Arm twist

Hiji gaeshi: Elbow twist (or *suisha gaeshi*)

10. *Shime Waza:* Strangle Techniques

Washi jime: Eagle choke
   Nodo jime: Adam's apple choke (single hand eagle choke to
        Adam's apple)
   Kin jime: Groin choke (single hand eagle choke to groin)
Hadaka jime: Bare choke (two hand bare choke)
Okuri eri jime: Collar choke (two hand collar choke)

86

Washi jime: Eagle choke

Hadaka jime: Bare choke (two hand bare choke)

Nodo jime: Adam's apple choke (single hand eagle choke to Adam's apple)

Okuri eri jime: Collar choke (two hand collar choke)

Chapter 5 Kata

1. Definition and Purpose of Kata

All the fundamental elements of karatedo have been put into formal sets of systematized sequences thoroughly developed, codified, and improved by dedicated karatedo Masters through the course of several centuries.

Each set, called a kata, is made up of carefully selected elements which all have a profound meaning both intrinsically, and in their context. Each posture, movement, or technique, is the most appropriate one under the circumstances for it has been repeatedly tested over hundreds of years in innumerable occasions of real fighting over matters of life and death. In recent days these principles have been scientifically rationalized by great karatedo Masters such as Doctor Kori Hisataka, who brought his expertise in the field of anatomy, physics, and psychology to the study of karatedo principles.

Kata are truly a microcosm of karatedo for they contain all of its essential principles, techniques, and traditions. The salutations with their philosophical implications (see Chapter 2), the proper postures and stances, body and foot movements, the control and use of breathing, the various techniques and their timing, the proper mental attitude, the *kiai* (spirit), and the search for perfection in the execution of each technique, are all included in the kata.

Until very recently, the kata were kept secret. They were never practiced publically by karatedo Masters, who were transmitting their knowledge only to a handful of trusted students through the practice of kata. Kata was then the sole and unique form of karatedo training. This gives a measure of the historical and practical importance of the kata in karatedo.

A kata is performed alone against imaginary opponents. Its purpose is to develop every aspect of karatedo: postures, body movements, techniques, and mental attitudes. The assiduous practice of kata leads to a deep understanding of the techniques of karatedo. It develops the ability to use these techniques and to respond almost automatically to any kind of attack, in any situation. In addition, kata contains all of the various strategies of fighting.

The practice of kata is most propitious to the development of the spirit and mental attitudes essential to karatedo. In kata, one must constantly imagine his opponent(s) and perform each movement and technique with all his spirit and force, as if death would result from improper execution. This kind of practice helps to achieve a complete union of mind and body.

Kata is also an excellent physical conditioning exercise. Its complete execution usually takes only one to two minutes and in any case less than five minutes. So even very busy people can practice it. Kata can be performed in an apartment or office or anywhere (there is a saying that the surface of one *tatami* (1 m × 2 m) is sufficient). There is no need for any special facility or equipment as in most other sports. However, the wearing of a *karatedogi* is recommended as it allows a greater freedom of movement. Kata can also be practiced at any time of the day and at any time of the year. Being practiced alone, kata can be performed according to one's physical or health condition. It is a particularly suitable exercise for women, older persons, and sick persons as it can be adjusted to their own needs and goals. In this sense, the practice of kata truly provides freedom of mind.

Another important aspect of the kata is that because of the danger of karatedo techniques, the practice of a kata allows the student to gain enough technical knowledge to be able to control his own techniques and to protect himself before practicing with another person.

Kata practiced assiduously and with dedication lead to an understanding of the purposes of the Masters who have created them. That is why the practice of kata is one of the most important aspects of karatedo.

2. Classification of Kata

In ancient times, there were only a few lengthy katas. As karatedo spread from China to Okinawa and Japan, giving birth to a number of different styles, kata underwent a series of transformations and adaptations reflecting the philosophy of great karatedo Masters who created various styles. The long original kata were split up into a number of shorter ones. Variations of the same kata appeared, in some instances, under different names.

More recently, *Shinan* Kori Hisataka, founder of Shorinjiryu Kenkokan Karatedo, has himself developed, modified, and adapted a number of kata. Some of those he elected to teach are presented here. They are classified into basic (*kihon*) kata, intermediate kata, and advanced (*tanren* or *kaite*) kata according to their technical complexity.

a. Basic Kata

Sanchin kata
This is the oldest kata in karatedo. Loosely translated, *sanchin* means "three points" or "three phases", a reference to the fact that *sanchin* seeks to develop three elements at a time: the mind, the body, and the techniques; the internal organs, the blood circulation, and the nervous system; and the three *ki* located in the top of the head (*tento*), the diaphragm (*hara*), and the lower abdomen (*tanden*). *Sanchin* is an isometric kata where each motion is performed in a state of complete tension accompanied with powerful, deep breathing. It is aimed at strengthening the muscles and developing a strong stance and proper breathing. Its practice leads to the development of the inner power (*ki*) and to the coordination of mind and body. It teaches basic footwork, basic hand techniques, and basic blocking techniques. This kata is taught to students from the rank of tenth *kyu* (white belt) to fourth *kyu* (green belt).

Naihanchin kata
Naihanchin means "sideways fighting" or "fighting within" because in this kata one fights against opponents on both sides. It is one of the oldest kata in karate. In China, it was the most outstanding kata of *Shorinji Kempo* and since then has been transmitted from Master to Master, from China to Okinawa. In recent days it has been adapted by *Shinan* Kori Hisataka and is now taught in Kenkokan Karatedo.

Naihanchin kata is the only kata which does not start with a defensive technique but with a surprise attack aimed at taking the lead in a fight and breaking away from the attackers. This kata teaches one how to fight in a narrow space, such as a hall or bridge, with opponents on each side. Thus *naihanchin* kata is performed in two phases, to the right side first, and then to the left, the second phase being a mirror image of the first phase.

Naihanchin kata emphasizes lateral stances (*naihanchin* and *sotobiraki jigotai* stances) and basic techniques useful in sideways fighting. It also teaches the combining of techniques into sequences of attacks, counterattacks, blocks, and pauses, etc. This develops a feeling for the rhythum of fighting.

Naihanchin kata is recommended for 10th and 7th *kyu* students (white belt).

Nijushiho kata
The original name of this kata is *niseishi* kata meaning "twenty four movements". It was developed by Okinawan karate Masters and was designed both for empty-hand and weapon fighting. It has since been adapted by *Shinan* Kori Hisataka in Kenkokan Karatedo.

In fact, there are not twenty four movements in *nijushiho*. There is a second hidden meaning to this name. *Nijushiho* stresses combinations of two techniques and 24 could be interpreted as 2 *and* 4, implying that 2-technique combinations are worth twice as much (4). This kind of double understanding was quite frequently used in naming kata.

In this kata, one faces two opponents and learns diagonal and circular body motions both to create an opening in the opponent's guard and to evade his attacks. It emphasizes rapid foot movements such as *neko ashi*, *hiraki ashi*, and *kosa ashi*, and flexible stances (cat stances).

Nijushiho kata is recommended for 8th and 7th *kyu* students (yellow belt).

Heian kata ichi (or shodan)
The original name of this kata is *pinan* (or *chanan*) *kata* meaning "peaceful mind". It is the first of the five *pinan* kata developed a century ago by Master Anko Itosu, one of the most prominent Masters of *Okinawa te*. This series of kata was aimed at teaching a student to respond to any kind of attack thus giving him a "peaceful mind".

Heian kata *ichi* is typical of *Okinawa te*: hard and powerful techniques executed with closed hands. It develops in the student a steady stance and teaches him combination attacks, blocking techniques, and armlocks.

It is recommended for 6th and 5th *kyu* students (orange belt).

b. Intermediate Kata

Sankakutobi kata
This kata, meaning "triangular jumping attacks" or "the triangular leap", has been developed by *Shihan* Masayuki Hisataka. It is a lengthy and flowing kata using long and powerful techniques against moving opponents. It develops stamina and body and foot movements. All-round techniques are displayed in a close succession of jumping attacks and counterattacks.

Sankakutobi kata is recommended for 4th and 3rd *kyu* students (green belt).

Heian yon (dan) kata
This *kata* is the most representative of the series of *heian kata*. It emphasizes the harmony of form and builds up balance and a sense for combination techniques. Unlike *heian shodan*, *heian yon* is performed with open hands. It is recommended for 4th and 3rd *kyu* students (green belt).

Happiken kata
This kata literally means "to use the fist like a monkey in eight directions." The creation of *Shihan*

Masayuki Hisataka, *happiken* kata is geared to close fighting situations as it uses a great many elbow strikes and emphasizes strong postures and stances. *Happiken* kata is recommended for 2nd and 1st *kyu* students (brown belt).

Koshiki naihanchin kata

This kata is a variation of the original *naihanchin* kata of *Shorinji Kempo*. *Shihan* Masayuki Hisataka undertook to modify the original form of *naihanchin* because it lacked body movements and kicking techniques. Like the first form it stresses sideways fighting techniques and strong stances. This kata is recommended for 2nd and 1st *kyu* students (brown belt).

c. Advanced Kata

Seisan kata

Like *sanchin* kata, *seisan kata* is aimed at developing footwork, strong stances, *ki*, and breathing control. It is also an isometric body building form of exercise, however, the techniques displayed in *seisan* are more advanced than in *sanchin*. Its stances are wider and the postures are 'half face front' (*hanmi*, body diagonal to the front).

Seisan kata has its origin in *Shorinji Kempo* and has been transformed by *Shinan* Kori Hisataka.

The first half of the kata consists of strong stances, slow motions, and powerful techniques, while the second half emphasizes fast body motions and techniques.

This kata is recommended for *shodan* (first degree black belt).

Bassai kata

The meaning of *bassai* is "how to break through a fortress." It is a beautiful kata with very fast and powerful techniques representative of the *shorin* style of karate. *Bassai* was one of the favorite kata of Master Chojun Kyamu of *Okinawa te*, one of the most prominent instructors of *Shinan* Kori Hisataka.

There are two forms of bassai kata practiced in Kenkokan Karatedo, one with closed hands and the other with open hands (*koshiki bassai*). This kata is recommended for shodan (first degree black belt).

Chinto kata

This kata, literally meaning "fighting towards the east," is also an extremely old kata representative of the shorin style. It emphasizes kicking techniques and one-leg stances (like a crane). It consists of quick, sudden attacks and counterattacks. It also contains armlock techniques and defenses against holding. *Chinto* also teaches how to take advantage of the natural environment (such as fighting with the sun to one's back, to dazzle the opponent) and the principles of fighting in the dark.

In Kenkokan Karatedo there is another version of *chinto* kata: *koshiki chinto*. *Chinto* is recommended for *nidan* (second degree black belt).

Sochin kata

This kata, using powerful and hard techniques, is representative of the *shorin* style. It teaches two-technique combinations and control of breathing.

Sochin kata is recommended for *nidan* (second degree black belt).

Jion kata

This kata is named for the Master who brought Shorinji Kempo to Okinawa. It is representative of the shorin style with its long and supple, but powerful motions inspired by the fighting attitudes of the tiger.

Jion kata is recommended for *sandan* (third degree black belt).

Kusoku (or *Kusokun*) kata

Kusoku is the title for a high government official in China. A priest from the Shaolin Temple (shorin in Japanese) who had this title was sent in the 18th century as an emissary of his country to Okinawa where he began to teach fighting techniques of the Shaolin Temple. After his departure, his Okinawan disciples regrouped all these techniques in a kata called *kusoku* in his honor.

In 1932 this kata was reintroduced in China at the celebration of China's Confederation by *Shinan* Kori Hisataka. This marked the first official recognition of Japanese karatedo by China.

Kusoku kata is one of the most complete and beautiful of all katas. It displays complex techniques against many enemies and stresses flowing motions and evading techniques. The first part of the kata concentrates on daytime fighting techniques, while the second part emphasizes fighting at night. There are three different forms of *kusoku* kata practiced in Kenkokan Karatedo.

Kusoku kata is recommended for *sandan* (third degree black belt).

3. Illustration of Kata

Two kata from each of the three levels are illustrated and described in detail in this section. In order to facilitate explanations, the cardinal points (north, south, east, west, northeast, northwest, southeast, and southwest) will be used to describe the direction of the movements, north (usually *shomen*) being the direction faced when starting.

Naihanchin kata

1–Stand in the "attention stance" (*musubi dachi*), facing *shomen*.
2–Bow with a *keirei* (ceremonial bow).
3–Call "*naihanchin*", loudly and with *kiai*.
4–Step forward, left foot first then the right, in a front natural stance (*shizen hontai dachi*).
5–Bow with a *kenko ritsurei* (fighting bow).
6–Be prepared: *zenshin* (or *kamaete*).
   These six steps are the standard salutation forms used for every kata.
7–Slowly extend your hands, joined together, in front of your body above your forehead. Inhale deeply and bring them down in an outward circular motion, pressing your right fist against the palm of your left hand in front of your navel, then exhale.
8–Adopt a defensive open stance (*sotobiraki jigo hontai* dachi, and rapidly turn your head to the right).
9–Move your right foot in the NE direction and cross your left leg behind the right (this is a *kosa ashi step*).
10–Moving your right foot east, deliver a right reverse knife-

hand strike (*gyaku shuto uchi*).

11–Follow with a left lunge punch (*oi zuki*), and pull your left fist back to the hip.

12–Rotate your body 180° clockwise, facing west, and execute a right knife-hand outward block (*shuto soto uke*).

13–Step to the SW corner with your left foot and cross your right leg behind in the *kosa ashi* stance, keeping your right hand in front of your body.

14–Stepping north with your left foot, deliver a left elbow strike (*yoko empi mawashi uchi*) from a left forward stance (*zenkutsu dachi*).

15–Execute a right knife-hand downward block (*shuto gedan barai*) in the SE direction.

16–Slide your left foot backward, close to the right, and then to the SW corner in a *zenkutsu* stance and execute a left downward block (*gedan barai*).

17–Shifting into a left cat stance (*neko ashi dachi*), execute a left outward knife-hand block (*shuto soto uke*).

18–Bringing your right foot close to the left in a *heisoku* stance, execute a right elbow strike (*yoko empi mawashi uchi*) to the palm of your left hand.

19–Without moving your feet, rotate your body 180° counter-clockwise, facing north, and execute an upper cross block (*morote jodan juji uke*).

20–Bring your arms down on each side of your body, hands open, in a right *zenkutsu* stance.

21–Look to the west side and execute a right twist punch (*hineri zuki*) or hook punch (*kagi zuki*) in this direction.

16

17

18

19

20

22–Pull your right fist to the hip, and facing north in a right cat stance (*neko ashi dachi*), execute a right knife-hand outward block (*shuto soto uke*).

21

22

23–Execute a right lunge kick (*oi geri*) using the heel of the foot.

24–Pull your right foot back in front of your body and execute a right *shuto soto uke*.

25–Execute a left twist kick (*hineri geri*) using the ball of the foot.

26–Bring your left foot to its starting position and execute a right knife-hand outward block (*shuto soto uke*).

27–Cross your right leg in front of the left, moving west, and bring your left foot back (*kosa ashi* step) into a natural position (*shizen hontai*).

28–Stamp on the ground with your right foot to surprise your opponent.

29–Cross your right foot behind the left.

30–Execute a right knife-hand downward block (*shuto soto gedan barai*) or a right *soto uke* in a *kosa ashi* stance.

31–Execute a left *sokumen zuki.*

32–Follow with a left outward block (*soto uke*).

33–Stamp on the ground with your left foot.

34–Step in the NW corner with your right foot and bring your left foot behind the right in *hiraki ashi.*

35–Adopting a *sotobiraki jigotai* stance, execute a left *shuto gedan barai* or a left *soto uke* in a *kosa ashi* stance.

36–From this position deliver a right *sokumen zuki*.

37–Follow with a right *soto uke*.

38–Bring your left foot forward in a *heisoku* stance, then slide your right foot to the SW corner in a left *sotobiraki jigotai* stance.

39–From this position execute a double-inverted block (*nidan uke*), the left hand in an upper outside block (jodan *soto uke*) and the right hand in a downward outward block (*gedan soto uke*).

40–Pull your left fist to your ear, elbow at the shoulder level and right hand extended downward in front of your body.

41–Deliver a left front *uraken uchi*, your right hand coming under your left elbow.

42–Slide your right foot forward and rotate your body 90° counterclockwise facing west and execute a left *uchi uke*.

43–Execute a left *oi geri* and pull your left foot back in front of your body.

44–Follow with a right *hineri zuki*.

45–Slide your right foot behind the left and execute a left *sokumen zuki*.

46–Pull your left fist back and execute a left *soto uke* in a *zenkutsu* or *sotobiraki jigotai* stance.

47–Cross your left leg in front of the right and bring your right foot back in a *shizen hontai* stance. Repeat steps 7 through 48 to the left side (west) in mirror image. After completion return to *zanshin*.

48–Adopt a *shizen hontai* stance.
49–Bow with a *kenko ritsurei*.

50–Step backward with the right foot first, then with the left,
   into a *musubi* stance.
51–Bow with a *keirei*.

Nijushiho kata

1–Stand in the "attention stance" (*musubi dachi*).

2–Bow with a *keirei* (ceremonial bow) to *shomen*.

3–Call "*nijushiho*" loudly and with *kiai*.

4–Step forward with the left foot first, and then with the right, into a front natural stance (*shizen hontai* dachi, 'full face front').

5–Bow with a *kenko ritsurei* (fighting bow).

6–Be prepared: *zenshin* (or *kamaete*).

7–Slide your right foot behind the left (using *hiraki ashi*) in a left cat stance (*neko ashi dachi*).

8–At the same time, execute a left open-hand inward block (*shotei uchi uke*).

9–Follow with a right twist punch (*hineri zuki*).

10–Bring your right foot close to the left, then slide it to the NE corner.

11–Execute a right upward cat-back, back hand wrist block, (*jodan nekoze ken uke*).

12–Bring your right foot close to the left and slide it to the SW corner.

13–Execute a left lower scooping block (*gedan sukui uke*).

14–Bring your right foot close to the left and slide it to the NE corner. Then cross your left leg behind the right in a crossed-leg stance (*kosa ashi dachi*) and execute a left outward block (*soto uke*).

15–Step to the NW corner with your right foot and deliver a right side roundhouse elbow strike (*yoko mawashi empi uchi*).

16–Move your left foot to the west and execute a right outside downward block (*soto gedan barai*).

17–Rotate your body 90° counterclockwise, facing south, and deliver a right back elbow strike (*ushiro empi ate*) to the north, keeping your eyes in this direction, while extending your left arm to the south to give power to the strike.

18–Cross your right leg in front of the left, moving to the SW corner; bring the left leg behind the right in the same direction.

19–Follow with a right knife-hand outside downward block (*shuto soto gedan barai*).

20–Move your left foot in the NW direction, then cross your right leg behind the left in a crossed-leg stance (*kosa ashi dachi*).

21—Step forward with the left foot and deliver a left knife-hand strike (*shuto yoko mawashi uchi*).

22—Move your right foot to the NE corner and cross your left leg behind the right in a crossed-leg stance (*kosa ashi dachi*).

23—Execute a left upper circular block (*jodan mawashi uke*).

24—Step forward with your right foot and execute a right upper side punch (*jodan sokumen zuki*).

25—Cross your left leg behind the right in a right crossed-leg stance (*kosa ashi dachi*).

26—Apply a groin choke with your open right hand describing an inward half-circle (*washi jime*).

27—Move your right foot forward and execute a right reverse knife-hand strike (*gyaku shuto uchi*).

28—From this position execute a left twist punch (*hineri zuki*).

29—Execute a cat step (*neko ashi*) to the SE corner and follow with two-fist downward punching block (*morote seiken otoshi uke*).

30—Adopt a right cat stance (*neko ashi dachi*) the right hand is open in front of the face and the left hand close to the solar plexus, palm upward.

31—Execute a right lunge kick (*oi geri*) to the NE, and bring your right foot back in front of your body.)

32–In a right cat stance, move your left foot west, then bring your right foot behind the left in an open-leg stance (*hiraki ashi*).

33–Execute a left cat-back block (*nekoze ken uchi age uke*).

34–Follow with a right downward knife-hand strike (*shuto uchi oroshi*). (Figs. 57–61)

35–Execute a left lunge kick to the north (*oi geri*).

36–Follow with a left outward block (*soto uke*) in a left *zenkutsu* stance.

37–Bring your right foot behind the left in a *kosa ashi* stance and rotate your body 180° clockwise (*hidari ushiro mawari*). You are now facing south in the natural position (*shizen hontai*). Repeat steps 7 through 36 in mirror image. After completion, return to *zanshin*.

38–Execute a right back-leg turn (*ushiro mawari*). You are now facing *shomen* in *shizen hontai*.

39–Bow with a *kenko ritsurei*.

40–Step backward, right foot first and then the left, into a *musubi* stance.

41–Bow with a *keirei*.

Sankakutobi kata

The first six steps are the standard salutation forms already described.

7–Slowly raise both open hands above your head in an outward, semi-circular motion. Inhale deeply and close your fists as both hands meet. Bring them down in front of your body, forearms together in *morote kamae* and tightening your knees inward. Exhale and slowly lower your hands on either side of your body.

8–Repeat the movements of step 7 twice.

9–Step forward with your right foot, stamp on the floor (*ashi fumikomi*), and adopting a right cat stance, execute a right *soto uke*.

10–Bring your left foot behind the right.

11–Execute a right *oi zuki*, and pull your right fist to the right hip.

12–Move with *neko ashi* to the SW corner and execute a right *soto uke*.

13–Bring your left foot forward, closing your feet together and slide your right foot to the NE corner.

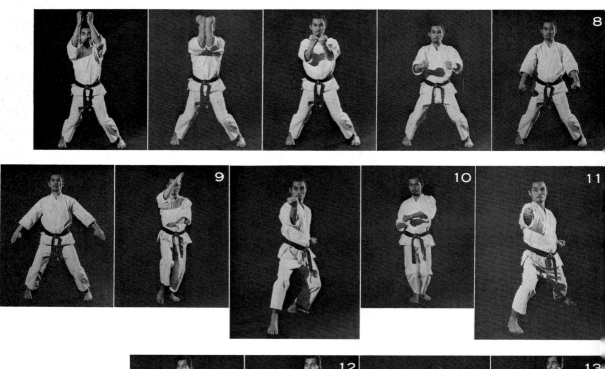

14–Deliver a left *hineri zuki.*

15–From this position execute a right *shuto uchi uke.*

16–Cross your right leg in front of the left, moving to the SW corner using *kosa ashi,* and bring your left foot behind the right.

17–Execute a right *shuto gedan barai* in the *soto biraki jigotai* stance.

18–Move with *neko ashi* to the SE corner and execute a right *sukui uke* (scooping block).

19–Cross your left leg in front of the right, moving to the NW corner, and turn clockwise facing the NE corner, bringing your right leg behind the left.

20–Deliver a left *sokumen zuki* to the NE.

21–Pull your right foot behind the left, then move your right foot back to the SE corner to assume a *sotobiraki jigotai* stance and duck, keeping your body straight and stretching out both arms on the sides of your body with the palms facing the ground to keep your balance.

22–Then move your body upward and execute a left *okuri geri.*

23–Bring your left foot to the right knee, then down in front of
   your body, and execute a left *sokumen zuki*.
24–Bring your left fist back to your left hip and deliver a right
   hineri zuki.
25–Bring your right fist back to your right hip and move your
   right foot east in the direction of your toes.
26–Extend both arms, crossed together, in front of your
   forehead and execute a *morote jodan juji uke* with open
   hands in a left *zenkutsu* stance.
27–Bring your arms down on either side of your body.
28–Switching into a left *neko ashi dachi*, execute a left *shuto
   uke*.
29–From this position, execute a right *hineri geri*.
30–Bring your right foot back to your left knee in front of your
   body, and deliver a right upper spear-hand strike (*oi nukite*).
31–Bring your right hand back to the hip and move yout left
   foot to the SW corner. Then bring your right leg behind the
   left in a *kosa ashi* stance.

32–Execute a right *soto uke*.

33–Follow with a left *empi mawashi uchi* to the NE corner.

34–Turn your body 90° clockwise (facing south). Move your right foot backward and deliver a right *empi ushiro ate*, clenching both hands together to give more power to your elbow and looking in the direction of the hit (north).

35–Switch to a *neko ashi* stance and execute a left *shuto soto uke*.

36–Move forward with a left *fumikomi ashi*. Assume a left *neko ashi* stance and once again execute a left *soto uke*.

This motion is similar to motion 9 but in mirror image. Motions 10 through 35 are now to be executed in mirror image. After completion you are in a right *neko ashi* stance, facing north.

37–Cross your right leg in front of your left, moving to the SW corner, and bring your left foot behind the right in a *kokutsu* stance, at the same time executing a right *soto gedan barai*.

38–Crossing your left leg behind (or in front of) the right leg, execute a right *yoko geri* to the NE corner.

39–Bringing your right foot to the left knee and then putting it down in front of your body, execute a right *shuto gyaku uchi*.

40–Bring your right arm back across your face and pivot clockwise in a 180° semi-circular motion around your left foot (you are now facing the SW corner). For advanced students this pivot can be accomplished by spinning 180° in the air (*sankaku tobi*).

41–Simultaneously execute a left *sukui uke* (scooping block) in a left *sotobiraki jigotai* stance.

42–Shifting the weight of your body forward, deliver a left upper *oi geri*, using the ball of the foot.

43–Bring your left foot to the right knee and then down in front of your body (but close to the right foot). Execute a small jump to your left front corner and block with both fists using *morote seiken gedan tome* (*otoshi uke*).

44–Stepping forward with your right foot, follow with a left *oi geri*, using the heel.

45–Bring your left foot to the right knee and then down in front of your body. Then execute a left *oi zuki*.

46–Deliver a right *empi yoko mawashi uchi* into the palm of your left hand extended in frotn of your body.

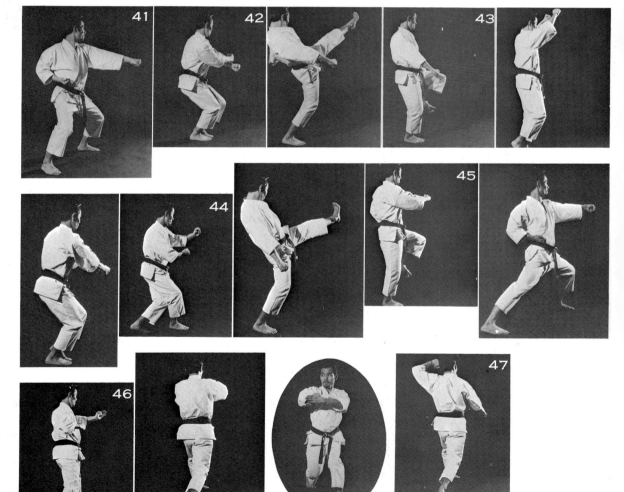

47–Block with your right fist at the groin level in *gedan barai*, at the same time bringing your left hand to your left ear.

48–Deliver a left *shomen uraken uchi* while your right hand comes across your body, below your left elbow.

49–Step in the SW direction, using a left *neko ashi* and duck, arms extended in front of your body. Turn your body 180° clockwise to the NE corner.

50–In a right cat stance execute a right *soto uke*.

51–Step forward to execute a left *oi zuki*.
Pull your left fist back.

52–Move your right foot to the east and cross your left leg behind the right, moving to the SE and pivoting your body 90° counterclockwise.

53–Execute a right *sukui uke* in a *sotobiraki jigotai dachi*.

54–Move your left leg in the NW direction and cross your right leg behind the left.

55–Step forward with the left foot and deliver a left *shuto yoko mawashi uchi*.

56–Move your left leg in front of the right and turn your body clockwise 180° (*hidari mae mawari*). You are now facing south.

57–Execute a left *soto uke*.

58–Now repeat steps 37 through 57 in mirror image. After completion, move your right leg back to a *shizen hontai* stance, facing *shomen*.

59–Repeat the respiratory movements described in step 7 three times and return to *zanshin*.

60–Bow with a *kenko ritsurei*.

61–Step backward with the right foot first, and then with the left, into a *musubi* stance.

62–Bow with a *keirei*.

Happiken kata

The first six steps of this *kata* are the standard salutation forms already described.

7–Slowly extend both hands in front of your body, above and slightly in front of the head, inhaling deeply. Bring them down in an outward circular motion, closing your left hand and pressing it against the right palm. Exhale and turn your head rapidly to the left.

8–Move your left foot slightly backward. Rotate your body to the left (west) while adopting a left cat stance.

9–Execute a left *soto uke* (with your right fist under the left elbow.)

10–Follow with a right *hineri zuki*.

11–Bring your right leg behind the left and slide your left foot (*okuri ashi*) to the west.

12–Deliver a left *shuto gyaku uchi* in a left *zenkutsu* stance.

13–Pull your left leg close to the right, rotate your body 80° clockwise to the east, and adopt a right cat stance.

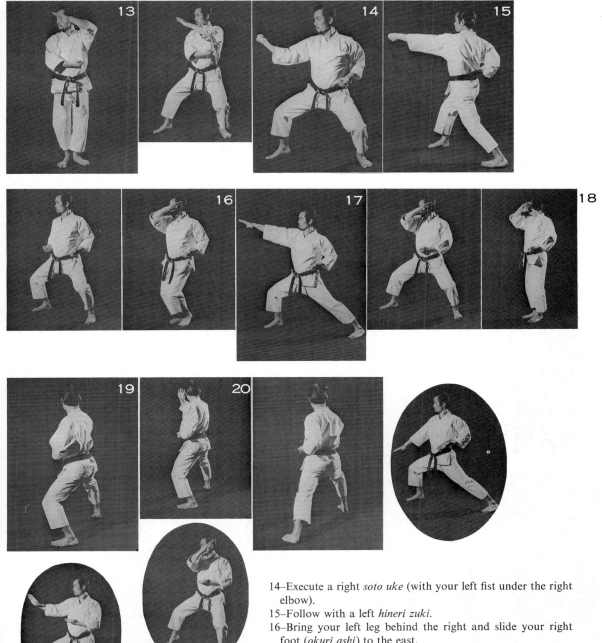

14–Execute a right *soto uke* (with your left fist under the right elbow).

15–Follow with a left *hineri zuki*.

16–Bring your left leg behind the right and slide your right foot (*okuri ashi*) to the east.

17–Deliver a right *shuto gyaku uchi* in a right *zenkutsu* stance.

18–Pivot 90° clockwise on your left foot, the right foot describing a circular motion. You are now facing south.

19–Adopting a right cat stance, execute a right *shuto uke*.

20–Switching to a right *zenkutsu* stance, execute a right *shuto gedan barai*.

21–Follow with a left *jodan nukite*.

22–Follow immediately with a left *hineri geri*.

23–Bring your left foot back to its starting position, switching to a right cat stance, and execute a right *uchi gedan barai*.

24–Rotate your head, then your body, 180° counterclockwise to the north, moving your left leg slightly to the west, and in a left cat stance execute a left *shuto uke*.

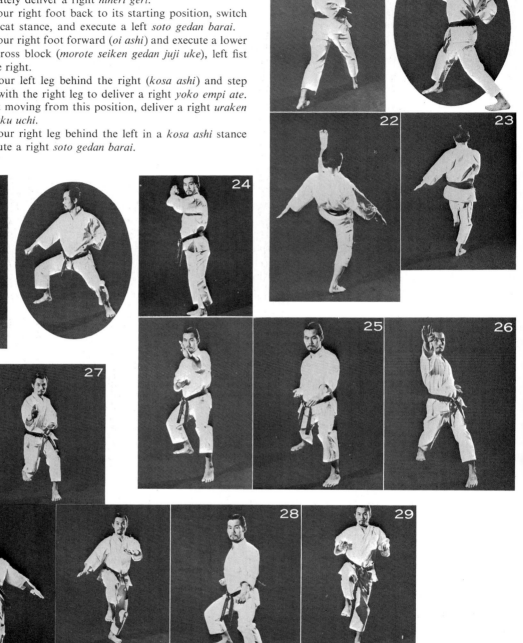

25–Switching to a left *zenkutsu* stance, execute a left *shuto gedan barai*.

26–Follow with a right *jodan nukite*.

27–Immediately deliver a right *hineri geri*.

28–Bring your right foot back to its starting position, switch to a left cat stance, and execute a left *soto gedan barai*.

29–Move your right foot forward (*oi ashi*) and execute a lower two-fist cross block (*morote seiken gedan juji uke*), left fist above the right.

30–Cross your left leg behind the right (*kosa ashi*) and step forward with the right leg to deliver a right *yoko empi ate*.

31–Without moving from this position, deliver a right *uraken jodan gyaku uchi*.

32–Cross your right leg behind the left in a *kosa ashi* stance and execute a right *soto gedan barai*.

33–Step forward with your left foot and deliver a left *empi yokò mawashi uchi*.

34–Follow immediately, without moving your feet, with a left *soto gedan barai*.

35–Without moving your feet, deliver a right *hineri empi uchi age* (upward elbow strike).

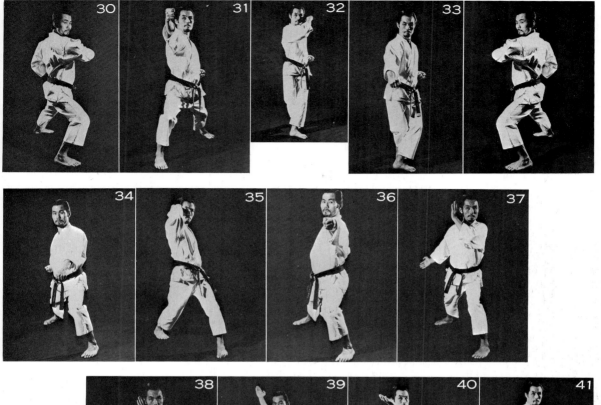

36–Switching to a *zenkutsu* stance, execute a left *sokumen* or *okuri zuki*.

37–Move your left hand across your face, executing a deflecting block with the palm (*shotei nagashi uke*).

38–Simultaneously, your right hand moves 45° downward in front of your body, palm upward (groin choke or leg grabbing movement).

39–Then the left hand moves downward, executing a *shuto soto gedan barai*, while simultaneously bringing the right hand upward behind your head, executing a *haito jodan soto uke*.

40–From this position, the right hand executes a *shuto yoko mawashi uchi*, while the left hand comes across the chest, parallel to the ground with the palm down.

41–Place the right forearm directly on the left one and execute a right *sokuto yoko geri* to the NW corner.

42–Pull your right foot back to the left knee. Then put it down on the ground in the NW direction and cross your left leg behind it in a *kosa ashi* stance.

43–Deliver a right *uraken mae uchi* to the north.

44–In the same position execute a right uppercut (*gyakuken tsuki age*).

45–Rotate 180° counterclockwise, facing south. Move your right foot forward in *neko ashi* and execute a right *uchi uke*.

46–Step forward with the left foot (*oi ashi*) and execute a lower .two-fist cross block (*morote seiken gedan juji uke*), right fist above the left.

47–Repeat steps 30 through 45 in mirror image.

48–Step forward with the left foot to the NW corner and

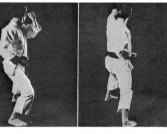

execute a left *soto gedan barai* in a *sotobiraki jigotai* stance.

49–Follow with a right *hineri zuki* in the NW direction.

50–Execute a right *hineri geri*. Bring your right foot back to the left knee and then put it down in front of your body in the NW corner.

51–In this position (right *neko ashi* stance), execute a right *soto uke*.

52–Rotate your body 90° clockwise on your left foot, your right foot coming in a circular motion to the NE corner.

53–Execute a right *soto gedan barai* in a *sotobiraki jigotai* stance.

54–Follow with a left *hineri zuki* in the NE direction.

55–Execute a left *hineri geri*. Bring your left foot back to the right knee and put it down in front of your body in the NE corner.

56–In this position (left cat stance), execute a left *soto uke*.

57–Bring your left foot aside your right foot in a *shizen hontai* stance.

58–*Zanshin.*

59–Bow with a *kenko ritsurei.*

60–Step backward (right foot first) into a *musubi* stance.

61–Bow with a *keirei.*

Bassai kata

The first six steps are the standard salutation forms already described.

7–Raise both hands above your forehead and bring them down in an outward circular motion. Clench your right fist in your left hand and tighten your knees inward in an *uchimata jigotai* stance.

8–Step forward slowly, with your left foot, in a *neko ashi* stance and raise both hands, clenched, in front of your body to your eye level.

9–Step forward with your right foot (*oi ashi*) and cross your left leg behind the right, knees deeply bent, in a *kosa ashi* stance.

10–Simultaneously execute a right *morote soto uke* while your left palm comes to press on the inside of your forearm.

11–Straighten up your body and use the upward motion to deliver a right *gyakuken tsuki age* (uppercut).

12–Rotate your head, and then your body, 180° counter-clockwise to face south, and slide your left foot forward in a left *neko ashi* stance.

13–Execute a left *shuto gedan barai* and simultaneously bring your right hand close to your right ear, the elbow being slightly above shoulder level.

14–Deliver a right *shuto yoko mawashi uchi*, at the same time pulling your left hand to the left side of your chest.

15–Simultaneously execute a right *hineri geri* and bring your right foot back to its starting position.

16–Rotate your right forearm around the elbow, palm down until parallel to the ground, and simultaneously deliver toward the front a left *nukite oi zuki* while standing in a left *zenkutsu* stance.

17–Rotate your head, and then your body, 180° clockwise facing the north. Move your right foot in a circular motion to the NE and adopt a right *neko ashi* stance.

18–Repeat steps 13 through 16 in mirror image.

19–Pivoting on the left foot, rotate your body 270° counterclockwise, your right foot moving in a circular motion to the SW corner. Adopt a left *neko ashi* stance, facing east.

20–Repeat steps 13 through 16. After completion, you are in a left *zenkutsu* stance, facing east.

21–Move your right foot forward using *hangetsu hoko* and adopt a right *neko ashi* stance.

22–Repeat steps 13 through 16 in mirror image.

23–Turn your head 90° counterclockwise, looking north. Pull both fists to your right hip (left fist above the right, right fist turned upward and left fist turned to the stomach) and rotate your body in the same direction as your head in the *shizen hontai*, facing north.

24–Execute a left *shuto uke*, tightening your knees inward in an *uchimata jigo hontai* stance.

25–Stamp on the ground with your left foot and simultaneously execute a right *shomen zuki*, immediately followed by a right *soto uke* in a low left *zenkutsu stance*, looking to the north.

26–Repeat step 25 in mirror image.

23

24

25

26

27

27–Move your right foot forward using *hangetsu* (half-circle) *hoko* and adopt a right *sotobiraki jigotai* stance. Execute a right *soto gedan barai* in a wide circular motion, the right hand coming above the right knee, and simultaneously execute a left *jodan age uke*.

28–Repeat step 27 in mirror image.

29–Repeat step 27.

30–Move your right foot backward using *hangetsu hoko* and adopt a left *neko ashi* stance. Execute a left *shuto soto uke* while your right hand comes in front of your solar plexus, palm upward.

31–Circle your right hand clockwise and bring it under your left wrist. Grab your right wrist with your left hand and pull both arms to your right hip, twisting your hips counterclockwise.

32–Raise your right knee in front of your body and from this position, deliver a right downward side-kick (*sokuto ke oroshi*).

33–Pull your right foot back to your left knee and then put it down in the NW corner.

34–Rotate your head, and then your body, 180° counterclockwise facing south. In a right *neko ashi* stance execute a left *shuto soto uke*, your right hand in front of your solar plexus, palm inward.

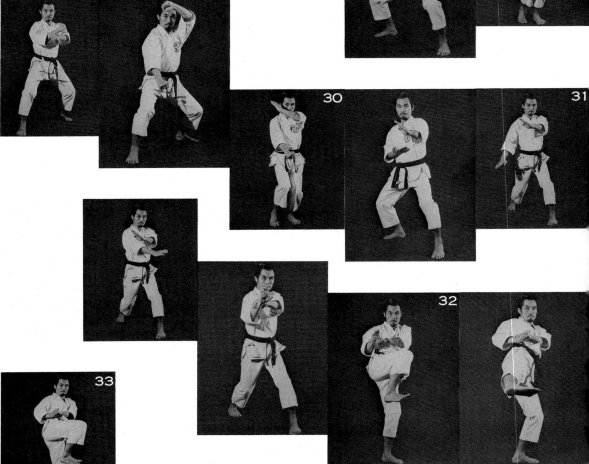

35–Move your right foot forward using *hangetsu hoko* and in a right *neko ashi* stance, execute a right *shuto soto uke*, your left hand in front of your solar plexus, palm inward.

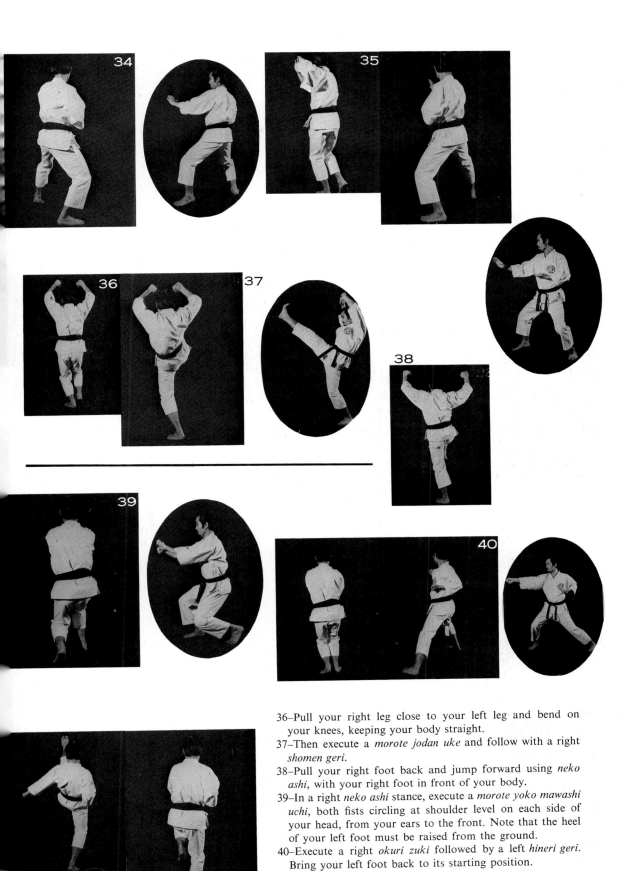

36–Pull your right leg close to your left leg and bend on your knees, keeping your body straight.

37–Then execute a *morote jodan uke* and follow with a right *shomen geri*.

38–Pull your right foot back and jump forward using *neko ashi*, with your right foot in front of your body.

39–In a right *neko ashi* stance, execute a *morote yoko mawashi uchi*, both fists circling at shoulder level on each side of your head, from your ears to the front. Note that the heel of your left foot must be raised from the ground.

40–Execute a right *okuri zuki* followed by a left *hineri geri*. Bring your left foot back to its starting position.

41–Standing in a right *neko ashi* stance, execute a right *shuto jodan soto uke*.

42–Rotate your head, and then your body, 180° counterclockwise facing north, and shift your left foot (with a circular motion) to the NW corner.

43–Execute a deflecting block across your face with your left palm (*shotei nagashi uke*).

44–Simultaneously, your right hand goes downward 45° in front of your body, palm upward (this is a groin choke or alternately a leg grabbing motion).

45–Your left hand then goes downward in a *shuto soto gedan barai*, while your right hand simultaneously goes upward behind your head in a *haito jodan soto uke*.

46–Keeping your hands in the same position, slowly bring your left foot close to your right foot in a *musubi* stance.

47–Execute a sweeping crescent-block with your right foot and put it down, stamping on the ground. Execute a right *soto gedan barai* in an *uchimata jigotai* stance.

48–Rotate your head counterclockwise to the south and deliver a left *gyaku kentsui uchi*.

49–Deliver a right *mikazuki geri* (crescent kick) into the palm of your left hand extended in front of your body and put your right foot down on the ground toward the south.

50–Adopting a right *uchimata jigotai* stance, deliver a right *empi yoko mawashi uchi* into the palm of your left hand.

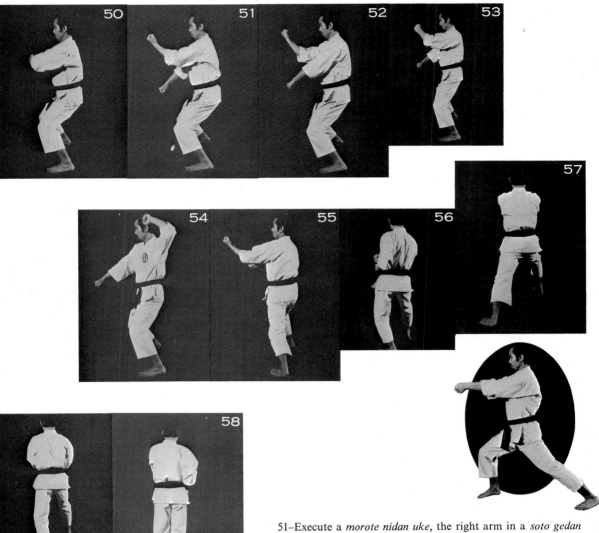

51–Execute a *morote nidan uke*, the right arm in a *soto gedan uke* and the left arm in a *soto uke*.

52–Repeat step 51 in mirror image.

53–Repeat step 51.

54–Pull your left fist to your left ear (elbow above the shoulder level) while your right hand is extended in front of your body.

55–Execute a left *uraken shomen uchi* while your right fist comes across your body below your left elbow (note that the fingers of your right fist face the ground).

56–Rotate your head 90° clockwise, at the same time bringing both fists to your left hip (as in step 23). Then rotate your body in the same direction. You are now in a right *neko ashi* stance facing south.

57–Pull your fists under your armpits, slide your right foot forward in a right *zenkutsu stance*, and execute a *morote awase zuki*.

58–Bring your right foot back next to the left in a *musubi stance*, at the same time drawing both fists to your right hip.

59–Deliver a left *shomen geri*, pull your left foot back to your right knee, and put it down in front of your body in a left *zenkutsu* stance.

60–Execute a *morote nidan zuki* (a right upper-level punch delivered simultaneously with a left middle-level punch).

61–Repeat steps 58 through 60 in mirror image.

62–Draw your fists to either side of your body. Rotate your head 180° counterclockwise facing north, and pull your left leg close to your right leg.

63–Slide your left foot to the west in a low left *zenkutsu* stance and simultaneously execute a *soto uke* with your right fist in a wide clockwise circular motion, while your left fist is pulled under your left armpit.

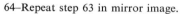

64–Repeat step 63 in mirror image.

65–Bring your left leg close to your right leg, bending on your knees. Then slide your right leg to the NE corner.

66–Execute a *soto gedan barai* with your right fist in a wide counterclockwise circular motion (at the end of this motion your right fist is above and slightly inside of your right knee) and simultaneously execute a left *jodan age uke*. During the execution of this motion you are in a right *sotobiraki jigotai* stance.

67–Slide your right leg backwards in the SE direction, rotate your head to the NW corner, and execute in this direction a left *okuri ashi* (or *fumikomi ashi*).

68–Repeat step 66 in mirror image.

69–Move your left leg back in a *shizen hontai* stance facing north, at the same time pulling both fists back in front of your thighs.

70–*Zanshin.*

71–Bow with a *kenko ritsurei.*

72–Step backwards with your right foot first into a *musubi* stance.

73–Bow with a *keirei.*

Seisan kata

The first six steps of this kata are the standard salutation forms already described.

7–Join your hands together down in front of your body, forefinger against forefinger, and thumb against thumb. Raise both hands slowly in an outward circle above your forehead, inhaling deeply.

8–Close your right hand around your left fist and bring both hands down in front of your body. Exhale and adopt an *uchimata jigo hontai* stance.

9–Move your left leg forward in a large half-moon step (*hangetsu hoko*) and slowly execute a left *soto uke*, tightening your knees and arms inward.

10–Execute a right *hineri zuki* and, without pulling your arm back, rotate your right forearm clockwise in a right *mawashi soto uke*.

11–Repeat steps 9 and 10 in mirror image.

12–Repeat steps 9 and 10.

13–Execute slowly, but with strength, a two-fisted punch (fists together) (*morote awase zuki*) in a left *zenkutsu* stance.

14–Pull both fists to your chest (the strength of the pull originating from the thumb, ring finger, and little finger), at the same time switching into a left cat stance.

15–Lift your elbows slightly above shoulder level, keeping your hands close to the nipples and forearms parallel to the ground. Deliver a double spear-hand strike (*morote nukite awase zuki*), switching into a left *zenkutsu* stance.

16–Pull your right hand across the left and pull your left foot slightly backward, bringing both hands in front of your forehead in a *shuto jodan juji uke*.

17–Keep moving the weight of your body backward and bring both hands apart on the side of your head, switching your stance from *zenkutsu* to *kokutsu*.

18–Rotate your hands, palms facing each other. Pull your arms back, chest expanded, and pause in *neko ashi* stance.

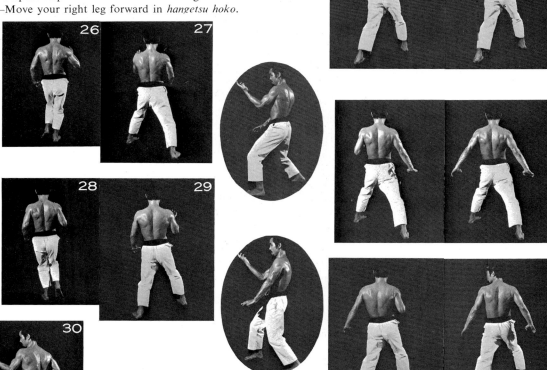

19–Switch to a *zenkutsu* stance, bringing your hands down in a circular motion in front of your body, and then pointing to the ground on either side of your body.

20–Stepping forward with a left *neko ashi*, execute a left *jodan age uke*.

21–Simultaneously deliver a right *gyakuken age zuki* (uppercut).

22–Bring your right foot close to the left in a *heisoku* stance and execute a right *yoko mawashi empi uchi* in the palm of your left hand.

23–Rotate your body 180° counterclockwise (you are now facing south) and move your left leg backwards in a right *uchimata jigotai* stance.

24–Your right arm moves in a circular motion, blocking upward with the outside edge of your hand (*haito mawashi soto uke*). Simultaneously your left arm circles downward, blocking with the inside edge of the hand (*shuto mawashi gedan otoshi*). Both blocks must be executed in front of your body.

25–Pull your right hand back to your chest (thumb and little finger joined together) while extending your left hand backwards in the NW direction. (During this motion, your hips are twisted clockwise, pivoting on your left foot with the heel towards the NW.) Then slowly extend your right arm towards the NE, moving the weight of your body forward in a right *zenkutsu* stance.

26–Move your left leg forward in *hangetsu hoko*.

27–Repeat steps 24 and 25 in mirror image.

28–Move your right leg forward in *hangetsu hoko*.

29–Repeat steps 24 and 25.

30–Rotate your head, and then your body, 90° counterclockwise, facing east, and shifting into a left *neko ashi* stance, execute a left *soto uke*.

31–From this position execute a right *hineri zuki.*

32–Then a left *sokumen zuki.*

33–Follow with a right *hineri geri* and simultaneously pull your right foot back to its starting position.

34–Execute a right *hineri zuki.*

35–Then a left *soto uke*, tightening the knees and arms inward in a left *uchimata jigotai* stance.

36–Rotating your head, and then your body, 180° clockwise, facing west, and shifting into a right *neko ashi* stance, execute a right *soto uke.*

37–Repeat steps 31 through 35 in mirror image.

38–Rotate your head, and then your body, 90° counterclockwise, facing south. Shift into a left *neko ashi* stance and excute a left *soto uke.*

39–Repeat steps 31 through 35.

40–Pull your right foot forward, close to the left, in a *heisoku* stance and rotate your head 180° clockwise (facing north). Bring your right hand across your face to your left ear, while your left hand comes in front of your solar plexus (palms down).

41–In this same position, rotate your body 180° clockwise, step forward (north) with your right foot, and cross your left behind the right in a *kosa ashi* (or *fumikomi ashi*) stance.

42–Then deliver a right *uraken shomen uchi*, pulling your left fist to your left hip.

43–Move your left foot backward into a right *neko ashi* stance and slowly raise your right fist from shoulder to eye level.

44–Then suddenly stamp on the ground with the heel of your right foot (without moving your toes) and step forward with your left foot to execute a right *oi geri*.

45–Pull your right foot back to your left knee and then put it down in front of your body. Execute a right *soto gedan barai*, your stance being a right *uchimata jigotai*.

46–Execute a left *hineri zuki*.

47–Follow with a right *jodan age uke*, tightening up your body, knees inward.

48–Repeat steps 40 through 47 in mirror image.

49–Repeat steps 40 through 45.

50–Follow with a left *hineri geri* and bring your left foot back to its starting position.

51–Move your right foot backwards, behind the left foot, using a cat-step.

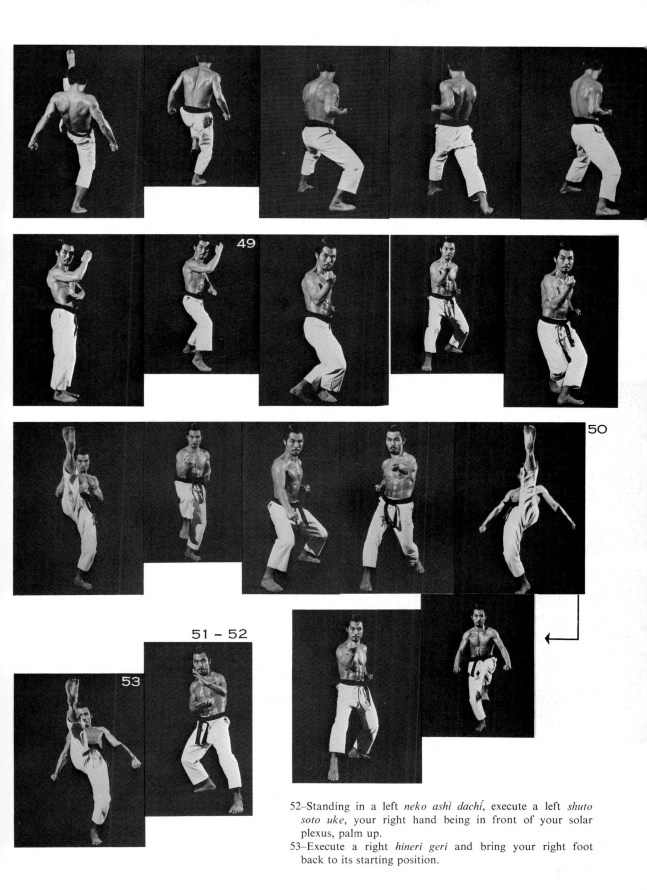

49

50

51 – 52

53

52–Standing in a left *neko ashi dachi*, execute a left *shuto soto uke*, your right hand being in front of your solar plexus, palm up.

53–Execute a right *hineri geri* and bring your right foot back to its starting position.

54–Follow with a right *hineri zuki.*
55–Bring your left foot backward, close to your right foot in a low left cat stance. Raise your hands above your head, and bringing them down in an outward circular motion, execute a low block with the palms of both hands (*morote shotei gedan awase uke*).
56–Move your left foot aside in a *shizen hontai* stance.
57–*Zanshin.*
58–Bow with a *kenko ritsurei.*
59–Step backward into a *musubi* stance.
60–Bow with a *keirei.*

4. Training for Kata

Kata is truly the essence of karatedo and there is no real progress possible without a thorough study of kata.

Since in kata one faces oneself, it must be practiced with sincerity and complete dedication. Each technique must be executed with *kiai* (a state of utmost concentration where mind and body are one). A kata must be repeated over and over again, not less than ten times at a practice, because it is only when the body gets exhausted, that the efficiency of the technique can be improved and the mind brought into play to support the failing strength. For this reason the student will, from time to time, have to push himself to the limit of his endurance. Each time the kata must be practiced a little better or a little faster.

At first each movement must be learned individually, slowly, and motion by motion, yet each time executing either a complete portion or the entire kata. Hundreds of repetitions of this type are necessary to learn the sequence of the techniques. Following this, the techniques should be executed in an expanded form using combined techniques with large exaggerated motion. This type of practice should then be followed by a practice of contracted form, using understated motion. This alternating practice develops a feeling for the right form.

In the same way kata must be practiced with alternating hard and soft executions. First maximum power is applied to each technique; then the sequence is repeated using minimum power (stressing form). This leads to an understanding of how much power should be used from motion to motion.

The rhythm of a kata is discovered in much the same way except alternating practice of fast and slow execution respectively, replaces hard and soft; thus displaying to the practitioner where speed is stressed and where it is not. This leads to a well-balanced and rhythmic kata. Kata should also be performed using different breathing sequences, retaining the breath during the execution of one technique, and then, through a plurality of techniques. In this way the student learns when to inhale and when to exhale.

Kata should also be practiced blindfolded to develop an acute sense of direction, balance, and concentration. This refinement of concentration increases the practitioner's awareness and ability to visualize the imaginary opponent.

Whenever possible, the various sequnses of techniques displayed in a kata should be put to a real test in kumite and shiai to develop their practical applications and to better understand them. Also, the observation of the fighting attitudes of various animals (even cats and dogs) is helpful to understand some of the stances, movements, and techniques used in katas.

The mental attitude to be observed in a kata is as important as the physical attitude. In particular, before executing a kata, one has to prepare oneself mentally with intense concentration (*zenshin*). During this concentration, one must empty the mind of all thoughts and visualize oneself performing the kata. During the execution, one must always try to maintain this same state of mental concentration (*tsushin*). Each time the kata must be performed maintaining this same state of mind. After completion of the kata one must bring about a state of mental quietness, calming down one's breathing and metabolism but at the same time being ready to answer any further attack. This state is called *zanshin*.

5. Kata Competition

Kata competition serves the purpose of stimulating and improving the practice of kata among students. It is also an excellent test of their technical proficiency.

There are two types of kata competition:

Kohaku (red-and-white system)

In this form of competition, two contestants wearing a red or white ribbon, or head-band, perform a kata selected beforehand or imposed by the judges. It is a direct elimination system where the winners of each phase compete until defeated.

Saiten (scoring points system)

In this type of competition, contestants perform their favorite kata, one at a time. They are awarded points by a referee assisted by four judges. The lowest and highest marks are nullified—except if given by the referee—and the other points are added up to make the score. When there are three or less judges, all the points are added up.

Points awarded range from 0.0 to 10.0. They are usually distributed in the following way by category:
–White belt: 3.0 to 5.0
–Yellow belt: 4.0 to 6.0
–Orange belt: 5.0 to 7.0
–Green belt: 6.0 to 8.0
–Brown belt: 7.0 to 9.0
–Black belt: 8.0 to 10.0

These two types of competition are judged by the same criteria. The factors taken into consideration are the following:
A. –postures and stances
B. –body and foot movements; the proper expansiveness and tightness respectively at the right time
C. –perfection of form
D. –the way the targets are aimed at (focus)
E. –control of breathing
F. –speed and power (capability and control)
G. –concentration of body and mind
H. –general attitude and manners (such as salutation forms)
I. –spirit
J. –performance line (direction) and sequence; gauging the over-all reality of the fighting situation being displayed.

In kata competition the following set of rules must be adhered to:
1–The *shiaijo* (contest area) must be entered from the side opposite the *shomen*.
2–When entering the *shiaijo*, bow with a *keirei* (ceremonial bow), and go to the center of the *shiaijo* (except for some katas, such as *sanchin*).
3–From the center, bow with a *keirei* to the referee.
4–Call loudly, and with *kiai*, the name of your kata. Begin when the referee calls "*Hajime!*"
5–Then bow with a *Kenko ritsurei* (fighting bow) to your imaginary opponent—in fact, to yourself.
6–After completion of the kata, bow with a *Kenko ritsurei* and wait until the referee renders his decision.
7–Then bow with a *keirei* to the referee and leave the *shiaijo* on the side opposite the *shomen* and bowing with a *keirei*.

chapter 6 Kumite

1. Definition and Purpose of Kumite

Kumite is an exchange of offensive techniques, defensive techniques, and motions between two, and sometimes several, karate practitioners. It is another form of practice of the art of karatedo. Like kata, it has been developed and codified by great Masters at a way of learning how to use karatedo techniques in real fighting situations, when facing one or several opponents.

If kata teaches the theory of karatedo, then kumite teaches the application of theory. In kumite, one learns how and when to attack and counterattack with a single technique or a combination of techniques. The practice of kumite leads to an understanding of all the basic principles of karatedo. Like kata, kumite develops body and foot movements, expansion and contraction of motions, control of breathing as a source of power, concentration of force, and stamina. Moreover, kumite develops a sense for the proper distance (*maai*), timing, reflexes, fighting strategies (*senjutsu*), and the psychological factors involved in an encounter with an actual opponent. The proper distance is one which is dictated by circumstances such as size, strength, and the technical level of the opponent. The timing of the attack, body movement, and counterattack mean the precise moment at which the technique must be executed. Good reflexes are necessary to be able to feel your opponent and reach him with a lightning-fast technique. *Kuzushi* is concerned with creating an opportunity to attack or counterattack, such as opening up the opponent's guard. The psychological factors involved in kumite are not only the fighting spirit, courage, and confidence in one's own ability, but also to take the initiative toward one's opponent, to anticipate his actions, and to develop a sixth sense with which to really feel not only the opponent's actions but also his mind and mental attitudes.

Unlike kata, in kumite one is pressed by an opponent so that its practice is more strenuous. There is an emulation between the two partners who are, in fact, helping each other to achieve greater results in the art of karatedo. This attitude is conducive to a mutual understanding of, and respect for each other, and thus becomes a source of harmony with others at large.

In ancient China, prearranged kumite were devised as a means of practicing the best proven techniques in a safe way by determining, in advance, the roles of attacker and defender and the number and types of techniques to be used, etc.

In Shorinji Kempo this form of practice was called *jaoshu* (meaning "crossing hands" or "exchange of techniques") or *dashu* (interspersing of blows). The Chinese art of *tai chi chuan*, in Japanese *toishu* (testing the techniques or hands), is a practice consisting of alternately pushing and pulling an opponent to develop a feeling for his body motion, strength, and *ki*.

In Okinawa, and then in Japan, kumite became known as *kumiai jutsu* or *kumi uchi*, but was mainly used to complement kata training, as a means of explaining the techniques displayed in kata. In modern days *shinan* Kori Hisataka, founder of Shorinjiryu Kenkokan Karatedo, developed a completely original form of *yakusoku randori* kumite (prearranged form of kumite sparring) which at once serves as application and training for kata, and as a preparation for *shiai* (competition) and for real fighting situations. In this form of kumite practice, the emphasis is on fast body motions, escaping techniques (sideways and in circular motions) as a superior form of blocking, and the coordination and combination of hand and foot techniques.

In Kenkokan Karatedo, kumite is practiced with either empty-hands or weapons (see Chapter 9), and with or without protective equipment.

2. Classification of Kumite

Kumite can be divided into two broad categories: yakusoku (pre-arranged form) kumite and jiyu (free form) kumite.

a) *Yokusoku kumite:* It consists of a sequence of techniques and motions practiced by two or more opponents in a completely predetermined way. Like kata, they contain all the basic elements of karatedo: salutation, stances, body movements, punching, kicking striking, blocking techniques, etc., but performed alternately by each partner. The techniques displayed in *yakusoku* kumite can be considered model techniques, successfully tested by karatedo Masters. These as well include lethal techniques which can be safely practiced because of the agreed upon rules not applicable in free-form kumite.

Because of these rules, *yakusoku* kumite can be learned and practiced by any karatedo student, regardless of his physical condition, and thus allows him to benefit from karatedo training without any risk.

Training in *yakusoku* kumite also permits the student to develop a comprehensive technical knowledge that he can then use in free-form kumite, in competition, or, if need be, in self-defense. Also, as mentioned before, the student will find in this type of kumite the practical application of the various kata techniques. *Yakusoku* kumite can be further divided into three categories.

***Tanshiki* (or *ippon*) kumite:** It consists of a single predetermined attack followed by a counterattack. This is the first step in the practice of kumite. It allows the student to learn a single technique at a time, fully concentrating on its execution, without having to worry about any related or subsequent techniques. It also illustrate the fundamental principle of karatedo which is to dispose of one's opponent immediately and with a single technique.

***Fukushiki* kumite:** The attacker executes a combination of two, three, four, or five offensive techniques which are blocked and evaded by the defender who then executes a counterattack. (*Nihon, sanbon, yonhon,* and *gohon* kumite.)

***Randori* kumite:** In this type of kumite each partner executes a series of single or combination attacking and counterattacking techniques. The order of execution of each technique is fixed and arranged in advance, as in a kata. The roles of each partner are then reversed and practiced in mirror image, to develop an all-round capability in the execution of each motion and technique. Each partner must be able to assume the role of the other(s) to fully understand his own role. He must also be able to perform his techniques in mirror image to achieve complete versatility.

Classification of *yakusoku randori* kumite

b) ***Jiyu* kumite:** In this type of kumite the techniques are not pre-arranged. In *tanshiki* and *fukushiki jiyu* kumite the roles of attacker and defender are still determined in advance but the choice of techniques is left to each partner. *Jiyu randori* kumite is the actual sparring where any partner can attack with any technique or combinations of techniques. The assault is called off when a decisive technique has been scored but resumes after the partners have returned to their starting positions.

Jiyu kumite develops real fighting attitudes, reflexes, and the sixth sense which is the feeling for one's opponent. It teaches how to maneuver one's opponent, and break up his position or guard. It is oriented to practice under real conditions. It allows the student to have a free mind, unconcerned with injuries or with losing. He will then be more inclined to try out and test different techniques or moves. By practicing *jiyu* kumite, the student will develop the efficiency of his techniques according to his own size, strength, speed, and other characteristics.

***Jiyu randori* kumite:** It is usually practiced with protective equipment so that blows can be delivered with full power and speed, without having to stop the motion yet not risk injury.

***Jiyu* kumite:** It is not illustrated in this chapter. It is intended that the illustration of *yakusoku* kumite will serve as a source of inspiration for the practice of *jiyu* kumite.

Classification of *yakusoku randori* kumite

***Go ho no* kumite:** This kumite derives its name "five techniques" from the fact that each *go ho no* kumite contains five of the most fundamental and outstanding techniques of karatedo which have been inspired from the basic fighting attitudes of five animals (tiger, snake, crane, monkey, and dragon, the last representing the spirit). There are five different go ho no kumite and they all are recommended for 10th and 9th *kyu* students (white belt).

***Renshu* kumite:** Renshu (training) kumite contain most of the basic techniques and principles of karatedo. *Renshu ichi* (No. 1) emphasizes the use of the front hand and is recommended for 10th and 9th *kyu* students while *renshu ni* (No. 2), which teaches the use of the back hand, is recommended for 8th and 7th *kyu* students (yellow belt). In the section entitled "Illustration of *yakusoku* kumite," *renshu ni* is demonstrated in a left stance to stress the necessity of practicing from the right as well as the left side. Similarily, renshu *ichi* is demonstrated using *okuri ashi* (sliding step) as the basic body and foot movement. Subsequently, *neko ashi* (cat step) is used because it is much faster and allows motions of wider amplitude than *okuri ashi*.

Nijushiho waza: This kumite was originally an application of the kata of the same name. It emphasizes diagonal and circular motions against one or two opponents, the former being recommended for 8th and 7th *kyu* students and the latter for more advanced students.

***Randori* kumite:** There are five of these "sparring" kumite specially designed for this purpose. They emphasize combination techniques and all-round fighting. They are recommended for students from the 6th *kyu* to the 2nd *kyu* (orange to brown belt.)

***Sankakutobi* kumite:** There are eleven different *sankakutobi* kumite, three of them practiced with weapons (*buki ho*). As their name ("jumping or leaping in triangular motions") implies, *sankakutobi* movements are quick and performed in a triangle, avoiding direct clashes with the opponents. *Sankakutobi* kumite are some of the most dynamic and representative of all kumite of Kenkokan Karatedo. Sankakutobi kata originated from this kumite. They are recommended for all students from the rank of 6th kyu and more advanced.

***Naihanchin* kumite (or *waza*):** This kumite comes from the kata of the same name. It also emphasizes sideways fighting techniques against one or two opponents and is recommended for 4th and 3rd *kyu* students (green belt).

Sanchin waza: This kumite is derived from sanchin kata. It teaches close-fighting techniques and armlocks. It is recommended for 1st kyu students (brown belt).

Gorin no waza (or **Itsutsu no waza**): As its name implies, *itsutsu no waza* illustrates the five basic fighting principles, practiced with protection in order to fully understand them:

I–A direct and unique attack to a *kyusho* (vital point); this is the first principle of a karatedo technique: to be unique and completely successful at once.

II–An evading motion using *tai sabaki* (body-evading motion). This is the first defensive principle. Do not oppose your strength to your opponent's strength but rather avoid his attack. In doing so, you cannot be overcome by any opponent however strong he may be.

III–Turn your opponent's attack against himself. After the opponent's attack has been avoided, he is either off balance or his guard is open. In a flowing motion the evading move should be transformed into a powerful counterattack.

IV–Application of the principle of contrast: a high attack should be answered by a low counterattack, a hard technique by a soft one, a hand attack countered by a foot technique, etc.

V–Sacrifice technique: in some cases it is best to sacrifice one's balance, such as throwing oneself on the ground or to fall upon one's opponent, rendering his attack ineffective.

3. Illustration of Yakusoku Kumite

a. *Tanshiki kumite*

The general scheme of *Tanshiki kumite* is:

Offensive side:
Attacking technique

Defensive side:
Evading-blocking technique counterattacking

Three different attacking techniques using the hand will be explained and three different counter techniques will be shown for each type of attack. Then three different attacking techniques using the feet will be presented. For each of the three, different counterattacks will be used.

As in *kata*, the cardinal points will be used to indicate the direction of movements.

Offensive (Facing east):
Stand in a left *neko ashi* stance, left fist in front of the body *(seiken chudan kamae).*

Defensive (facing west):
Stand in a left *neko ashi* stance, left open hand in front of the body *(shuto chudan kamae).*

1st Hand Technique

Offensive Side
Stepping forward with a left *okuri ashi*, execute a left *okuri mae zuki* to the face *(men).*

Defensive Side
a–Step back with a left *okuri ashi* to the NE and execute a left *age uke.*
 –Counter with a right *empi yoko mawashi uchi* to the ribs *(do).*
b–Step back with a left *neko ashi* to the NE and execute a left *shuto soto uke.*
 –Counter with a left *sokuto yoko geri* to the ribs *(do).*
c–Step back with a left *hiraki ashi* to the SE and execute a left *shuto uchi uke.*
 –Counter with a right *ushiro mawashi geri* to the face *(men).*

2nd Hand Technique

Offensive Side
Stepping forward with a right *oi ashi*, execute a right *oi mae zuki* to the face *(men).*

Defensive Side
a–Step back with a right *yoko tobi* (lateral leaping motion) to the north and execute a left *shuto soto uke.*
 –Counter with a *shuto uchi otoshi* to the top of the head *(men).*
b–Step back with a left *neko ashi* to the NE and execute a left *shuto soto uke.*
 –Counter with a right *hineri mawashi geri* (using the ball or instep of the foot) to the solar plexus *(do).*
c–Step back with a left *hiraki ashi* to the SE and execute a left *shuto uchi uke.*
 –Counter with a right *hineri mae zuki* to the ribs *(do).*

199

3rd Hand Technique
Offensive Side

Stepping forward with a left *neko ashi*, execute a right *hineri mae zuki* to the solar plexus *(do)*.

Defensive Side

a–Step back with a *hiraki ashi* to the SE and execute a left *ude uchi uke*.

– Counter with a right *hineri mae zuki* to the face *(men)*.

b–Step back with a left *neko ashi* to the NE and execute a left *shuto soto uke*.

– Counter with a right *hineri mawashi geri* to the face *(men)*.

c–Step back with a left *hiraki ashi* to the SE and execute a left *shuto uchi uke*.

– Counter with a left *sokuto yoko geri* to the solar plexus *(do)*.

1st Foot Technique
Offensive Side

Stepping forward with a left *oi ashi*, execute a left *oi mae geri* to the solar plexus *(do)* using the heel of the foot.

Defensive Side

a–Step back with a left *neko ashi* to the NE and execute a left *ude soto gedan barai*.

– Counter with a right *hineri mawashi geri* to the face *(men)*.

b–Step back with a left *neko ashi* to the NE and execute a left *ude soto gedan barai*.

– Counter with a right *hineri mae zuki* to the face *(men)*.

c–Step back with a left *hiraki ashi* to the SE and execute a left *ude uchi gedan barai*.

– Counter with a left *oi mawashi geri* to the solar plexus *(do)*.

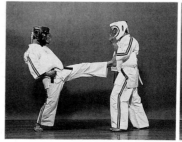

2nd Foot Technique
Offensive Side
Stepping forward with a left *neko ashi*, execute a right *hineri mae geri*, using the heel or ball of the foot, to the solar plexus *(do)*.

Defensive Side
a–Step back with a right *yoko tobi* to the north and execute a left *ude soto gedan barai*.
  –Counter with a right *hineri mawashi geri*, using the instep, to the solar plexus *(do)*.
b–Step back with a left *hiraki ashi* to the SE and execute a left *uchi sukui uke nagashi*.
  –Counter with a right *hineri mae zuki* to the solar plexus *(do)*.
c–Step back with a left *neko ashi* to the NE and execute a left *ude soto gedan barai*.
  –Counter with a left *sokuto yoko geri* to the solar plexus.

3rd Foot Technique
Offensive Side
Stepping forward using a *kosa ashi*, deliver a left *sokuto yoko geri* to the solar plexus *(do)*.
Defensive Side
a–Step back with a left *hiraki ashi* to the SE and execute a left *ude uchi gedan barai*.
  –Counter with a right *ushiro mawashi geri* to the face *(men)*.
b–Step back with a left *ushiro mawari ashi* to the SE and execute a left *ude gedan uchi*.
  –Counter with a right *shuto ushiro mawashi uchi* to the face *(men)*.
c–Step back with a left *neko ashi* to the NE and execute a left *ude soto gedan barai*.
  –Counter with a right *shuto uchi otoshi* to the head *(men)*.

b. *Fukushiki kumite*

This multiple-technique *kumite* can be further subdivided into *Nihon kumite* (two techniques), *Sanbon kumite* (three techniques), *Yonhon kumite* (four techniques), and *Gohon kumite* (five techniques).

Nihon and *Sanbon kumite* will be illustrated in this section. *Yonhon* and *Gohon kumite* can be viewed as a combination of two *Nihon kumite* and of a *Nihon* and *Sanbon kumite*.

Nihon kumite

The general scheme of this *kumite* is the following:

Offensive	Defensive
1–Attack	2–Evade and Block
3–Attack	4–Evade and Block
	5–Counterattack

Five "foot-hand" and five "hand-foot" combination techniques will be described and illustrated as they are the most representative of the various possible combinations of hand and foot techniques.

Offensive	Defensive
Stand in a left *hiraki ashi* or *neko ashi* stance with a left *seiken chudan kamae*.	Stand in a left *hiraki ashi* or *neko ashi* stance with a left *seiken chudan kamae*.

1st "foot-hand" Combination Techniques
1–Execute a left *chudan oi mae geri*, using the heel of the foot, to the right of your opponent's centerline *(do)* making him move to his left.
3–Follow through with a right *jodan hineri mae zuki* to the face *(men)*.
2–Step back with a left *neko ashi* to the NE and execute a left *ude soto gedan barai*.
4–Step back with a left *neko ashi* to the NE and execute a left *jodan ude soto uke*.
5–Counter with a right *hineri mae zuki* to the face *(men)*.

2nd "foot-hand" Combination Technique
1–Execute a right *chudan hineri mae geri*, with heel of the foot, to the left of your opponent's centerline *(do)*.
3–Follow through with a left *jodan hineri mae zuki* to the face *(men)*.
2–Step back with a left *neko ashi* to the NE and execute a left *ude soto gedan barai*.
4–Step back with a left *hiraki ashi* to the SE and execute a left *jodan ude uchi uke*.
5–Counter with a right *jodan ushiro mawashi geri* to the face *(men)*.

3rd "foot-hand" Combination Technique

1–Execute a left *chudan sokuto yoko geri* to the right of your opponent's centerline *(do)*.

3–Follow through with a *jodan shuto gyaku uchi* to the temple or jugular vein *(men)*.

2–Step back with a left *neko ashi* to the NE and execute a left *ude uchi gedan barai*.

4–Step back with a right *hiraki ashi* 180 degrees backward to the NE and execute a right *shuto uchi nagashi uke*.

5–Counter with a left *chudan hineri mawashi geri* to the solar plexus or kidney *(do)*.

4th "foot-hand" Combination Technique

1–Execute a right *chudan hineri mawashi geri* to the solar plexus or liver *(do)*.

3–Follow through with a left *uraken jodan ushiro mawashi uchi* to the face *(men)*.

2–Step back with a left *neko ashi* to the NE and execute a left *ude soto gedan nagashi uke*.

4–Assume a one-leg stance *(sagi ashi)* and execute a left *shuto jodan soto uke*.

5–Counter with a left *chudan sokuto yoko geri* to the solar plexus *(do)*.

5th "foot-hand" Combination Technique

1–Execute a right *chudan ushiro kaiten geri* to the solar plexus *(do)*.

3–Follow through with a right *shuto jodan gyaku uchi* to the temple or jugular vein *(men)*.

2–Step back with a left *hiraki ashi* to the SE and execute a left *ude uchi gedan nagashi uke*.

4–Step back with the left leg into a right *hiraki ashi* 180 degrees backward to the SE and execute a right *shuto jodan soto uke*.

5–Counter with a left *jodan hineri mae zuki* to the face *(men)*.

1st "hand-foot" Combination Technique

1–Execute a left *jodan okuri mae zuki* to the left side of your opponent's face *(men)*.

3–Follow through with a right *chudan kaiten geri* to the solar plexus *(do)*.

2–Step back with a left *neko ashi* backward to the NE and execute a left *shuto jodan soto uke*.

4–Step back with a left *hiraki ashi* to the SE and execute a left *shuto uchi gedan sukui uke*.

5–Counter with a right *jodan hineri mae zuki* to the face *(men)*.

2nd "hand-foot" Combination Technique

1–Execute a right *jodan oi mae zuki* to the left side of the face *(men)*.

3–Follow through with a left *chudan hineri mawashi geri*, using the ball or instep of the foot, to the solar plexus *(do)*.

2–Step back with a left *neko ashi* to the NE and execute a left *shuto jodan soto uke*.

4–Step back with a left *hiraki ashi* to the SE and execute a left *shuto uchi gedan nagashi uke*.

5–Counter with a right *jodan ushiro mawashi geri* to the face *(men)*.

3rd "hand-foot" Combination Technique

1–Execute a right *jodan hineri mae zuki* to the left side of the face *(men)*.

3–Follow through with a left *chudan oi mawashi geri*, using the ball or the instep of the foot, to the solar plexus *(do)*.

2–Step back with a left *hiraki ashi* to the SE and execute a left *shuto jodan uchi nagashi uke*.

4–Step back with a left *neko ashi* to the SE and execute a left *shuto gedan soto mawashi uke*.

5–Counter with a right *jodan hineri mae zuki* to the face.

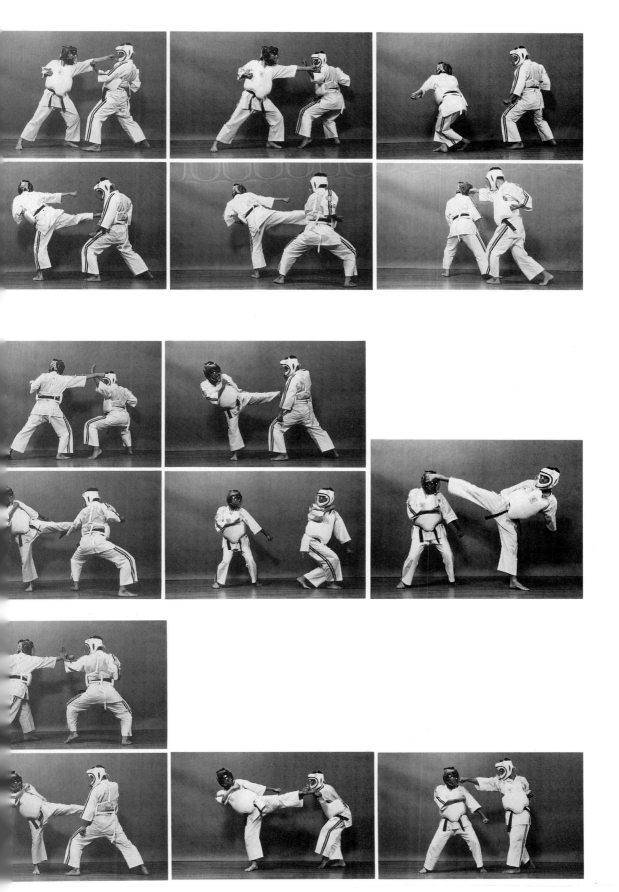

4th "hand-foot" Combination Technique

1–Execute a left *jodan uraken gyaku uchi* to the face *(men)*.

3–Follow through with a left *chudan sokuto yoko geri* to the solar plexus *(do)*.

2–Step back with a left *neko ashi* to the NE and execute a left *shuto jodan soto uke*.

4–Step back with a left *neko ashi* to the NE and execute a left *shuto soto gedan barai*.

5–Counter with a right *jodan hineri mawashi geri* to the face *(men)*.

5th "hand-foot" Combination Technique

1–Execute a right *jodan shuto uchi otoshi* to the left side of the head *(men)*.

3–Follow through with a left *chudan hineri mawashi geri*, using the ball or instep of the foot, to the solar plexus *(do)*.

2–Step back with a left *neko ashi* to the NE and execute a left *shuto jodan mawashi uke*.

4–Step in with a left *fumikomi ashi* to the east and execute a right *ude gyaku soto gedan barai*.

5–Counter with a left *jodan choku zuki* to the face *(men)*.

Sanbon kumite

The first technique of *sanbon kumite* is aimed at opening the opponent's guard *(kuzushi)*. The second is the decisive technique that must destroy the opponent *(kime)*, while the third is a supporting technique *(engo)*, in case the opponent has not been completely disposed of.

Offensive:
Stand in a right *neko ashi* stance with a right *seiken chudan kamae*.

Defensive:
Stand in a right *neko ashi* stance with a right *seiken kamae* (or a right *shizen hontai kamae*).

Five "foot-hand-hand" and five "hand-foot-foot" techniques will be illustrated and described in detail. From these examples, many other combinations can be worked out.

1st "foot-hand-hand" combination technique

1 –Execute a right *chudan oi mae geri*, using the ball or heel of the foot, to the left of your opponent's centerline *(do)*, making him/her move to his/her left.

3–Follow through with a right *jodan choku zuki* to the face *(men)*.

5–Execute a left *chudan hineri zuki* to the solar plexus *(do)*.

2–Step back with a right *hiraki ashi* to the NE and execute a right *ude uchi gedan barai*.

4–Execute a right *ude jodan uchi uke*.

6–Step back with a right *neko ashi* to the SE and execute a right *ude soto gedan barai*.

7–Follow with a left *jodan hineri mae zuki* to the face.

2nd "foot-hand-hand" combination technique

1—Execute a left *chudan hineri mae geri*, using the heel or ball of the foot, to the right of your opponent's centerline *(do)*, making him/her move to his/her left.

3—Follow through with a left *jodan choku zuki* to the face *(men)*.

5—Execute a right *chudan hineri mae zuki* to the solar plexus *(do)*.

2—Step back with a right *neko ashi* to the SE and execute a right *ude soto gedan barai*.

4—Execute a right *ude jodan uchi uke*.

6—Step back with a right *hiraki ashi* to the NE and execute a right *ude uchi gedan barai*.

7—Follow with a left *jodan hineri mawashi geri*, using the instep, to the face *(men)*.

3rd "foot-hand-hand" combination technique

1—Execute a right *chudan sokuto yoko geri* to the right of your opponent's centerline *(do)*.

3—Follow through with a right *jodan shuto gyaku uchi* to the temple or jugular vein *(men)*.

5—Execute a left *chudan hineri mae zuki* to the solar plexus *(do)*.

2—Step back with a right *neko ashi* to the SE and execute a right *ude soto gedan barai*.

4—Execute a right *shuto jodan soto uke*.

6—Step back with a right *neko ashi* and execute a right *ude soto gedan barai*.

7—Follow with a right *chudan oi sokuto yoko geri*.

4th "foot-hand-hand" combination technique

1—Execute a left *chudan hineri mawashi geri* to the right side *(do)*.

3—Follow through with a right *jodan uraken ushiro kaiten uchi* to the face *(men)*.

5—Execute a left *chudan hineri mae zuki* to the solar plexus.

2—Step back with a right *neko ashi* to the NE and execute a left *shuto soto mawashi gedan barai*.

4—Execute a right *shuto jodan soto uke*.

6—Step back with a left *hiraki ashi* to the SE and execute a left *ude uchi gedan barai*.

7—Follow with a right *jodan ushiro kaiten geri*, using the ball of the foot, to the face *(men)*.

5th "foot-hand-hand" combination technique

1–Execute a left *chudan ushiro kaiten geri* to the left side *(do)*.

3–Follow through with a left *jodan uraken gyaku uchi* to the temple *(men)*.

5–Execute a right *chudan hineri mae zuki* to the solar plexus *(do)*.

2–Step back with a right *neko ashi* to the NE and execute a right *shuto soto mawashi gedan barai*.

4–Execute a right *shuto jodan uchi uke*.

6–Step back with a *neko ashi* to the NE and execute a right *ude uchi gedan barai*.

7–Follow with a left *jodan ushiro kaiten geri* to the face.

Sanbon kumite: "hand-foot-foot"

The "hand-foot-foot" combination techniques will be demonstrated with the attacker standing in a right *neko ashi* stance with a right *seiken chudan kamae*, the defender still assuming a right *neko ashi* stance (or *shizen hontai kamae*) with a right *seiken* (or *shuto*) *chudan kamae*.

1st "hand-foot-foot" combination technique

1–Execute a right *jodan choku zuki* to the right side of your opponent's face *(men)*.

3–Follow through with a left *chudan ushiro kaiten geri* to the solar plexus *(do)*.

5–Execute a right *jodan hineri mawashi geri* to the face *(men)*.

2–Step back with a right *neko ashi* to the SE and execute a right *shuto jodan soto uke*.

4–Step back with a right *hiraki ashi* to the NE and execute a right *shuto soto mawashi gedan barai*.

6–Step back with a left *hiraki ashi* to the NE and execute a left *shuto jodan soto uke*.

7–Follow with a right *jodan hineri mae zuki* to the face.

2nd "hand-foot-foot" combination technique

1–Execute a left *jodan choku zuki* to the right side of your opponent's face *(men)*.

3–Follow through with a right *chudan hineri mawashi geri* to the solar plexus *(do)*.

5–Execute a left *jodan ushiro kaiten geri* to the face *(men)*.

2–Step back with a right *neko ashi* to the SE and execute a right *shuto jodan soto uke*.

4–Step back with a right *hiraki ashi* to the NE and execute a right *shuto mawashi soto gedan barai*.

6–Step back with a left *hiraki ashi* to the NE and execute a left *shuto jodan soto uke*.

7–Follow with a right *chudan ushiro kaiten geri* to the solar plexus *(do)*.

3rd "hand-foot-foot" combination technique

1–Execute a left *jodan hineri mae zuki* to the right side of your opponent's face *(men)*.

3–Follow through with a right *chudan oi mawashi geri*, using the instep or ball of the foot, to the solar plexus *(do)*.

5–Execute a left *jodan hineri mawashi geri*, using the instep, to the face *(men)*.

2–Step back with a right *hiraki ashi* to the NE and execute a right *shuto jodan uchi uke*.

4–Step back with a right *neko ashi* to the NE and execute a right *shuto mawashi soto gedan barai*.

6–Step back with a right *neko ashi* to the SE and execute a right *shuto jodan soto uke*.

7–Follow with a left *chudan hineri mae zuki* to the solar plexus *(do)*.

4th "hand-foot-foot" combination technique

1–Execute a right *choku zuki* or *jodan uraken gyaku uchi* to the face *(men)*.

3–Follow through with a right *chudan sokuto yoko geri* to the ribs *(do)*.

5–Execute a left *jodan ushiro kaiten geri* to the face *(men)*.

2–Step back with a right *neko ashi* to the SE and execute a right *shuto jodan soto uke*.

4–Step back with a right *neko ashi* to the SE and execute a right *shuto soto gedan barai*.

6–Step back with a left *hiraki ashi* to the NE and execute a left *shuto jodan soto uke*.

7–Follow with a right *jodan hineri mawashi geri*, using the instep, to the face *(men)*.

5th "hand-foot-foot" combination technique

1–Execute a left *jodan kentsui uchi otoshi* to the top of your opponent's head *(men)*.

3–Follow through with a right *chudan hineri hiza geri* to the solar plexus *(do)*.

5–Execute a left *chudan hineri hiza geri* to the kidney *(do)*.

2–Step back with a right *neko ashi* to the SE and execute a right *shuto jodan soto uke*.

4–Step back with a right *hiraki ashi* to the NE and execute a *nidan uke*.

6–Step in with a right *fumikomi ashi* to the west and execute a *nidan mawashi uke*. Grab his/her left leg *(kata ashi tori)*, pull up with the right hand while pushing down on the neck with the left hand, and prepare for a front foot sweep with your left foot *(de ashi barai)*.

7–Simultaneously twist and throw.

8–Follow with a right *hineri otoshi zuki* to the face.

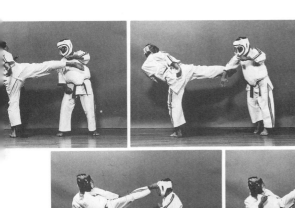

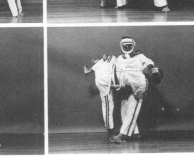

Randori Kumite

Renshu kumite *ichi*

Offensive:

–Standing in a *musubi ashi* stance, bow with a *keirei* (ceremonial bow) to *shomen* (north).

–Loudly call the name of the kumite with *kiai*.

–Bow with a *kenko ritsurei* (fighting bow) to your opponent (west).

–*Kamaete*.

1–Slide your right foot forward, your right fist in front of your body, in a right *neko ashi* stance (*seiken chudan kamae*). (Fig. 1)

3–Move forward using *okuri ashi* and execute a right *sokumen zuki* (or *oi zuki*) to the solar plexus of your opponent. (Figs. 2–3)

6–Move backward using *okuri ashi* to the SW corner and execute a right *uchi uke* in a right *sotobiraki jigotai* stance. (Figs. 4–5)

7–Step forward in the NE direction and execute a right *oi geri* with your heel to the opponent's groin. Draw your right foot back in front of your body. (Figs. 6–8)

9–Sliding your right foot to the SE corner, deliver a right *gyaku kentsui uchi* in a right *zenkutsu* stance to your opponent's left temple. (Fig. 9)

12–Pull your right leg back close to the left and then slide it backward to the NW corner, executing a right *gyaku gedan barai*. (Figs. 10–11)

13–Move forward to the SE corner using *okuri ashi* and deliver a left *shuto yoko mawashi uchi* to your opponent's neck (jugular vein). Then draw your left hand close to your left ear. (Figs. 12–13)

16–Draw your left leg close to the right, then slide your right foot in the SE direction and twist your body to face the north, pivoting around your left foot in a circular motion. Then, in a right *neko ashi* stance, execute a right *shotei yoko nagashi uke*, pushing your opponent's left shoulder. (Figs. 14–15)

18–Stand in a right *neko ashi* stance with a right *seiken chudan kamae* (right fist in front of your body). (Fig. 16)

Then:

a–Pull your right leg backward into a *shizen hontai* stance.

b–Observe *zanshin*.

c–Bow with a *kenko ritsurei* to your opponent.

d–Step backward with your right foot first into a *musubi ashi* stance.

e–Bow with a *keirei* to *shomen*.

Defensive:

–Stand in a *musubi ashi* stance and bow with a *keirei* to *shomen* (north).

–Bow with a *kenko ritsurei* to your opponent (east).

–*Kamaete.*

2–Slide your right foot backward into a left *neko ashi* stance, keeping your left fist in front of your body (*seiken chudan kamae*). (Fig. 1)

4–Slide your right foot backward to the NE corner and in a *sotobiraki jigotai* stance, execute a left *soto uke*. (Figs. 2–3)

5–Follow with a right *oi zuki* to your opponent's face and draw your right foot back in front of your left foot. (Figs. 4–5)

8–Slide your right foot backward (*hiraki ashi*) to the SE corner and in a *sotobiraki jigotai* stance, execute a left *uchi gedan barai*. (Figs. 6–7)

10–Move backward to the SE corner using *okuri ashi* and execute an upper two-fisted block (*jodan morote awase uke*) in a *sotobiraki* (or *uchimata*) *jigotai* stance. (Figs. 8–9)

11–From this position, execute a right *hineri geri* with the ball of the foot to your opponent's ribs, drawing your right foot back close to the left. Then move your left leg backward to the SE corner and into a right *neko ashi* stance. (Figs. 10–12)

14–Bend low on your knees (*otoshi mi*), body straight, arms extended in the direction of your toes (to keep your balance), and continue to look at your opponent's eyes. (Fig. 13)

15–Stepping forward with your left leg, cross your right leg behind it (in a *kosa ashi* stance) and slide your left leg to the NW corner, at the same time delivering a left *empi yoko mawashi uchi* to your opponent's solar plexus. (Figs. 14–15)

17–Turn your head to the west, looking at your opponent's eyes, and move your right leg slightly to the north, adopting a left *neko ashi* stance. Your left fist is in front of your body in a *seiken chudan kamae*. (Fig. 16)

·Then:

a–Pull your right leg forward into a *shizen hontai* stance.

b–Observe *zanshin*.

c–Bow with a *kenko ritsurei* to your opponent.

d–Step backward with your right foot first into a *musubi ashi* stance.

e–Bow with a *keirei* to *shomen*.

Renshu **kumite** *ni*

Offensive:

Standard salutation forms—*kamaete.*

1–Stand in a left *neko ashi* stance, your left fist in front of your body (*seiken chudan kamae*). (Fig. 1)

2–Step forward using *neko ashi* and execute a left *sokumen zuki* to the solar plexus (or face) or your opponent. (Figs. 2–4)

5–Step backward to the SW corner with *neko ashi* and execute a left *soto uke*. (Fig. 5)

6–Step forward to the NE corner with *neko ashi* and execute a right *hineri zuki* to your opponent's ribs. (Figs. 6–7)

9–Moving backwards to the SW corner with *kosa ashi* (left leg crossing in front of the right leg), execute a left *soto gedan barai*. (Fig. 8)

10–Execute a right *hineri geri* with the heel to the solar plexus and draw your right leg back in front of your body. (Figs. 9–10)

13–Step to the NW corner with a right backward *neko ashi* and execute a right *soto gedan barai*, standing in a right *kokutsu* stance. (Figs. 11–12).

14–Execute a left *mawashi geri* with the ball of the foot to the ribs, rotating 315° to face east in a left *neko ashi* stance. (Figs. 13–17)

16–Stand in a left *seiken chudan kamae*, facing your opponent (east). (Fig. 18)

Then execute the standard salutation forms already described (steps 'a' to 'e' in *renshu* kumite *ichi*).

Defensive:

Standard salutation forms—*kamaete.*

1–Stand in a right *neko ashi* stance, your right fist in front of your body (*seiken chudan kamae*). (Fig. 1)

3–Step backward to the NE corner with *neko ashi* and execute a right *uchi uke*. (Figs. 2–3)

4–Follow with a left *oi zuki* to the face of your opponent (in the SW corner). (Figs. 4–5)

7–Bring your left leg behind the right in a circular motion to the NE (*hiraki ashi*) and, in a right *neko ashi* stance, execute a right *uchi uke* (Fig. 6).

8–Moving to the SW corner, your left leg crossing in front of the right (*kosa ashi* step), execute a right *sokuto yoko geri* to your opponent's left knee (or ribs). Draw your right foot back in front of your left leg. (Figs. 7–9)

11–Shift your left foot to the SE corner and execute a right *soto gedan barai*. (Fig. 10)

12–Execute a left *hineri geri* with the heel to your opponent's ribs and draw your left foot back to its starting position. (Figs. 11–13).

15–Step backward to the SE corner with a right *neko ashi* and execute a right *soto gedan barai* standing in a right *kokutsu* stance, then execute a left *mawashi geri* with the ball of the foot to your oppohent's ribs, rotating 180° to face west in a right *neko ashi* stance (Figs. 14–17).

16–Step forward with a right *neko ashi*, facing your opponent in a right *seiken chudan kamae*. (Fig. 18)

Then execute the standard salutation forms already described.

Randori **kumite** *go*

Offensive:

Standard salutation forms—*kamaete.*

1–Stand in a left *neko ashi* stance, facing your opponent in a left *seiken chudan kamae.* (Fig. 1)

2–Shift your left foot to the NE corner, opening your guard to induce your opponent into attacking you. (Fig. 2)

4–Step backward to the SW corner with a left *neko ashi* and deliver a left *kentsui gyaku uchi* to the solar plexus of your opponent, at the same time stepping forward with your left foot in a *zenkutsu* stance. (Figs. 3–5)

7–Move your left leg backward to the SW corner using *hiraki ashi*, and in a *sotobiraki jigotai* stance, execute a right *uchi gedan barai.* Then again move backward to the SW corner, using a right *okuri ashi*, and execute a right *jodan uchi uke.* (Figs 6–8)

8–Execute a right *okuri geri* with the heel to your opponent's groin. Draw your right leg back to your left knee and step with your right leg to the NE corner, at the same time delivering a right *kentsui gyaku uchi* to your opponent's right temple. (Figs. 10–12)

11–Move backward to the SW corner using a right *okuri ashi* and execute a right *shuto uchi uke.* (Figs. 13–14)

13–Shift your left leg to the west, cross your right leg behind the left, and execute a right *gyaku soto gedan barai.* (Figs. 15–16)

14–Execute a left *sokumen zuki* (toward the east) to your opponent's face. (Figs. 17–18)

16–Execute a left *oi geri*, in the SE direction, to your opponent's groin. (Figs. 19–20)

19–Step backward to the SW corner with a left *neko ashi* and execute a left *gedan barai* in a *kokutsu* stance. (Figs. 21–22)

20–Execute a right *mawashi geri*, with the heel, to your opponent's ribs, rotating 360° to face east in a right *neko ashi* stance. (Figs. 23–24)

23–Shifting into a right *kokutsu* stance, execute a right *shuto gedan barai.* (Figs. 25–27)

24–Moving your left leg to the north, rotate your body to the east and face your opponent in a left *seiken chudan kamae.* (Figs. 28–29)

Then execute the standard salutation forms.

Defensive:

Standard salutation forms—*kamaete*.

1–Stand in a right *neko ashi* stance, facing your opponent in a right *seiken chudan kamae*. (Figs. 1)

3–Step forward to the NW corner using a right *okuri ashi* and execute a right *sokumen zuki* to the solar plexus of your opponent. (Figs. 2–3)

5–Move your left leg backward to the NE corner, using *hiraki ashi*, and in a *sotobiraki jigotai* stance, execute a right *uchi gedan barai*. (Figs. 4)

6–Execute a right *oi geri* with the heel to your opponent's ribs and draw your right foot back to your left knee. Then execute a right *oi zuki* to the face of your opponent. (Figs. 5–8)

7–Move your right leg to the NE corner using *hiraki ashi* and in a left *sotobiraki jigo tai* stance, execute a left *gedan barai*. Move again to the NE corner using a left backward *okuri ashi* and duck, keeping your body straight and extending your arms in the direction of your toes, while looking at your opponent's eyes. (Figs. 9–12)

10–Step forward to the SW corner using *okuri ashi* and execute a right *shuto hineri uchi* to the solar plexus of your opponent. (Figs. 13–14)

12–Execute a left *oi geri* with the ball of your foot to your opponent's ribs and draw your left leg back in front of the right. (Figs. 15–16)

15–Move your right leg backward to the SE corner and execute a left *jodan uchi uke* in a left *neko ashi* stance. (Figs. 17–18)

17–Shift your right leg to the NE corner and move your left leg behind it, using *hiraki ashi*. Execute a right *uchi gedan barai*, standing in a right *sotobiraki jigotai* stance. (Figs. 19–20)

18–Deliver a left *hineri geri* with the ball of the foot (in the SW direction) to your opponent's ribs and pull your left foot back in front of the right (Figs. 21–22).

21–Step backward to the NE corner using a left *neko ashi* and execute a left *soto gedan barai* (Figs. 23–24).

22–Execute a right *mawashi geri* with heel to your opponent's ribs, rotating 315° to face, after completion, the SW corner in a left *neko ashi* stance. (Figs. 25–27)

24–Shift your right leg to the south and twist your body to the west, facing your opponent in a right *seiken chudan kamae*. (Figs. 27–29).

Then execute the standard salutation forms.

Sankakutobi shodan

Offensive:

Standard salutation forms—*kamaete*.

1–Face your opponent in a right *seiken chudan kamae*. (Fig. 1)

2–Step forward using a right *neko ashi* and execute a right *sokumen zuki* to your opponent's solar plexus. (Figs. 2–3)

5–Step backward to the NW corner using a right *neko ashi* and execute a right *soto uke*. (Figs. 4–5)

7–Step backward to the SW corner using a right *neko ashi* and execute a right *uchi gedan barai* or *sukui uke*, standing in a right *sotobiraki jigotai* stance. (Figs. 6–7)

8–Jump north with your left leg and cross your right leg behind in a *kosa ashi* stance. Execute a left *sokumen zuki* to the solar plexus of your opponent. (Figs. 8–9)

11–Shift your right leg to the SW corner and duck low, keeping your body straight and arms extended in the direction of your toes (*otoshi mi*), while looking at your opponent's eyes. (Figs. 10–11)

12–Execute a left *oi geri* in the NE direction to the groin of your opponent with the heel. (Figs. 12–13)

14–In the same direction, execute a right *hineri geri* with the ball of your foot to your opponent's solar plexus. Pull your leg back in front of your body. (Figs. 14–15)

Defensive:

Standard salutation forms—*kamaete*.

1–Face your opponent in a left *seiken chudan kamae*. (Fig. 1)

3–Move your left leg backward to the SE corner and simultaneously execute a right *sokumen zuki* to your opponent's ribs. (Figs. 2–3)

4–Execute a left *oi zuki* to your opponent's face, in the NW corner. (Figs. 4–5)

6–Execute a left *oi geri* with the heel to the ribs of your opponent and pull your left leg back in front of the right. (Figs. 6–8)

9–Step backward to the SE corner with a left *neko ashi* and execute a left *shuto uchi uke*. (Fig. 9)

10–Jump north with your right leg and cross your left leg behind it. Then slide your right leg forward to the SW corner to execute a right *shuto yoko mawashi uchi*. Pull your right hand back to your ear. (Figs. 10–12)

13–Step backward to the NE corner with a right *neko ashi* and execute a right *uchi gedan barai*. (Fig. 13)

15–Jump south with your left leg and cross your right leg behind it. Then execute a left *uchi gedan barai* in the SE direction. (Figs. 14–15)

Off.

17–Step backward to the SW corner with a right *neko ashi*, swinging your left hand in this direction (to counterbalance your body motion). (Figs. 16–17)

18–Step forward to the NE corner and execute a right *sokumen* (or *okuri*) *zuki* to your opponent's face. (Figs. 18–19)

21–Step forward to the NE corner with a right *neko ashi* and duck forward with your arms extended in the direction of your toes *mae kagami*. Then get up and rotate your body 180° counterclockwise, facing the SW corner. Shift into a left *neko ashi* stance, your left fist in front of your body (*seiken chudan kamae*). (Figs. 20–21)

22–Execute a right *oi zuki*, towards the west, to your opponent's face. (Figs. 22–23)

25–Shift your left leg to the south, then bring your right leg behind it to the SE corner (*hiraki ashi*) and execute a left *uchi gedan barai*, standing in a *sotobiraki jigotai* stance. (Figs. 24–25)

26–Execute a right *shuto oi yoko mawashi uchi*, in the NW direction, to the solar plexus (or jugular vein) of your opponent. (Figs. 26–30)

28–Move your left leg forward to the NW corner and rotate your body clockwise to the east, facing your opponent in a right *seiken chudan kamae*. (Fig. 31)

Then execute the standard salutation forms.

Def.

16–Execute a left *oi geri*, with the heel, to your opponent's ribs. Then pull your left foot back in front of the right. (Figs. 16–18)

19–Step backward to the SE corner with a left *neko ashi*, swinging your right hand in this direction as in motion 17. (Fig. 19)

20–Cross your right leg behind the left and move your left leg to the west, executing a left *shuto gyaku uchi* in a left *zenkutsu* stance, to the jugular vein of your opponent. Bring your right foot behind the left in an 180° circular motion (clockwise) to face the east in a left *seiken chudan kamae*. (Figs. 20–21)

23–Move your right leg to the NW corner (*hiraki ashi*) and execute a left *uchi uke*. (Figs. 22–23)

24–Execute a right *hineri geri* with the ball of the foot to the ribs of the opponent (SE corner) and pull your right leg back in front of the left. (Figs. 24–26)

27–Jump with your left leg to the NE corner and bring your right leg behind it in a clockwise circular motion, facing the SW corner in a left *neko ashi* stance. (Figs. 27–30)

28–Shift your right leg slightly to the east, facing your opponent in a left *seiken chudan kamae*. (Fig. 31)

Then execute the standard salutation forms.

Naihanchin waza

Offensive:

Standard salutation forms—*kamaete*.

1–Step forward with your right leg, facing north in a *naihanchin* stance. Pull both fists to your hips (*ryoken koshi kamae*).

2–Raise your hands in front of your body and bring them down in an outward circular motion. Press your right fist against your left palm and rotate your head 90° clockwise to the east (Fig. 1).

3–Move east with a rapid *okuri ashi* and deliver a right *shuto gyaku uchi* to your opponent's neck (Figs. 2–3).

5–Slide your left leg to the north and cross your right leg behind it in a *kosa ashi* stance (Fig. 4). Then slide your left leg to the NE corner and execute a left *empi yoko mawashi uchi* to the solar plexus of your opponent, in a left *zenkutsu* stance (Fig. 5).

8–Moving to the SW corner, cross your left leg in front of the right and rotate your body 180° clockwise, facing the NE corner in a right *zenkutsu* stance. Execute a right *shuto soto gedan barai*. (Figs. 6–7)

9–Step forward with a right *neko ashi* to the north and grab your opponent with your right arm around his body, holding his right arm under your left armpit and pushing him forward with your right shoulder. Keep your body straight in a *shiko* stance. (Figs. 8–9)

10–Push your opponent in the NW direction, shifting into a right *zenkutsu* stance. (Fig. 10)

11–Now pull your opponent with your right hand in the SW direction, at the same time shifting into a right *kokutsu* stance (Fig. 11). Then execute a right *hineri kagi zuki* to his solar plexus. (Fig. 12)

14–Move your right leg behind the left using *kosa ashi*. Execute a left *nekozeken jodan uke* in a left *zenkutsu* stance. (Fig. 13)

16–Move your left leg behind the right (*hiraki ashi*) to the SE conrner and shifting into a right *neko ashi* stance, execute a right *uchi gedan barai*. (Figs. 14–15)

17–Execute a right *oi geri* with the heel to your opponent's groin (in the NW direction) and pull your leg back in front of your body. (Figs. 16–17)

Defensive

Standard salutation forms—*kamaete*.

1–Step backward with your right leg, facing north in a *naihanchin* stance, both fists at your hips.

2–Raise your hands in front of your body and bring them down in an outward circular motion. Press your left fist against your right palm and rotate your head 90° counterclockwise to the west. (Fig. 1)

4–Duck and step forward with your right foot to deliver a left *shuto jodan uke* in a left *neko ashi* stance. (Figs. 2–3)

6–Move your left leg backward to the NE corner, using *hiraki ashi*, and execute a right *shotei nagashi uke* in a right *neko ashi* stance. (Figs. 4–5)

7–Cross your left leg in front of, or behind the right (using *kosa ashi*) and execute a right *sokuto yoko geri* (in the SW direction) to your opponent's knee. Then pull your right leg back to the left knee and put it down in front of your body. (Figs. 6–7)

9–Move with a right forward *neko ashi* to the south and grab your opponent as described for the offensive side, but in reverse. (Figs. 8–9)

10–Pull your opponent to the NE, shifting into a right *kokutsu* stance (Fig. 10). Then push him to the SE with your right shoulder in a right *zenkutsu* stance. (Fig. 11)

12–Without moving your feet, twist your body clockwise to the NE, shifting into a right *neko ashi* stance. Then execute a left *haito gyaku uchi uke*. Draw your right hand to your right ear. (Fig. 12)

13–Deliver a right *shuto yoko mawashi uchi* to your opponent's jugular vein. (Fig. 13)

15–Execute a right *shuto soto gedan barai* in a large circular motion in front of your body and in a right *neko ashi* stance (Figs. 14). Follow with a right *shomen geri* with the ball of the foot and pull your right leg in front of the left. (Figs. 15–16)

18–Move your left leg to the NE corner and bring your right leg behind with *hiraki ashi*, facing the SW corner in a left *neko ashi* stance. Execute a left *uchi gedan barai*. (Fig. 17)

Off.

20–Step backward to the SE corner using a right *neko ashi* and execute a right *uchi gedan barai*. (Figs. 18–19)

21–Execute a left *hineri geri* with the ball of the foot to your opponent's ribs (in the NW direction) and pull your foot back to its starting position. Assume a right *neko ashi* stance. (Figs. 20–23)

24–Move to the SE corner with a right backward *neko ashi* and execute a right *uchi gedan barai*. Then slide your left leg to the SW corner, facing north in a right *neko ashi* stance. (Figs. 24–26)

26–Move your right leg to the west, using a *naihanchin hoko*, and assume a *naihanchin* stance, facing north in a right *seiken chudan kamae* (Figs. 27–28).

27–Stamp strongly on the ground with your right foot (to surprise your opponent). (Figs. 29–30)

29–Cross your right leg behind the left in a *kosa ashi* stance, and execute a right *gyaku soto uke* followed by a left *sokumen zuki* to your opponent's face (in the NE direction). (Figs. 31–32)

20
21
22
23
24

17
18
19

25
26
27
28
29

30
31
32

Def.

19–Execute a left *oi geri* in the SW direction with the heel to your opponent's ribs and pull your left leg back in front of the right. (Figs. 18–20)

22–Move to the NW corner with your right foot and bring your left foot behind, using *hiraki ashi*, to face the SE corner in a right *neko ashi* stance. Deliver a right *uchi gedan barai*. (Figs. 21–22)

23–Deliver a left *hineri geri* with the ball of the foot to the solar plexus of your opponent and draw your left leg back in front of the right. (Figs. 23–25)

25–Shift your right leg backward to the NW to assume a left *neko ashi* stance with a left *seiken chudan kamae*. (Fig. 26)

26–Move your left leg west using a *naihanchin hoko* and assume a *naihanchin* stance, facing north with a left *seiken chudan kamae*. (Figs. 27–29)

28–Execute a right *sokumen zuki* (in the SE direction) to the solar plexus of your opponent. (Figs. 30–31)

30–Shift your left leg east and cross your right leg behind it (Fig. 32). Then slide your left leg towards the SW and execute a left *sokumen zuki* to your opponent's solar plexus. (Figs. 33–35)

Off.

31–Move east using a left backward *neko ashi* and execute a *morote shuto uke* in a left *zenkutsu* stance, pushing your opponent in the NW direction. (Figs. 33–35)

33–Slide your left leg in the SW direction to face north in a *naihanchin* stance. (Fig. 36)

34–Stamp strongly on the ground with your left foot. (Figs. 37–38)

36–Cross your left leg behind the right in a *kosa ashi* stance and execute a left *gyaku soto uke* followed by a right *sokumen zuki* to your opponent's face (in the NW direction). (Figs. 39–40)

39–Move west using a right backward *neko ashi* and execute a *morote shuto uke* in a right *zenkutsu* stance, pushing your opponent in the NE dirction. (Figs. 41–42)

41–Slide your right foot backward to face north in a *naihanchin* stance. (Fig. 43)

43–Move to the SE corner using a left backward *neko ashi* and execute a *nidan uke* with your right hand in a *gyaku gedan soto uke* and your left hand in a *jodan soto uke*. During the execution of this technique, you are in a left *uchimata jigotai* stance. (Figs. 44–45)

44–Pull your left fist to your left ear, extending your right arm downward on your right side (Fig. 46). Then execute a left *uraken shomen uchi* to your opponent's face (towards the north). (Fig. 47)

46–Shift your right leg to the NE and twist your body to face west in a left *neko ashi* stance with a left *seiken chudan kamae*. (Fig. 48)

47–Execute a left *oi geri* with the heel to the solar plexus of your opponent (towards the west) and pull your left foot back in front of the right. (Figs. 49–51)

35

36

37

38

39

40

33

34

Def.

31–Move your right foot to the NW corner and move your left leg backward to the NW in a *naihanchin* stance facing south. (Figs. 36–37)

35–Step forward to the SW corner and execute a left *sokumen zuki* to your opponent's solar plexus. (Figs. 38–39)

38–Move your right leg west and cross your left leg behind it (Fig. 40). Then slide your right leg to the SE and execute a right *sokumen zuki* aimed at your opponent's solar plexus. (Figs. 41–42)

40–Pull your right leg behind the left to the NW corner and assume a left *neko ashi* stance. (Fig. 43)

42–Execute a left *oi geri* (to the groin) and simultaneously, a right *hineri zuki* (to the face). Pull your left leg back in front of the right. (Figs. 44–46)

45–Immediately move your left leg backward, twisting your body to face east, and execute a right *jodan uchi uke* standing in a right *neko ashi* stance. (Fig. 47)

48–Shift your left leg to the north and move your right leg behind it to the NW corner. Execute a left *uchi gedan barai*. (Figs. 48–50)

Off.

50–Move to the SE coerner using a left backward *neko ashi* and standing in a left *neko ashi* stance, execute a left *uchi gedan barai*. (Fig. 52)

51–Move to the NW corner with a left forward *okuri ashi* and execute a *nidan zuki* (left fist to the face; right fist to the solar plexus of your opponent). During the execution of this technique, you are standing in a left *zenkutsu* stance. (Figs. 53–56)

55–Execute a left *yoko uke mi* (side break-fall). (Figs. 57–61)

57–After the fall, sit up with your left knee bent and right leg stretched out (Fig. 62). Stand up on your right leg then left, rotating your body to the west in right *neko ashi* and with a right *seiken chudan kamae*. (Fig. 63–64)

Then execute the standard salutation forms.

Def.

49–Execute a left *oi geri* with the heel to your opponent's groin (in the SE direction) and pull your left leg back in front of your body. (Figs. 51–53)

52–Step backward to the NW using a right *neko ashi*. Then step into a right *zenkutsu* stance in the SE corner and execute a *nidan uke*, your right hand executing a *jodan soto uke* and your left hand simultaneously a *gedan soto uke* (Figs. 54–55).

53–Bring your right hand to your right ear, extending your left hand downward on your side, and execute a right *uraken shomen uchi* to your opponent's face (to the SE). (Figs. 56–57)

54–Execute a right *o-goshi* throw. (Move your right foot in front of your opponent's legs and grab him with your right hand around his waist. Pull him to the NE and twist your body to the left. Bring your left foot close to the right, bend on your knees, and flip him over your hips.). (Figs. 58–59)

56–Pull your opponent's right arm with both hands. Shift your left leg slightly to the west and deliver a right *shuto uchi oroshi* to his solar plexus. During the execution of this motion you are in a left *kata hiza* stance, your right knee on the ground. (Figs. 60–61)

59–Stand up in a left *neko ashi* stance, facing west with a left *seiken chudan kamae*. (Figs. 62–64)

Then execute the standard salutation forms.

Randori kumite ni

Offensive:

Standard salutation forms—*kamaete*.

1–Move your right foot forward to assume a right *neko ashi* stance with a right *seiken chudan kamae*. (Fig. 1)

2–Execute a right *oi geri* with the heel to your opponent's solar plexus (towards the east) and pull your foot back in front of your body (Figs. 2–3).

5–Move to the NW corner with a right backward *neko ashi* and execute a right *soto uke*, standing in a *zenkutsu* stance. (Figs. 4–5)

7–Move to the NW corner with a *kosa ashi*, crossing your right leg in front of the left (in order to escape the foot sweep being delivered to your forward leg). Simultaneously rotate your body 180° counterclockwise to face the SE corner in a left *neko ashi* stance. (Fig.s 6–8)

9–Move your right leg in the SW direction until facing the NE corner and duck, keeping your body straight and your arms extended in the direction of your toes (Figs. 9–10).

10–Move to the NE corner with a left forward *neko ashi* and execute a right *hineri zuki* to the solar plexus of your opponent. (Figs. 11–12)

12–Follow with a left *oi geri* with the heel to your opponent's solar plexus and draw your left leg back in front of the right. (Figs. 13–14)

Defensive:

Standard salutation forms—*kamaete*.

1–Move your left foot backward to assume a left *neko ashi* stance with a left *seiken chudan kamae*. (Fig. 1)

3–Shift your right leg to the SE corner and execute a left *uchi gedan barai*. (Figs. 2–3)

4–Move west with a left forward *neko ashi* and deliver a right *hineri zuki* to the solar plexus of your opponent. (Figs. 4–5)

6–Slide your right leg forward in the NW direction and execute an *ashi barai* (sweeping your opponent's right leg at the level of his knee). Put your left foot down in the NW corner. (Figs. 6–7)

8–Move forward with your right foot in this direction and bring your left foot behind it (Fig. 8). Then, sliding your right foot to the west, deliver a right *shuto yoko mawashi uchi* to the jugular vein of your opponent and draw your right hand back to your right ear. (Figs. 9–11)

11–Move to the NE corner with a right backward *neko ashi* and execute a right *shuto uchi uke*. (Fig. 12)

13–Shift your left leg to the SE, facing the NW corner in a right *zenkutsu* stance, and execute a right *shuto soto gedan barai*. (Figs. 13–14)

14–Execute a left *hineri geri* to your opponent's groin and pull your left leg back to your right knee (Figs. 15–16). Then step forward with your left leg and deliver a left *shuto uchi oroshi* to the top of the head (*tento*) in a left *zenkutsu* stance. (Figs. 17–18)

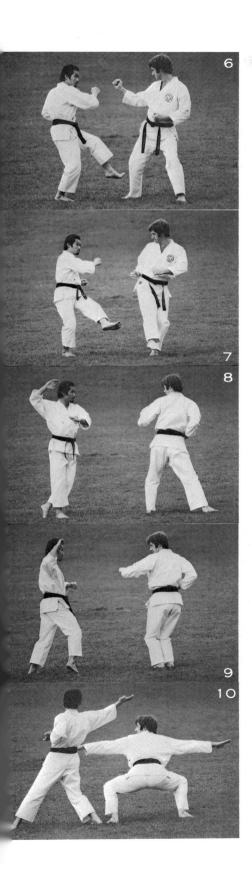

Off.

15–Move to the NW corner with a left backward *hiraki ashi* and in a left *zenkutsu* stance, execute a left *uchi gedan barai* (Figs. 15–16). Move your left leg backward, using *hangetsu hoko* (Fig. 17), and shift into a right *naihanchin* stance to execute a *morote jodan juji uke* (Fig. 18). Then grab your opponent's wrist with your right hand and your own wrist with your left hand. Pull both hands to your right hip, twisting your hips clockwise until facing south. (Fig. 19)

16–Execute a left *hineri zuki* to your opponent's face (in the SE direction). (Fig. 20)

19–Assuming a right *neko ashi* stance, execute a right *jodan uchi uke*. (Figs. 21–22)

20–Follow with a left *hineri geri*, with the ball of the foot to the solar plexus of your opponent, and pull your left leg back in front of the right. (Figs. 23–24)

22–Move to the NW corner with a left backward *neko ashi* and execute a *morote jodan awase uke* in a left *neko ashi* stance. (Fig. 26)

23–Follow with a right *mawashi geri*, spinning 180° counterclockwise to face east after completion of the motion. Bring your right leg close to the left. (Figs. 2 29)

25–Move to the SW corner with a right backward *neko ashi* and execute a *morote awase uke* from a right *neko ashi* stance. (Fig. 30)

26–Assume, in the same stance, a right *seiken chudan kamae* facing east. (Figs. 31–32)

Then execute the standard salutation forms.

Def.

17–Step to the NW corner with a left forward *neko ashi* (Fig. 19), pushing downward on your opponent with your left hand to break his grip on your wrist. Shifting into a left *neko ashi* stance, execute a left jodan *uchi uke*. (Fig. 20)

18–Execute a right *hineri zuki* (in the NW direction) to your opponent's face. (Figs. 21–22)

21–Shift your right leg to the SE corner and execute a left *uchi gedan barai* (Figs. 23–24). Then rotate your head and body 180° clockwise to face the SE corner, your right leg pivoting around the left foot to stop in the NW corner. Simultaneously deliver a right *uraken gyaku uchi* (in a right *zenkutsu* stance) to the right temple of your opponent. (Figs. 25–26)

24–Move to the NE corner with a right backward *neko ashi* and in a right *neko ashi* stance, execute a *morote awase uke* (Figs. 27–28), followed by a left *kaiten geri* (or *ushiro mawashi geri*) to the solar plexus of your opponent (Figs. 29–30). Then face the SW and draw your left leg back in front of the right. (Fig. 31)

26–Assume a left *neko ashi* stance with a left *seiken chudan kamae*. (Fig. 32)

Then execute the standard salutation forms.

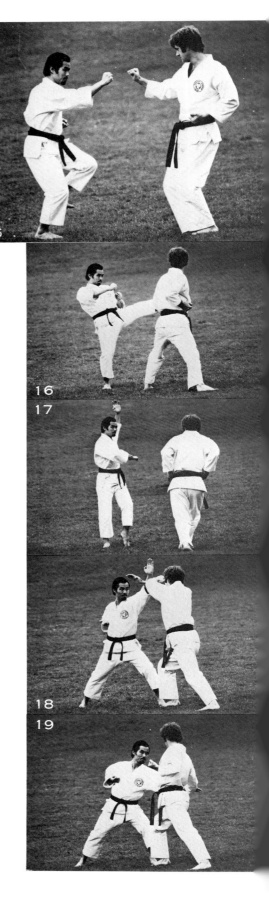

4. Training for Kumite

Most of what has been said for kata training is applicable to kumite training with a few additional considerations.

Each individual technique must first be learned, strictly following the teaching of the instructor without altering the form. The student should try to understand the meaning of each technique and motion and not only memorize them. He should practice each kumite hundreds of times with different partners, adjusting the execution of the techniques and motions to the opponent's size, speed, and power. Each punch, kick, or block has its own requirements for distance and timing which vary according to the physical characteristics of each individual and the technique that the opponent is using.

In practicing kumite one should learn to control his form, power, and breathing, performing each kumite alternately fast then slow—with full power and then normally—contracting and then expanding each form.

After having learned each individual technique, the student must then learn to combine them in a sequence of techniques executed with proper timing, harmonizing his action with the behavior of his opponent.

In the actual practice of kumite, the student must first prepare his mind by concentrating fully. Then he must perform each kumite with full power and speed, from the beginning to the end, as if it were a real fight. Performing with spirit is essential, particularly in a prearranged kumite, which otherwise becomes a futile exercise. The student should not be afraid to be hit because even in a *jiyu* kumite, his opponent is controlling the execution of his techniques. He can then concentrate on properly practicing his technique and motions with full speed, power, and spirit, in complete harmony with his partner's own techniques and motions. It is very important in the practice of kumite that each partner respects and trusts the other for their mutual benefit. Both partners must alternately assume the offensive and the defensive. They should also practice from the right and the left side, for kumite is a preparation for real fighting. In contrast to shiai (sport competition), where one faces only one frontal opponent, in kumite the student must develop an ability to fight any number of opponents in any direction. So his techniques should be executed equally well from the right and the left side. He must also develop "eyes" in every direction. This means learning to anticipate any offensive action originating from any direction.

There are three different ways of practicing kumite. Each complements the other:

–Each technique can be stopped short of the target so that the student learns to properly focus his technique and develops a sense for the right distance (*maai*).

–Each technique can be followed through completely but executed a few inches aside the target to teach the student to put all his speed and power into the technique.

–Finally, kumite can be practiced with protective equipment so that each technique can be fully executed without risk of injury. This kind of practice allows the student to really test his techniques and allows him to develop the proper balance, distance, timing, and power of karatedo techniques.

There are also three different attitudes in the practice of kumite:

–One consists of being constantly on the offensive, attacking with determination in order to prevent the opponent from taking the initiative or even from counterattacking. This attitude, called *shin*, is aimed at winning before the opponent can attack.

–Another attitude, *gyo*, on the contrary, is a defensive one. It consists of carefully studying the opponent's moves, inducing him to attack and then, in a quick motion, evading his technique and counterattack.

–The third attitude, *so*, is a combination of *shin* and *gyo*. It consists of adapting one's attitude to his opponent's attitude: an offensive technique is met by a defensive technique, a soft one by a hard one, etc.

These three attitudes should all be practiced in kumite.

5. Kumite Competition

As in kata competition, kumite competition can be disputed according to the *ko haku* or *saiten* system. The former is a direct elimination system where contestants usually perform an imposed kumite. In the latter system, points are awarded by a referee and four judges for the performance of a kumite chosen by the contestants themselves.

Points or decisions by the referee and judges are based on the following criteria:

a. proper manners and general attitudes.
b. smooth and harmonious exchange of techniques.
c. perfect execution of form.
d. understanding of the techniques by both partners.
e. timing, distance, postures, and breathing.
f. seriousness displayed in the execution of the kumite.
g. concentration of body and mind.
h. control of power, speed, and body motions.
i. effectiveness of the techniques.
j. fighting spirit.

The point system is the same as that for kata, as is also the etiquette of kumite competition..

chapter 7 Shiai

1. Definition and Purpose of Shiai

Shiai used to be actual fights to the death between two opponents challenging each other. There were usually not any rules in such fights, which could be with any type of weapon or with "bare hands" Later a shiai became a challenge where opponents fought in a pre-determined place, usually a square or circle area surrounded by ropes of straw, until one opponent was knocked out, or abandoned the fight by jumping over the ropes. There usually was no restriction on the type of techniques to be used. The contestants sometimes oiled their bodies to make themselves more difficult to grab and also to reduce injuries.

As shiai became more tightly governed, they were usually conducted in *dojos* but full contact rules still prevailed, though some dangerous techniques (*nukite* to the eyes, etc.) were prohibited. Nowadays, a shiai is a sporting competition administered by strict rules in order to prevent injuries, and is conducted in a fair atmosphere of true sportsmanship. Its main purpose is to enhance the human quality of the contestants through a test of determination, endurance, and skill.

In a shiai, both contestants attempt to deliver a decisive technique to a vulnerable or vital point with enough power to disable the opponent. However, blows are either stopped short of the target or fully delivered to protective equipment strong enough to sustain any impact.

A shiai is a real test of the technical ability of the student, the seriousness of his training, and his fighting spirit. It is one of the ways to progress in karatedo and to learn one's weaknesses and correct them. Although one should always try to win in a shiai, the most important thing is to participate to the best of one's ability, not to win at all costs. Shiai should be courteous encounters following the rules of good sportsmanship. If one is thinking only of winning, the mind will become oriented only towards achieving good results in competition and thus will not achieve the true objectives of karatedo. The student will start hating his opponents, become very aggressive, and lose his self-control. Thus he will achieve results completely opposed to the principles and philosophy of karatedo. The winner should not boast of his victory nor should the loser be discouraged, for the essential thing is to perfect one's mind and body.

2. Training for Shiai

More than anything, a shiai is a test of proficiency in the practice of karatedo. Therefore, only students who train thoroughly in the other aspects of karatedo—basic techniques, kumite, and kata—should compete in shiai.

The approach to a shiai should be made rationally under the guidance of a competent and professional instructor who should establish a well scheduled program of training fitted to the student's abilities, physical characteristics, and goals in karatedo. The student should receive a medical checkup to ascertain that he can safely take up such a program. Beginners should start with short and frequent practices, gradually building up their physical condition and concentrating on everything they learn, while trying to see it in its whole context. Frequency and planning of training are of the utmost importance. A proper sequence of training would be to start each practice session with basic techniques followed by *tanshiki* kumite in order to test one's basic techniques. After that, perform a basic kata to loosen up the body and to work out proper form, breathing, and combinations of techniques. Then practice *fukushiki* kumite to test and develop these combination techniques. Next perform a training kata and practice *jiyu randori* kumite.

The program should encompass mental as well as physical training. The student must learn to control his excitability and fears through breathing exercises and meditation. In a competition, in fact in any tense or critical situation, the mind becomes numb and the body stiff. The heart-beat quickens, the throat dries up, and the general attitude becomes negative. It thus becomes impossible to win. It is only through hard practice that one gains enough confidence in oneself to overcome these problems. The student must also understand the purpose of shiai, which is to win against himself and to help him become a better karatedo practitioner and a better human being. Upon understanding this, he will lose his fears of losing a competition. Then his mind will be free to concentrate on improving his techniques and attitude.

The student must also prepare mentally for shiai through meditation. He should mentally picture himself competing against all types of contestants using various techniques. He should "feel" his techniques coming out of himself and must develop a strong positive fighting spirit, reaffirming his goals and aspirations with determination.

It is said that "training for shiai should be aimed at developing a mind quiet and serene *like water*, a spirit (*ki*) fiery *like fire*, techniques fast and powerful *like lightning*, a body strong and steady *like a large tree*, and the whole being free and omnipresent *like the air*."

Good conditioning of the body is essential, for without heightened stamina, shiai are soon lost through weariness, however good one's techniques are. During practice, the student should train for twice the competition time at least. If each bout lasts two minutes and there are five rounds to reach the final, the student should be able to practice free sparring thoroughly for twenty minutes, almost without interruption, to develop enough stamina for the competition.

During the practice sessions, the student will also have to learn to relax readily through proper breathing exercises, in order to be able to fully recover in the rest period between each bout of a shiai.

The student should concentrate on developing a set of favorite techniques, usually one or two offensive and defensive techniques that are particularly appropriate for him and that he will be able to execute automatically and with good chance of success in any situation. These favorite techniques must be practiced repeatedly, and once mastered, should be used almost exclusively when competing in shiai. Their importance cannot be overemphasized for they are the key to winning at shiai.

Different Forms of Training

Uchikomi geiko: This is a basic offensive training against a passive partner. At first your opponent does not move and you execute the same technique several times, then moving on to a combination of techniques practiced for much speed and power as possible, using different angles and rhythms of attack, perfecting your stance, body motion, and the execution and precision of your techniques, without any respite until breathless. Then change the roles, your partner now assuming the offensive. This entire practice is to be repeated with the defensive partner escaping with, one step at first, and then freely. It develops basic and combination techniques. This kind of practice is similar to *uchikomi renshu* in judo and in kendo.

Kakari geiko: This is an exclusively offensive training where you concentrate only on attacking your opponent, trying to land effective blows regardless of his blocking and counterattacking techniques. It is usually performed with higher-ranked students and against successive opponents. It develops a strong offensive attitude.

Sute geiko: This form of training is aimed at

learning to master and transcend oneself, overcoming the pain and weariness of dozens of successive fights. At the Kenkokan *dojo* in Japan, such training can last a whole day. The student soon reaches a state of complete exhaustion which he eventually overcomes, thus reaching the "top of the mountain".

Hikitate geiko: This is a defensive training where one faces attacking opponents, each time counterattacking. It develops in the student strong defensive techniques and a feeling for the opponent's actions. Like *sute geiko*, it is practiced hundreds of times until exhausted.

Tokushu geiko: These different forms of training for shiai usually take place during special winter (*kan geiko*) and summer (*shochu geiko*) training camps and special training sessions which may last for several days. These camps allow the student to fully concentrate on the practice of karatedo. The students develop great confidence in themselves and their physical ability through hard and long hours of practice under extreme climatic conditions. In addition to drills in basic techniques, kata, kumite, and shiai, a number of other exercises are practiced. These are: fighting blindfolded, to learn to feel the attack; feet tied, to develop blocking and hand techniques; or hands tied, to develop body motion and foot techniques.

To develop proper distancing, students also fight attached together by a five- or six-foot cord. To learn sideways evading motions, a student takes a position against a wall and practices *hikitate geiko* (not being able to escape backwards he learns to escape sideways with great speed).

3. Strategies and Tactics of Shiai

To win shiai, as in winning a battle, one has to devise good strategies and tactics. Strategy is concerned with having a good knowledge of the forces present in oneself and the opponents, and a "plan of battle." Therefore one should first analyze one's techniques, knowing their strong points and how to effectively use them, as well as their weaknesses and how to cover them up by overshadowing them. One should also ascertain one's mental attitude and determination to win.

Next, one should find out about one's opponents. If already familiar with them, one should analyze their techniques and tactics and train accordingly, seeking the advice of one's instructor or coach. One should inquire about unknown opponents or go and observe the way they fight. Most fighters have habits: before attacking, some grin, blink, or move their head forward; often the shoulder is lowered before punching and kicking. These signs should be carefully observed for they may allow one to anticipate an opponent's action. One should try to find out the weaknesses of other fighters and develop strategies to exploit them. Also, one should carefully watch one's opponent's eyes and Adam's apple, for before an attack there is always a perceptible contraction of the Adam's apple and a dilatation of the pupils.

Then one should devise plans of action; firstly, determining the opportunities for attacking or counterattacking. This is called *tsukuri kuzushi*. It consists of either opening up the opponent's guard, breaking up his stance or rhythm of attack, or alternately forcing him to move. *Kuzushi* is created either actively or passively:

Actively:

a–Move to get around his guard; your movement has to be executed extremely fast, using short cat steps (*neko ashi*), in order to catch the opponent off-guard.

b–Attack with a feint or a setting-up technique that the opponent will block, thus opening up his guard; use contrasting techniques such as a combination of *oi zuki* to the face (*jodan*) and *hineri geri* to the solar plexus (*chudan*).

Passively:

a–Take advantage of the opponent's motion; firstly, if your opponent is in a left stance and moves to his right or steps backward, observe his rear foot and attack when it touches the ground; secondly, if he moves to his left or steps forward, attack as his front foot touches the ground; thirdly, if he does not move but goes up and down, attack when he is up (in extension).

b–Block or evade his attack and counterattack; attack either just before he attacks, or right after.

In general, the best opportunity for attacking is the very moment when the opponent moves or attacks, or immediately afterwards; also when he is blocking or hesitating, blinking, inhaling, or immediately after he exhales, etc.

Before attacking one has to have made up one's mind on the following points:

Where to attack: one must have decided which part of the opponent to attack: face, solar plexus, groin, etc.

Which technique to use: one must know whether to attack with a kick or punch, etc.

How to attack: direct frontal attack, combination, feint, etc.

What distance: how close to the opponent one should be to attack (proper distancing: *maai*).

How to terminate the attack: one must know which technique to use if one's first attack has failed, in order to win or to disengage from the attack. Schematically an attack starts with *kuzushi* (setting-up technique), followed by *kime waza* (scoring technique) and finally, *engo waza* (a supporting technique) aimed at securing the *kime waza*.

Most fighting tactics can be classifiesd as follows:

1–Attacking to the utmost, overwhelming the opponent with combination techniques, *like a tide*.

2–Letting the opponent attack, avoiding to the side at the last moment and simultaneously delivering a counter-technique, *like a wave flowing on a rock*.

3–Breaking away from the opponent's attack and counterattacking immediately without any rupture of rhythm, *like the surf*.

4–Attacking or counterattacking, using circular motions and techniques, *like a swirl*.

5–Jumping up and forward when the opponent is moving backward or diving to the ground to stop or avoid a rushing opponent, *like a wave rolling over a reef or under too large an obstacle*.

Tactics also include the combination of several techniques. Many combinations have been illustrated in Chapter 6 on kumite. They are particularly necessary in a shiai to overcome an opponent who adopts a very strong defensive stance, or is ready to counterattack after your first attack. Let your opponent block, thus opening his guard, then follow with a combination technique.

Combination techniques must also be utilized to get closer to or further away from your opponent if he is not moving or moving too fast, and also against taller opponents.

4. Advice for Shiai

A shiai should be prepared for as described in Section 2. It is usually best to stop the intensive training one week prior to competition, keeping at your top physical condition by training lightly, and eating and sleeping well. If the place where the competition is held is unknown to you, it is advisable to go and get acquainted with it (disposition, lighting, etc.) because everything which could disturb your mental concentration on the day of the competition should be avoided. Also prepared your equipment carefully. Get to know the competition rules and avoid arriving late for the shiai. As already mentioned, get some advice from your instructor or coach as to what strategies you should use. If you are not fighting immediately, carefully study the other contestants and prepare yourself mentally for the competition. Warm up thoroughly before your fights and punch and kick several times, using protective equipment.

During the competition, rigorously observe the prescribed rules and behave respectfully towards the judges and referees and courteously with the other contestants. Take command of the fight by showing a strong offensive spirit, anticipating your opponent's actions and looking deep into your opponent's eyes. When an opportunity presets itself, attack with determination until the referee calls off your action. In a three full-point system *(sanbon shobu)*, getting the first point is a considerable advantage, both materially and psychologically.

During the rest periods between matches, perform a few cooling off exercises, relax by breathing smoothly and deeply. Rub your bruises with a balm. Do not drink but eat a few lemons if you are thirsty. If you are hungry have some honey or other light but high energy food.

Calmly accept the referee's decision, whatever it may be. Thank your opponent and then mentally review your fight, analyzing your performance and seeking ways for improvement.

Shiai can only be learned through experience. Effective strategies and techniques must be developed individually, according to one's physical and mental characteristics. But strategies and techniques are not sufficient to win in shiai. A number of other points must be taken into consideration, some of which are presented below.

▶ When fighting, always keep your eyes on your opponent's eyes, not fixed on him but looking "through" him. In this way you can see all of his body and detect all of his motion. Do not tense up, or else your motions will be slowed down by the muscular contraction. Be economical in your motions and do not waste your energy. Keep yourself "cool" and breathe deeply but smoothly with your *tanden* (diaphragm) to dissimulate and slow your breathing.

▶ Do not rush, take your time, and never attack without a precise goal.

▶ Maintain the proper distance between yourself and your opponent, moving rapidly and with agility on the tips of your toes.

▶ Avoid an attack, rather than blocking it, so that you can counterattack more rapidly. Do not move back but rather move sideways.

▶ Against a taller opponent, get close to him to "kill" his foot techniques, using your front hand and foot to protect yourself by faking or blocking, and your rear hand and foot to score; use a fast combination of techniques in close succession.

▶ Against a rushing opponent, try to catch him before he throws his techniques or step sideways and counterattack using contrasting combination techniques (high/low, hand/foot, etc.).

▶ If your opponent is getting too close, throw him by sweeping his leg or push him to get enough distance to punch or kick. To get closer to your opponent, particularly a larger opponent, use combination techniques or dive to the ground with a forward *ukemi* or a cartwheel, or raise up one knee in a *sagi ashi* stance and jump forward.

▶ If your techniques are not successful or if you are tired, return to basic techniques. Try to score with what you can and are certain of.

▶ Cover up your weaknesses, particularly your fatigue; do not show your injuries and never give up your fighting spirit.

5. Use of Protective Equipment

As shiai evolved into a sport competition, rules were drawn up to prevent injuries. In many systems it was decided that the safest way would be to have the competitors stop their blows before making actual contact. However, it is extremely difficult in most cases to fully appreciate the potential of techniques executed with full speed and power, in close succession, and sometimes simultaneously. Under such rules it is often impossible to accurately determine the actual winner of a match. This system has thus become a source of frustration for contestants as well as spectators of karate competitions. Furthermore, some techniques were discarded for competition purposes because of the difficulty of stopping them short of the target. This resulted in a limitation of the techniques to frontal or sideways techniques. Some forty years ago, Kaiso Kori Hisataka introduced the use of protective equipment derived from kendo making it possible to deliver each technique with full speed and power. Hanshi Masayuki Kukan Hisataka further developed this concept when he created Supersafe body protectors and headgear. Supersafe's unique design protects the head and body allowing praticioners to make solid contact with their techniques without risking serious inury to their partners.

Protective equipment should be of such a nature as to cover the vulnerable and vital points, but not the natural weapons. Natural weapons can and should be developed into strong offensive weapons. Covering them with gloves or other safety equipment for fighting means that they are not used for their primary purpose which is to punch, hit, strike, and kick with as small and as hard a surface area as possible. Furthermore, it is not possible to safely cover all of the natural weapons, particularly the heel, elbow, and knee. Without protective equipment these natural weapons cannot be fully utilized and if the blows are stopped short, then the technique loses its efficacy. Vulnerable and vital points of the body cannot, and should not, be trained to sustain high impact blows. There are some physical limitations to what the human body can endure and organs such as the heart, liver, eyes, etc. cannot be conditioned to receive punishing blows. This kind of practice is, in fact, not only dangerous but also contrary to the spirit of karatedo, which is to positively condition the individual by perfecting one's techniques and body motions, and by building up a strong, positive mind. Teaching an individual to receive blows would be a rather negative way to educate him/her, since it does not contribute to any kind of progress and even contradicts the laws of nature.

Hanshi Masayuki Kukan Hisataka has devoted two decades to the development of Supersafe safety equipment and the Koshiki Karatedo competitive system. In so doing, he has brought kung fu, tae kwon do, *kempo,* and karate practitioners together to compete and learn with one another. With this standardization of rules and unification of competitors, the dream of Olympic karate is fast becoming a reality.

6. International Koshiki Karatedo Competition Rules

The Ethics of Refereeing

Referees and judges must always bear the following points in mind:
1. Referees and judges must always be absolutely neutral and impartial.
2. Referees and judges must always conduct themselves with dignity and self-possession.
3. Referees and judges must, with the utmost attentiveness and concentration, watch and observe every detail of the competition or contest they attend, and pass correct judgment on every move of the contestants.
4. During a match, the arbitrator, referees, and judges shall speak only to each other. They shall not speak to spectators or other persons. The referee shall give all commands and make all announcements. In principle, judges shall communicate exclusively by the use of their flags. However, they may speak to attract the referee's attention or if called to conference by the referee.
5. The quality of the judgment and attitude shown by the referees and judges has a profound effect on the progress of Koshiki Karatedo match operation. It is therefore required that every referee and judge demonstrates exemplary efficiency, speed, and refined behavior.

In summary it is absolutely necessary for officials of true martial arts (budo) competitions to not only arbitrate and safeguard, but to educate. To do this, they must be superior in training, experience, and knowledge to the contestants, and in this way, and only in this way, can the true spirit of budo, true combat, be controlled and maintained to the highest possible standards. This is the spirit that forms the basis of Koshiki Karatedo.

The Rules of Kumite Competition

Article 1: Match Area
1. The match area (shiaijo) shall have a flat surface and will, in principle, have Supersafe Anzen Tatami, or equivalent safety matting. The area is to be provided with proper hazard-prevention measures.
2. The size of the shiaijo shall, in principle, be nine square meters or equivalent.
3. As a general rule, all the line markings on the floor shall be of a distinct white color and five centimeters in width. The warning track shall have a minimum width of one meter, marked by a red line or tatami.
4. All measurements shall be made between the outer sides of the lines.
5. In the event that the match is to be elevated from the floor level, the height shall be one meter and the floor space 9.2 x 1.5 meters square. The chair for the arbitrator should be placed in this elevated area.

6. Two parallel lines perpendicular to the front side line, each one meter long, shall be drawn at a distance of 1.6 meters from and on both sides of the center point of the shiaijo. These lines shall be the standing lines for the contestants.
7. A fifty centimeter-long line shall be drawn parallel to the back-side line, two meters away from the center point, towards the back-side line. This line shall designate the regular position of the referee.
8. The arbitrator and the record keeper(s) shall, as a rule, be seated at the front of the shiaijo, facing the referee, and more than two meters removed from it.
9. The coaches' box shall be one meter from the parameter of the shiaijo adjacent to the players' box on the side closest to the arbitrator. The box shall be one meter in length and fifty centimeters in width.
10. A Safety Supervisor shall be appointed to oversee the overall safety of all conditions at each tournament. This person should be a high-ranking referee, and in conjunction with the Chief Referee, should ensure the safety of all aspects of the tournament.

Article 2: Official Attire
1. The contestants shall wear clean official Supersafe karatedogi or equivalent clean white karatedogi. Each contestant may wear on his/her chest a designated identification mark of his/her country and the emblem of his/her style on the left sleeve midway between the elbow and shoulder. The opposite sleeve shall only be used to display the official W.K.K.F. Badge.
2. When tightened around the waist, the belt must be of an even length covering the hips.
3. The sleeves must not only cover the elbows, but also at least half of the forearm.
4. The pants shall cover at least three-quarters of the skin down from the knees.
5. The length of the belt from knot to end shall be no less than fifteen centimeters.
6. The red and white strings that will be worn by contestants for a kumite match must be approximately five centimeters wide and of a length sufficient enough to allow fifteen centimeters of it to hang from the knot at both ends. They must be distinctly colored, one red and one white, so as to be easily identifiable during the match. This requirement shall be waived when red and white Supersafe face protectors are available.
7. Hair should be clean, reasonable in length, and should not interfere with the competition. The referee can, under certain circumstances, with the approval of the chief referee, declare a competitor who violates this rule to be disqualified.
8. The use of bandages, pads, fist guards, and kick guards for reasons of injury, must be approved by the referee, in consultation with the chief medical officer.
9. Referees, judges, and arbitrators shall wear the official Supersafe karatedogi, with the official W.K.K.F. Referee's Crest worn on the left side of the chest. The

standard official W.K.K.F. Crest should be worn on the right sleeve. In addition, a black *hakama* shall be worn over the *karatedogi*. Finally, the karatedo *obi* shall be worn over the *hakama*. No footwear of any kind is to be worn.

Article 3: Protective Equipment

1. All contestants are required to wear the standard Supersafe Guard shiai protectors, consisting of the main body protector *(do)*, face protector *(men)*, and groin guard *(kin-ate)*. For safety reasons, only certified Supersafe protectors are approved as the official shiai protectors for tournaments. It is mandatory for contestants to wear the official shiai protectors unless prior certification has been obtained from the W.K.K.F.
2. Supersafe equipment will be certified for use in competition for a maximum of three years from the year of manufacture. Supersafe equipment manufactured from 1993 bears a label indicating the year of manufacture. Undated Supersafe equipment will not be valid for use in competition after 1995.
3. The Safety Supervisor will ensure that Supersafe equipment used at a tournament is valid. In addition, the Safety Supervisor will have the responsibility to ensure that equipment used is safe, even if valid. Any equipment deemed by the Safety Supervisor to be unsafe, regardless of whether it is still within three years of manufacture, cannot be used in competition unless it is repaired to the satisfaction of the Safety Supervisor.
4. The use of any type of supporting bandages or protectors by contestants is strictly forbidden unless prior permission has been sought from and given by the proper tournament authorities. The use of such items will normally only be allowed for medical reasons. A decision of the tournament Chief Medical Officer shall be regarded as final.
5. All female contestants may wear official Supersafe mitts and shin guards. An additional chest protector under the *dogi* may be worn by female contestants, as long as it has been endorsed by the W.K.K.F. or has the approval of the Chief Referee prior to being worn.
6. The use of a mouth guard is optional.

Article 4: Matches

1. The types of shiai are as follows:
    a individual-title shiai
    b team shiai
2. The shiai shall in principle be decided by *"ippon shobu"* (one full point) and *"sanbon shobu"* (three full points).
3. The number of persons composing a team shall be an odd number.
4. A team shiai shall be considered complete if a minimum of three out of five, four out of seven, or two out of three are present for the match. However, any team with less than half of the required members present shall automatically forfeit the match. Three wins out of five matches

(or equivalent) shall end a team shiai in a championship tournament.
5. Shiai *(ippon shobu)* between individual members of each team shall be held in a pre-determined order and the winning team shall be decided on the basis of these individual shiai.
6. The order of the shiai for each member of the team cannot be changed once the official order list has been submitted. In case a recorded member fails to show up for the fight, he/she shall be automatically awarded *kiken*, and the opposing contestant shall be the winner.
7. Failure of the player or the team to arrive on time for the tournament may result in disqualification *(shikkaku)*.
8. If a team or individual fails to attend a tournament after sending in an application form, or quits during the match, the W.K.K.F. Executive Board may bar that team or individual from future events.
9. Competitors attempting to compete without having completed the appropriate application procedures may be refused.
10. There shall be one method of conducting a shiai, being the "number of winners method."
11. In the "number of winners method," the winning team is the one that has had the greater number of winning contestants. If both teams have an equal number of winning contestants, the points of both contestants shall be counted. First, the number of *ippon* each team has been awarded will be the criteria. If there is still no clear result, the number of *waza-ari* awarded shall be compared. If the final points are still equal, a final deciding shiai shall be held between two chosen representatives of the contending teams. In case the deciding shiai exceeds two rounds, the representatives of each team shall be replaced by other team members. Victory through a foul or disqualification is counted as an *ippon*.
12. No competitor may compete in more than two successive shiai. Once withdrawn, a contestant shall not compete again until the entire team has competed their matches.
13. The official W.K.K.F. weight categories shall be as follows:

MEN
LIGHTWEIGHT Less than or equal to 63.5 kg
MIDDLEWEIGHT Greater than 63.5 kg and less than or equal to 73 kg
CRUISERWEIGHT Greater than 73 kg and less than or equal to 82 kg
HEAVYWEIGHT Greater than 82 kg.

WOMEN
LIGHTWEIGHT Less than or equal to 54 kg
MIDDLEWEIGHT Greater than 54 kg and less than or equal to 61 kg
CRUISERWEIGHT Greater than 61 kg.

14. The correct composition and order for team events is as follows:

MEN Lightweight, Middleweight, Cruiserweight, Heavyweight

WOMEN Lightweight, Middleweight, Cruiserweight

MIXED Lightweight, Female Lightweight, Male Middleweight, Female Middleweight, Male Cruiserweight, Female Cruiserweight, Male Heavyweight

Article 6: Conduct of Matches

1. When the referee calls *"nyujo,"* the contestants waiting to compete in the next match shall bow and enter the *shiaijo,* taking up their positions behind the prescribed lines. They shall then bow to the referee and judges *(shinpan ni rei)* and then to each other *(otagai ni rei).* The match commences on the referee's command of *"shobu ippon hajime."*

2. When the referee calls *"yame,"* the contestants will stop and return to their prescribed positions *(motono ichi),* to await the referee's decision. They shall continue the shiai on the referee's command of *"tsuzukete hajime."* When the referee announces *"yame soremade,"* the contestants shall again return to their prescribed positions *(motono ichi)* to await the referee's awarding of the match. When this is given, the contestants shall again bow to each other, to the referee, and then shake hands with each other. The shiai is then over, and the competitors should leave the *shiaijo (taijo)* by backing out of the contest area and bowing toward it upon reaching the perimeter.

3. The shiai shall be conducted exclusively under the instructions of the referee.

Article 7: Match Time

1. Shiai time shall be three minutes in principle. The panel of judges, in consultation with each other, may specify that the shiai time for specific events (e.g. female and/or junior events) be two minutes or one-and-a-half minutes, as deemed appropriate.

2. When there is thirty seconds remaining in the match, the timekeeper shall announce *"ato san-ju byo,"* to which the referee shall respond by announcing *"ato shibaraku."*

3. An *encho-sen* (first extension) of one minute shall be staged if no decision is reached or if no conclusive judgment can be reached in the main bout. In this case, the rules of shiai shall be followed in the normal manner. Prior to the extension, the contestants may be given a short rest period as deemed appropriate by the referee, based on his/her assessment of the contestant's conditions.

4. If no conclusion is reached after the *encho-sen,* a *sai encho-sen* (final extension) shall be staged, again following all normal rules of the match. Only one *sai encho-sen* shall be staged, after which the judges must indicate a decision. No draw shall be permitted in a final extension.

5. The *sai encho-sen* shall take the form of *sagidori,* in which the first point scored *(ippon* or *waza-ari)* from a technique or foul shall determine the winner.

6. Shiai time shall be taken from the referee's signal to commence the shiai, and shall be counted until the final cessation of the match. However, any time spent in discussion among the referee and judges, or in connection to an injury, shall not be included in the shiai time. The command *"jikan"* must be called by the referee to stop the counting of shiai time.

7. An effective technique delivered simultaneously with the time-up signal shall be counted as part of the score. No technique executed after the referee has signaled *"yame, soremade"* shall be counted as part of the score.

Article 8: Victory and Defeat

1. Victory or defeat shall be awarded on the basis of *ippon,* the greatest number of *waza-ari,* decision, or defeat due to a foul or disqualification.

2. Areas of attack:
   a. Controlled contact attacks may only be delivered to Supersafe-protected areas.
   b. Contact to the *jodan* area must be light, controlled contact.
   c. Non-contact controlled techniques may be executed to the back of the torso area. If successfully executed and recognized, such an attack may be awarded a single *waza-ari.*

Article 9: Criteria for Deciding an Ippon

1. An *ippon* shall be awarded when an accurate, well controlled, powerful and effective punch *(tsuki),* kick *(keri),* or strike *(uchi)* is executed to a recognized target area with the following conditions: good form, good attitude, strong vigor, *zanshin,* proper timing, and adequate distance *(ma-ai).*

2. An *ippon* may be awarded for a technique that meets the above criteria and was preceded by a throwing or sweeping technique.

3. Techniques delivered outside the prescribed *shiaijo* shall be invalid. If however the attacking contestant was entirely within bounds at the time of executing a technique, it shall be considered valid provided it was delivered prior to the referee's *"yame"* signal.

4. A sequence of three or more effective techniques in an unbroken combination *(renzoku waza)* shall be awarded *ippon.*

5. In the event that the opponent has lost the will to fight, the other contestant shall be awarded an *ippon.*

6. Techniques that force the opponent to submit, such as strangulation *(shime waza),* joint locking *(kansetsu waza),* and throwing techniques *(nage waza)* may, at the discretion of the referee, be awarded an *ippon,* provided that such techniques are fully controlled, and applied with full regard to the opponent's safety. Techniques executed in violation of this rule are subject to penalties.

Article 10: Criteria for Deciding a Waza-ari

1. The criteria for deciding a *waza-ari* (one point as opposed to a full point) are the same as those for deciding an *ippon,* except that the techniques are judged to be slightly less powerful and perfect in execution. Such techniques must in all other ways be comparable to an *ippon.*

2. In the case of overtime extensions *(encho-sen)* and final extensions *(sai-encho-sen)*, all points shall be counted cumulatively.

3. Kicking techniques *(keri waza)* to Supersafe-protected areas shall be counted as two *waza-ari,* except when they are considered suitable for an *ippon.*

4. Non-contact controlled techniques (punches, strikes, and kicks) delivered to the back of the torso area shall only be awarded a single *waza-ari,* if judged to be suitable.

5. Techniques scored simultaneously by both contestants and recognized by the referee shall be awarded *ai-uchi* and a *waza-ari* awarded to each contestant.

Article 11: Criteria for Judgment

In the absence of an *ippon* or victory due to a foul or disqualification during the prescribed *shiai* time (including extensions), a decision shall be made based on the following:
  a. Which contestant has scored the greatest number of *waza-ari*
  b. The relative excellence of fighting attitudes
  c. Ability and skill
  d. The degree of vigor and fighting spirit
  e. The number of valid attacking moves
  f. Relative excellence in strategy

Article 12: Prohibited Acts and Techniques

1. Direct attacks to unprotected areas, including joints.
2. Striking while holding onto the Supersafe equipment.
3. Attacks to the groin area.
4. Attacks to the head without correct pullback.
5. Excessive contact to *jodan.*
6. Unnecessary grabbing, clinching, and bodily crashing against the opponent.
7. Any unsportsmanlike, discourteous behavior, such as name-calling, provocation, and unjustifiable utterances.
8. Kicking techniques executed to the legs. However, foot sweeping techniques are allowed, provided that they are immediately followed by another valid attacking technique.
9. Elbow strikes to the head *(jodan hiji-ate).*
10. Knee kicks to the head *(jodan hiza-geri).*
11. Any stalling or avoiding of competition.
12. Any stepping or moving outside of the designated *shiaijo.*
13. Any attack directed to the area of the ear.

Article 13: Fouls and Disqualification

1. When a contestant is about to commit a prohibited act, or has just done so, the referee shall give him/her a warning or a foul.
2. In case a contestant, after having once been warned, repeats prohibited techniques, the referee may award an *ippon* to the opponent.
3. In the event that a contestant willfully violates the rules by executing a prohibited technique, the referee may award *hansoku* or *hansoku chui* as deemed necessary. In the event that a *hansoku* is awarded, an *ippon* shall be awarded to the opponent. In the event that a *hansoku chui* is awarded, a *waza-ari* shall be awarded to the opponent.

4. In the event that a contestant is deemed to have deliberately committed a prohibited technique, that contestant shall be awarded a *hansoku* or *shikkaku.* In either case the opponent shall be awarded an *ippon.* In the event that a *shikkaku* is awarded, the offending contestant may face exclusion from future events at the discretion of the Referee's Council.

5. If a contestant is deemed by the referee and judges to be stalling or avoiding competition, he/she will be given a warning *(mukogeki keikoku).* Following the reprimand, the offending contestant must deliver an attack within ten seconds, after which time a *mubobi chui* shall be awarded and a *waza-ari* awarded to the opponent if no attack is executed.

6. When a contestant commits any of the following acts, he/she shall be awarded a *hansoku* or *shikkaku,* and the referee shall award an *ippon* to the opponent. If a *shikkaku* is awarded, the contestant may be barred from participating in the remainder of the tournament in progress at the discretion of the Chief Referee, and from future events at the discretion of the Referee's Council. These actions are:
  a. Acting maliciously and/or willfully violating the rules.
  b. Failing to obey the instructions of the referee.
  c. Becoming overexcited, to the extent that the contestant is considered unfit for engagement in the *shiai.*

7. If a contestant crosses the outside line of the contest area with both feet, he/she shall be given a *jogai chui* and the opponent a *waza-ari.*

8. A contestant who steps out of bounds shall automatically be given a *jogai chui,* and the opponent awarded a *waza-ari.*

9. In the event that a contestant is pushed, hit, or thrown out of bounds, a *jogai chui* shall not be awarded. If it is deemed that a contestant deliberately pushed an opponent out of bounds, a *hansoku chui* shall be awarded, and a *waza-ari* awarded to the opponent.

The Rules of Kata Competition

Organization of the Competition

1. The kata contest shall be performed by individuals only.

2. The contest shall be divided into the following categories:
  Junior Female
  Junior Male
  Senior Female
  Senior Male

3. The contestants may be asked to perform either a *toroku* kata (registered kata) or a *tokui* kata (favorite kata). For the elimination round, a *toroku* kata shall be performed. In the following rounds, a *tokui* kata may be

performed, which may be any of the *toroku* kata, or any other kata of the contestant's style or school. The list of registered kata shall be updated regularly by the World Koshiki Karatedo Federation.

Contest Operation

1. When a contestant's name is called by the announcer, the contestant shall enter the contest area from the area directly opposite the referee. Prior to entering the contest area, the contestant shall bow *(nyujo)* and proceed to the designated starting position. The contestant shall then bow to the referee *(shomen ni rei)* and announce the name of the kata to be performed in a loud voice with *kiai*. At the referee's call of *"hajime"* (start), the contestant shall commence the performance.
2. Upon completion of the performance, the contestant shall return to the designated position, and wait for the referee's announcement of the results. The contestant shall then bow to the referee *(shomen ni rei)* and withdraw, bowing upon exiting the contest area.
3. All matters relating to the performance during its conduct shall be handled under the exclusive direction of the referee.

Victory and Defeat

1. The results for each contestant shall be determined by adding the points awarded by each member of the judging panel. Each judge shall have up to ten points to award each contestant, in a mark range designated by the referee.
2. The highest and lowest scores awarded to each contestant by a member of the judging panel shall be subtracted prior to adding the total score. The score awarded by the referee shall not be eliminated.
3. At the end of the elimination round, a pre-determined number of competitors shall be selected to proceed to the next round. This is repeated until the final round, when the winner will be determined. The sole criterion for selection to proceed to the next round, or selection of finalists, will be the scores calculated using the above process.
4. In the event of a tie for a placing, the eliminated scores of the tied contestants will be compared to determine the result. Firstly the lower scores eliminated shall be compared. If there is still no result, the higher score eliminated shall be compared. In the event that the results are still tied, the contestants shall be requested to perform another kata to determine the outcome. This shall be a *tokui* kata, and shall be judged according to the standard criteria.

chapter 8 Self-defense Techniques

1. Introduction of Self-defense Techniques

Goshin jutsu is truly the act of protecting one's self and one's own against any harm or destruction of human origin. Thus it encompasses self-defense techniques as well as self-preserving attitudes and acts applicable to everyday situations. It must be stressed that self-defense and self-preservation are complementary, to avoid getting into trouble is undoubtably the most efficient self-defense technique. But this failing, self-defense may constitute the best, and perhaps last, self-preserving act. This chapter will cover some applications of karatedo as a self-defense technique and also as a prevention of aggression of human origin.

Self-defense and self-preservation constitute the most basic and common elements of nature. Examples abound in the vegetable and animal kingdom: roses have thorns, porcupines spines, octopuses spit a jet of ink, birds peck or fly rapidly, stags have antlers, etc. Other animals (tigers, etc.) and plants (carnivorous flowers) have a more offensive type of defense.

Throughout the centuries man has developed offensive and defensive weapons and also unarmed methods of fighting (because weapons were not always readily available) mostly as a means of survival.

In our modern societies, such a need for basic survival does not exist anymore, with perhaps a few exceptions. However, violence has not been completely stamped out of our societies and even under normal circumstances, there is still a need for man to protect himself and his near relations against unexpected aggressions. Everybody—men, women, and children—could carry a weapon but this would undoubtably result in an escalation of violence as demonstrated time and again. Furthermore, one cannot carry a weapon all the time and there would still be some need for unarmed self-defense. Karatedo provides certainly the most viable means of self-defense. One learns how to turn each part of his body into a weapon and also to make use of his environment to protect himself. In addition, the length of time and discipline required to achieve proficiency in karatedo provides some assurance as to the moral character of the individual. Through karatedo training one learns to know and control oneself better, thus not needing to prove oneself in futile fights.

Self-defense techniques are only specific applications of karatedo to special circumstances but cannot be dissociated from karatedo techniques. It is only through an assiduous practice of karatedo that one can learn to develop ones strong points to compensate for weaknesses and to apply them in protection oneself when needed.

Self-defense techniques can be either with or without weapons, against armed or unarmed aggressors. This chapter will deal only with empty-handed self-defense techniques. The next chapter will introduce two typical weapons, a short weapon, the *sai*, and a long weapon, the *bo*. The practice of these two weapons will suffice to cover all the applications of self-defense with weapons.

The self-defense techniques presented below have been selected on the basis of their simplicity of execution and their efficiency. It must be kept in mind that under the stress of a dangerous attack basic techniques are always the most efficient because they are more straightforward and have normally been practiced more often. It must also be remembered that in karatedo, self-defense techniques are aimed at completely disabling the aggressor in the shortest possible time and in the safest possible way. The practice of self-defense techniques must then reflect this goal.

Prevention of attacks

Like medicine, self-defense should be preventive rather than curative. This means that it is better to prevent an attack rather than to have to fight it off, especially if the aggressor is armed. Even a well-trained person should avoid going where he knows he will run into trouble. Women should avoid walking late at night in deserted or insecure streets. When going into a bar or *discotheque*, one should always study the place, locate the exists, and mentally figure out how to protect oneself or get out if attacked. Usually the safest place is against a wall close to the exit. In many cases a chain, umbrella, or even a tightly rolled newspaper can provide an adequate weapon to ward off an attack. At night, one should avoid or be very cautious of underground tunnels, scaffoldings, and other sites propitious to an ambush.

When pulling a door open, one should step a few feet backwards from the door; when pushing the door open, push it completely open before stepping in. One should never walk through a door in a suspicious place without first checking to see if there is anything beyond it. In a deserted parking lot, approach your car keeping away from other parked cars, looking under the cars to see if somebody is hiding behind them. Lock the doors as soon as you get into your car. If attacked, lean against a car to avoid being jumped from behind.

In summary, one should always be on one guard so that if attacked, one will not panic and one's mind will be free to think about defensive action. One should always try to prevent an attack rather than to respond to it and even a well-trained person would be well advised not to confront an armed aggressor.

Moral rectitude, self-respect, and respect towards others are the best protections in our societies where man's future rests in his own hands.

In the presentation of self-defense techniques, the usual notation will be used: the attacker is assumed to stand in a right stance, facing east, while the defender is in a *shizen hontai*, facing west.

2. Illustration of Self-defense Techniques

Defense against body holding (I)

The opponent grabs you over the arms in a front tackle (Fig. 1).
—Step backward with your right leg to the NE, lowering your position.
—Tighten your elbows inward and clasp his arms against your body with your hands. (Fig. 2)
—Then deliver a right *hiza geri* to his solar plexus. (Fig. 3)
—Move your right leg to the SE, using *hiraki ashi*, and break his hold by pulling your elbows outward and twisting your body. (Fig. 4)
—Then deliver a right *kentsui uchi* (or *empi uchi oroshi*) to his face. (Fig. 5)

Defense against body holding (II)

The opponent grabs you from behind over the arms. (Fig. 6)
—Bend your body forward, to break his balance, and clasp his arms. (Fig. 7)
—Stamp on the toes of his right foot with your right heel (Figs. 8–9) and raise your elbow up and outward to break his hold. (Fig. 10)
—Now rotate your body to your left and deliver a left *empi ushiro ate* to his solar plexus. (Fig. 11)
—Follow with a right *shotei uchi* to his nose or chin. (Fig. 12)

Defense against collar grappling (I)

The opponent grabs you with two hands and pulls you. (Fig. 13)
—Step forward with your right foot (Fig. 14) and execute a left *hineri geri* to the shin of his right leg with the ball of your foot. (Fig. 15)
—Pull your left foot back and cross it behind your right, using *hiraki ashi*. Execute a right *uchi sukui uke* to break his hold. (Fig. 11)
—Follow with a right *empi yoko ate* to his solar plexus. (Fig. 17)
—Then deliver a right *uraken uchi* to his nose. (Fig. 18)

Defense against collar grappling (II)

The opponent grabs you with one hand and pushes you. (Fig. 1)

—Bring your right leg behind the left, using *hiraki ashi*, and execute a left *uchi uke* to break his hold. (Fig. 2)

—Follow with a left *sokuto yoko geri* to his right knee. (Fig. 3)

—Then deliver a right *hineri zuki* to his face. (Fig. 4)

Defense against hair grabbing

The opponent grabs your hair from behind. (Fig. 5)

—Clasp his hand with both of your hands to prevent him from pulling your hair. (Fig. 6)

—Execute a left *ushiro kagi geri* to his right shin. (Fig. 7)

—Still holding his hand, bend forward and move backward in the SW direction to break his hold. (Fig. 8)

—Then deliver a right *hineri geri* with the ball of your foot to his solar plexus or ribs. (Fig. 9)

Defense against wrist grabbing (I)

The opponent grabs both your wrists from the front. (Fig. 10)
—Step backward to the NE with your right leg (to prevent him from kicking you) and bring your arms down on each side of your body, opening your hands. (Fig. 11)
—Execute a right *hineri geri* with the ball of the foot to his solar plexus (Fig. 12).
—Follow with a right *shotei oi uchi* to his nose or chin. (Fig. 13)

Defense against wrist grabbing (II)

You are facing north; the opponent grabs your left sleeve (or wrist or elbow). (Fig. 14)
—Shift your left leg backward to the south, bringing down your left arm, hand open.
—Deliver a right *shuto yoko mawashi uchi* to his jugular vein. (Fig. 15)
—Grab him behind the neck with your right hand and catch his sleeve or wrist with your left hand. (Fig. 16)
—Pull him to you and then twist your body to your left to break his balance in the direction of his right back corner. (Fig. 17)
—Sweep his right leg, using a right *osoto gari*. (Fig. 18)
—Then follow with a right *hineri zuki oroshi* to the solar plexus of your fallen opponent. (Fig. 19)

Defense against choking (I)

Frontal attack with both hands. (Fig. 1)

—Roll your tongue in your mouth, tuck your chin, and tighten your neck; hold your breath. (Fig. 2)

—Move your right leg backward to the SE, using *hiraki ashi*, and execute a left *uchi mawashi uke*, swinging your arm above his arms and twisting your body to your right. (Figs. 3–4)

—Then follow with a left *shuto gyaku uchi* to his face. (Fig. 5)

—Move with a left forward *neko ashi* and grab your opponent, your right arm to his right shoulder. (Fig. 6)

—Deliver a right *hiza hineri geri* to his groin. (Fig. 7)

Defense against choking (II)

The opponent attacks from behind, choking you with the outside of his forearm.

—Roll your tongue in your mouth, tuck your chin, and tighten your neck; hold your breath. (Fig. 8)

—Grab his forearm with both your hands and pull it down to prevent him from choking you further.

—Bend forward and deliver a left *kentsui ushiro uchi* to the groin. (Fig. 9)

—Rotate your body to your left and move backward to the SE with your body still bent forward. (Fig. 10)

—Holding his wrist with your left hand and his elbow with your right, pull him down and forward to the ground. (Figs. 11–12)

—Then execute a right *shuto uchi oroshi* to the back of his neck. (Figs. 13–14)

Defense against a knife attack

Even a well-trained person should avoid having to respond to a knife attack and would be best advised to walk away from such a situation. If, however, there is no other choice but to defend one's life, then one should try to find any kind of defensive weapon (stick, chair, rock). A jacket could also be used for protection either by swinging it at the knife to sweep it away or to encircle it, or by rolling it tightly against one's arm to block the attack in a safer way. A shoe could also be used in much the same way. In the absence of everything, spitting in the attacker's face may distract his attention for a fraction of a second, thus providing an opportunity to counterattack.

In all the situations described, one has to let the attacker commit himself before evading his attack and counterattacking.

The attacker steps in to thrust

—Move to the NE with a left backward *neko ashi* and execute a left *shuto soto uke*. (Figs. 15–17)

—Deliver a right *mawashi geri* with the ball of your foot to his solar plexus. (Figs. 18–19)

—Execute a right *shuto uchi otoshi* to his right wrist to make him drop his knife. (Fig. 20)

—Follow with a right *uraken gyaku uchi* to the face. (Figs. 21–23)

The attacker steps in to stab

—Move forward using *neko ashi*. Block his attack with a left *age uke*. (Figs. 1–3)

—Deliver a right *empi yoko mawashi uchi* to his ribs. (Fig. 4)

—Push his arm upward with your left forearm and grab his wrist with your right hand from underneath to execute an *ude garami* (arm warp). (Fig. 5)

—Throw your opponent with a right *osoto otoshi*. (Figs. 6–8)

—Follow with a right *empi uchi otoshi* to the solar plexus of your fallen opponent. (Figs. 9–10)

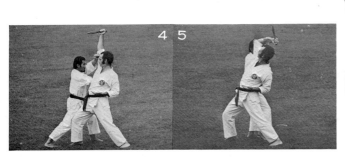

Slashing attack to the face

—Step backward with your right foot to the NE, rotate your body to your right and duck, bending your body forward. (Figs. 11–13)

—Execute a left *sokuto yoko geri* to his ribs. (Fig. 14)

—Step forward with your left foot and grab his hand with both of yours. (Fig. 15)

—Tuck his arm under your left armpit in a *waki katame* (armpit armlock) and rotate your body and right foot to your right, around your left foot. (Fig. 16)

—Step forward in the NE direction and apply pressure to his elbow joint with all your weight. (Figs. 17–18)

—Take your opponent down to the ground and deliver a right *kentsui uchi oroshi* to the back of his head. (Figs. 19–20)

Defense against a stick

Overhead strike to the head

—Move your right leg behind the left, using *hiraki ashi*, to avoid the strike. (Figs. 1–3)

—Move forward with a left *neko ashi*.

—Deliver a left *shuto gyaku uchi* to the attacker's face. (Fig. 4)

—Slide your right arm over his arms to catch his hand between your forearm and biceps, and clench both hands together. (Fig. 5)

—Slide your left foot towards the SW to break your opponent's balance and choke him with a *hadaka jime* (bare strangle). (Figs. 6–7)

Swinging attack to the face

—Move forward with a left *neko ashi* and execute a *jodan morote awase uke* behind his right arm or shoulder. (Figs. 8–9)

—Deliver a right *hiza geri* to the solar plexus of the attacker. (Fig. 10)

—Grab his right shoulder with both hands, step forward with your left foot (Fig. 11), and throw him, using *ushiro hiza guruma*, by applying the sole of your right foot to his left knee and rotating your body to your right. (Fig. 12)

—Then execute a right *hineri zuki oroshi* to the face of your fallen opponent. (Figs. 13–14)

The attacker thrusts his stick forward

—Move your right foot backward to the SE, using *hiraki ashi*, and execute a *morote uke nagashi* or *uchi sukui uke*. (Figs. 15–16)

—Follow with a left *sokuto yoko geri* to his right knee. (Fig. 17)

—Grab the stick with both hands and pull it to you, twisting it counterclockwise. (Figs. 18–19)

—Then push the stick to the NW, twisting clockwise, and sweep the opponent's legs with a circular motion of the stick. (Figs. 20–21)

—Take the stick away from your opponent and move forward to the NW with a right *oi ashi*. (Fig. 22)

—Twirl the stick on your right side (*fusha gaeshi*) to deliver a blow to your opponent's head. (Fig. 23)

Defense against a pistol

It is, in any case, extremely dangerous to attempt to disarm an aggressor with a pistol. However, if he stands no more than one step away from you, some self-defense techniques can be successfully utilized.

Hold-up position from the front

If the aggressor asks for your money, satisfy his demand first (Figs. 1–3). Then:

—Execute a left *shuto uchi otoshi* to the aggressor's wrist to deflect or make him drop his pistol (Fig. 4), and move forward to the NW, using a left *neko ashi*, to deliver a right *shuto mawashi uchi* to his eyes or temple. (Fig. 5)

—Grab his wrist from underneath with your right hand (Fig. 6), and the barrel of the pistol (if he still holds it) with your left hand, fingers down. (Fig. 7)

—Bend his wrist to the SW to snatch the pistol away from him. (Fig. 8)

—Deliver a strike to his temple with the butt of the pistol. (Fig. 9)

Hold-up position from behind

If the aggressor tries to pick your wallet, wait until his hand is busy searching your pockets (Figs. 11–13). Then:

—Execute a right *shuto gedan uchi oroshi* to his right forearm or wrist, rapidly rotating your body to your right. (Fig. 14)

—Follow immediately with a left *shuto yoko mawashi uchi* to his right temple or jugular vein. (Fig. 15)

—Follow with a right *hiza geri* to his groin. (Fig. 16)

—Step forward (west) with your right foot and deliver a right *shuto uchi oroshi* to his right elbow. (Figs. 17–19)

—Grab his wrist from underneath with your left hand and bend his arm to his face and snatch his pistol.

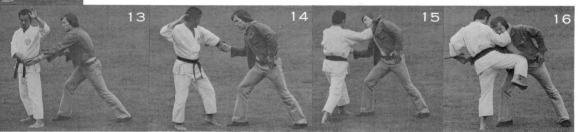

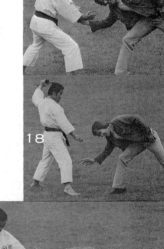

The aggressor points a pistol at your left temple (you are facing north). (Fig. 20)

—Execute a left *shuto jodan soto uke* to the pistol and simultaneously a right *shuto yoko mawashi uchi* to the jugular vein of the aggressor. (Figs. 21–22)

—Follow with a right *hiza mawashi geri* to his solar plexus. (Fig. 23)

—Grab his wrist with both hands and pull it upward in the SE direction. (Fig. 24)

—Step forward to the SW with your right foot and pivot to your left under his arm, bending it and pointing the pistol at his stomach. (Fig. 25)

—Execute an *ude garami* (arm wrap) and take away his pistol with your right hand. (Fig. 27)

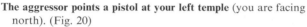

Special self-defense techniques for women

Women may have to deal with specific types of aggression such as purse-snatching and forcible assaults. Purse-snatching can be treated as in section "defense against wrist grabbing." Self-defense techniques against the most common cases of assaults will be discussed in this section. The aggressor is usually a stronger person who is overconfident. The defender should make use of the overconfidence of an unsuspecting assailant and must then deal with him very harshly, because if she does not disable her attacker at once, he may become much more violent and she will not be able to catch him off guard.

In a critical situation where her life is in danger, a woman should not hesitate to make use of what most women carry in their handbags, scissors, needles, hair spray, etc. She can also scratch or poke her fingers into her aggressor's eyes. She must of course resort to such things only as a last recourse, keeping in mind that she cannot afford to give her aggressor another chance to attack.

Front hugging

—Move backward with your right foot, resisting your opponent's pull, then give in. (Figs. 1–2)
—Deliver a right *hiza geri* to his groin. (Fig. 3)
—Grab his hair with your left hand and pull him downward to you, moving your right foot backward. (Fig. 4)
—Then execute a right *empi uchi age* to his face. (Fig. 5)

Hugging from behind

—Move your right foot backward, bend on your knees, and raise your elbows above your shoulders to break his hold. (Figs. 6–7)

—Twist your body to your left and execute a right *shotei hineri zuki* to his chin. (Fig. 8)

—Grab his hair with your right hand and pull his head downward. (Fig. 9)

—Then deliver a right *hiza geri* to his face. (Fig. 10)

Sitting on a bench and grabbed around the shoulders from your right side.

—Plant your left foot firmly on the ground and deliver a right *empi yoko ate* to the solar plexus of your attacker, pushing your right elbow in with your left hand. (Figs. 11–13)

—Then stand up and grab his hair with your right hand. Pull his head to you and deliver a left *empi hineri uchi age* to his face. (Figs. 14–15)

In these examples of self-defense techniques for women, the emphasis has been put on the use of the palm, elbow, and knee because they are very strong and do not require any prior strengthening. Furthermore, they are best suited for close-contact situations.

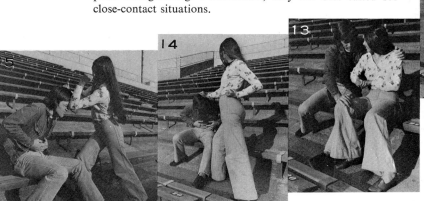

chapter 9 Practice of Weapons

1. The Development of Weapons in Karatedo

Man started carving clubs out of wood as an extension of his arm, to protect himself against wild animals and other men, and to secure his own property. Man was weak compared to other creatures and had no natural defenses except his brain. Clubs were stronger than his own hands and provided more reach. Soon he was able to sharpen wood and later stone. He had thus a cutting and spearing instrument that he could lengthen to give him even more reach or throw with his hands. Later he developed a bow which could send an arrow even farther away. At the same time he was developing defensive weapons against the inclemency of weather and animals (clothing, houses, etc.) and against offensive weapons (shields, helmets, etc.).

Methods of fighting were also devised in many parts of the world, particularly in China. They seem to have been imported from India. However, it was not until the T'ang period (A.D. 618–907) that methods of fighting were codified by a monk of Indian origin at the Shaolin Temple. This first form of unarmed practice was part of the monks' ascetic meditation (*zazen*). As the monks went throughout the province evangelizing the population, they had to walk along unsafe roads where numerous highwaymen robbed the travelers. These religious men could certainly not carry arms so they learned to turn their walking sticks into effective weapons.

There is a story of one such monk who with a *bo*, trounced a hundred army deserters who had attacked the Shaolin Temple. As Zen Buddhism spread throughout China, so did the use of implements as weapons. The population, mostly farmers and fishermen, used their long carrying rods or the shafts of their forks or fishspears as defensive weapons. But the development of weapons reached its peak when Okinawa became a protectorate of China in 1405 under the reign of King Satsudo. Okinawa was at that time divided into three kingdoms. In 1422 Shoashi became king of the Southern Mountain Kingdom and undertook to conquer the two other kingdoms. In 1429 he prohibited the possession of any weapon in an effort to bring the whole country under his sway. Again, in 1609, the Shimazu clan of the Kyushu Islands conquered Okinawa and placed much stricter restrictions on all weapons and martial arts than ever before. The population reacted both times by secretly practicing self-defense techniques with their working tools: sticks (*bo*), forks, scythes, flails (*nunchaku*), harpoons, etc. The three-pronged ends of the forks and harpoons (*sai*) were separated from the shaft and hidden behind the forearms; they were used to block a sword attack, breaking its blade with a rapid twist of the wrist; they could also be thrown at an opponent.

The handles of millstones (*tonfa*) were also carried two at a time, hidden behind the forearms, and were used to ward off a sword attack. The scythe was the reaping-hook used to harvest the rice and the *kusari kama* was a sickle attached to a chain and used for the same purpose by the farmers.

2. Value of the Practice of Weapons

All these instruments became truly martial weapons in Okinawa, but they were used only for self-defense purposes and not to attack others.

Although there is no longer need to defend oneself against the sword. The practice of weapons is still essential to karatedo training. The weapon augments the reach of the arm and, as a result, motions and techniques must have a wider amplitude. Proper distance becomes a critical factor. The mental attitudes of the karatedo practitioners are sharpened because one becomes more cautious when confronted by an armed opponent. *Sai* and *bo* practice are excellent for self-defense purposes because substitutions can usually be found easily in any kind of environment.

Also, the practice of weapons serves to illustrate and cause to come alive the karatedo concept that hands and feet should be considered as true weapons and that one should exercise the same caution in the practice of karatedo as in the practice of *buki ho*.

3. Illustration of the Practice of Weapons

Sai kata

The *sais* are always carried three at a time: one in each hand with the third slipped in the belt on the left hip as a replacement when one of the others is thrown.

Standard salutation forms, with both *sais* in the right hand. Place a *sai* in each hand, hiding them behind your forearms, points inward, to execute a *kenko ritsurei*.

1–Move your right leg backward to the south using *hiraki ashi*, assuming a left *neko ashi* stance, and execute a left *uchi uke nagashi*.

2–In the same position, rotate your left forearm until parallel to the ground in front of your body (*suihei kamae*).

3–Move forward (north) with a right *oi ashi* and execute a thrust using the butt-end of the right *sai* (to the throat).

4–Step forward to the NE with your left leg and execute a *morote tsuki oroshi* (to the legs) with the butt-end of the *sais*, bringing your right leg immediately behind the left.

5–Rotate your body 180° clockwise, to face the south, and in a right *zenkutsu* stance, execute a *jodan age uke nagashi*.

6–Move to the south with a left forward *oi ashi* and execute a left *oi zuki* with the butt-end of the left *sai*.

7–Move forward with a right *oi ashi*, twirling the *sais* to point forward, and execute a *morote heiko zuki*. Then twirl the *sais* inward in a *morote kakushi kamae* (hidden-position guard).

8–Turn your head to the north and execute a left *mae mawari*, then bring your left leg behind the right, using *hiraki ashi*, and in a right *neko ashi* stance, execute a right *uchi uke nagashi*.

9–Jump west with your left leg and slide your right leg behind it, using *hiraki ashi*. In a left *neko ashi* stance, execute a left *uchi uke nagashi*.

10–Jump to the SE with your right leg and bring your left leg behind it, using *hiraki ashi*. Then in a left *zenkutsu* stance, execute a *morote gedan barai*, twirling the *sais* forward. Bring your left foot close to the right in a *musubi ashi* stance and twirl both *sais* inward, hands down on the sides of your body.

11–Step forward with your left leg to the NW and bring your right leg behind it, using *hiraki ashi*. Execute a *jodan morote yoko mawashi uchi*, twirling both *sais* forward in a left *zenkutsu* stance.

12–Bring your left leg back close to the right in a *musubi ashi* stance and twirl both *sais* inward, hands down on the sides of your body.

13–Step forward to the NE with your right leg and bring your left leg behind, using *hiraki ashi*. Then twirl both *sais* forward and execute a *jodan morote mawashi yoko uchi* in a right *zenkutsu* stance. Twirl both *sais* inward and bring your right leg back close to the left in a *musubi ashi* stance.

14–Step to the SW with your left leg and bring your right leg behind it, using *hiraki ashi*. Twirl both *sais* downward in a left *zenkutsu* stance and execute a *morote uchi gedan barai*. Twirl both *sais* inward.

15–Bring your right leg forward, close to the left in a *musubi ashi* stance.

16–Rotate your body clockwise to face south and execute a left *empi uchi* to the north, extending your right hand to the south with both *sais* pointed inward in a hidden position.

17–Step backward to the south with your left leg and execute a left *gyaku gedan barai*, twirling the *sais* downward. Then execute a right *oi zuki* with the butt-end of the right *sai* and twirl it outward. Then execute a *jodan age nagashi uke* and twist the right *sai* to hook the blade of the sword (or the *bo*). Pull to your upper right, simultaneously twirl the left *sai* outward, and execute a left *oi zuki*.

18–Execute a right forward *oi ashi* and follow with a *morote hasami uchi* (scissors strike) to the temple, both *sais* still pointing forward.

19–Slide your right leg backward to the south and execute a *morote uchi gedan barai*, in a large circular motion above your head from the SE to the NW corner.

20–Execute a left foreward *okuri ashi* to the NW and follow with a *morote jodan mawashi uchi*, both *sais* pointing forward.

21–Step forward to the NE with your right leg and bring your left leg behind the right, using *hiraki ashi*, then twirl both *sais* forward and execute a *morote jodan mawashi uchi* in a large circular motion above your head from the NE to the NW corner.

22–Step to the SW corner with your left leg and cross your right leg behind the left, using *kosa ashi*.

23–Execute a right *gyaku soto gedan barai* or rotate your right forearm until parallel to the ground in front of your body (*suihei kamae*).

24–Move forward NE corner with a left *oi ashi* and execute a left *oi zuki* to the throat, in the NE direction, with the butt-end of the left *sai*. Follow with a left *oi geri*, using the heel to attack the groin, and draw your left leg back to the right knee. Then jump forward with your left leg and, twirling the left *sai* forward, deliver a left *mawashi uchi oroshi* (to the crown of the head).

25–Move with a left backward *neko ashi* to the SW and simultaneously execute *jodan juji uke* in *zenkutsu* stance, then adopt a left *neko ashi* stance with both *sais* pointing forward in a *chudan juji kamae*, twirl both *sais* inward.

26–Slide your right leg to the SE and cross your left leg behind it using *hiraki ashi*. Twirl the left *sai* downward and execute a left *gyaku gedan barai* or rotate your left forearm until parallel to the ground in front of your body (*suihei kamae*).

27–Execute a right *oi zuki* with the butt-end of the right *sai* to the throat. Follow with a right *oi geri*, using the ball of the foot, to the NW. Pull your foot back and quickly jump with your right leg forward, twirling the right *sai* forward, and execute a right *mawashi uchi oroshi* to the head.

28–Move to the SE with a right backward *neko ashi*, simultaneously execute a right *jodan juji uke* in *zenkutsu* stance and with both *sais* pointing forward in a *chudan juji kamae*. Twirl both *sais* inward.

29–Slide your right leg backward to the SE and execute a *morote gedan barai* in large circular motion above your head from the SE to the NE corner.

30–Execute a left forward *okuri ashi* to the north. Twirl both *sais* forward and swing them clockwise above your head to deliver a *morote jodan mawashi uchi* to the head. Then twirl both *sais* inward and follow with a left *oi geri* with the heel to the groin. Pull your left leg back and jump forward (on the same leg). Then execute a right *oi ashi* to the north and twirl the right *sai* in throwing position. Throw it to the north.

31–Cross your left leg behind the right, moving to the NE, and execute a right *ushiro mawari*, facing south.

Perform steps 1 through 30 in mirror image.

32–Assume *zanshin*.

33–Execute the standard salutation forms, holding both *sais* in your right hand.

31

32

33

Bo kata

The *bo* is held in its center with the right hand and hidden behind the right arm, pointing to the ground. Execute the standard salutation forms.

1—Step backward with your right foot in a left *neko ashi* stance. Twirl the *bo* in front of your body (*fusha gaeshi*: wind mill) and shift it into your left hand. Then drive it vertically into the ground in front of your left foot in a left *shuto chudan kamae* to stand in a left *zenkutsu* stance behind the *bo*. Hold this position for a few seconds.

2—Suddenly, step forward with your right leg, using *oi ashi*. Put your right hand on the *bo* above the left and slam it down (attacking the crown of the head) with a *shomen uchi oroshi*, standing in a right reverse *neko ashi* stance.

3—Then thrust the *bo*, using a right *oi zuki*, and stand in a right *zenkutsu* stance.

4—Shift into a right *neko ashi* stance by pulling your right foot back and rotate the *bo* into a vertical defensive stance, right hand down at the level of the belt, left hand at shoulder level, hiding behind the *bo*.

5—Move with a right forward *neko ashi* to the NE and execute a *jodan yoko mawashi uchi* in a right *zenkutsu* stance, twisting the *bo* counterclockwise with both arms and tightening it under your left armpit, the right arm being extended on top of the *bo*.

6—Move with a right backward *neko ashi* to the SW, then bring your right leg behind the left, using *kosa ashi*. Step north with a quick left forward *neko ashi* and execute a *gedan yoko mawashi uchi oroshi* (attacking the legs).

7–Execute a left forward *okuri ashi* and twirl the *bo* on your right side along a north-south line (*suisha gaeshi*: water wheel) attacking the head. After completion, you are in a left *zenkutsu* stance with the left hand extended on top of the *bo*, tightening it under your right armpit.

8–Move with a left backward *neko ashi* to the SE. Cross your left leg behind the right, using *kosa ashi*, and then reverse the grip of your hands on the *bo* and execute a *gedan yoko mawashi uchi*.

9–Move with a right backward *neko ashi* to the SW, then execute a thrusting and sweeping motion with the *bo* to the NE, standing in a low right *sotobiraki jigotai stance*.

10–Move with a left forward *oi ashi* to the north, thrusting the *bo* forward with a left *oi zuki*.

11–Cross your left leg behind the right, using *kosa ashi*. Then circle the *bo* around and behind your hips, inverting your hands on the *bo* with your right hand coming in front of the left.

12–Move with a right forward *neko ashi* to the north and thrust the *bo* with a right *oi zuki*.

13–Move to the SW with a right backward *okuri ashi* and dodge in a low right *sotobiraki jigotai* stance. Then reverse the grip of your hands and slide your right hand down to grasp the closest end of the *bo*. Move to the NE with a left *oi ashi* and sweep the *bo* in a large circular motion parallel to the ground (*kuruma gaeshi*), at the same time sliding your left hand on the *bo* close to the right in a low left *sotobiraki jigotai* stance.

14–Move forward with a left *okuri ashi* and twirl the *bo* on your right side (*suisha gaeshi*), attacking the top of the head while standing in a left reverse *neko ashi* stance.

15–Raise your left knee and then jump forward with your left leg. At the same time, reverse the grip of your hands on the *bo* and raise it above and behind your head before thrusting it downward at 45° in a left *sotobiraki jigotai* stance.

16–Move with a right forward *neko ashi* to the NE and cross your left leg behind the right, using *kosa ashi*. Then twirl the *bo* above your head and slide your right leg to the NW to execute a *jodan yoko mawashi uchi*.

17–Step west with your right leg and cross your left leg behind it with a *kosa ashi*. Slide your right leg to the south, twirling the *bo* above your head, and execute a *jodan yoko mawashi uchi*.

18–Hold the *bo* with your left hand and bring it behind your body in a right *zenkutsu* stance with a right *shuto jodan kamae*.

19–Step forward to the SE with your left leg and bring your right foot behind it, using *hiraki ashi*. Then execute a left *gedan yoko mawashi uchi oroshi* to the west.

20–Execute a right forward *oi ashi* to the SW. Cross your left leg behind the right using *kosa ashi*, and deliver with the *bo*, a *yoko mawashi uchi* in a circular motion, parallel to the ground, towards the east.

21–Move with a left backward *neko ashi* and execute a left *jodan uchi oroshi*. Facing the NE, hide the *bo* with your right hand behind your body with a left *shuto jodan kamae*, standing in a left *zenkutsu* stance.

22–Raising your right knee, step forward with a right *oi ashi* and raise the *bo* above your head to deliver a right *jodan uchi oroshi* from the upper right to the lower left while standing in a right *zenkutsu* stance.

23–Twirl the *bo* on your left side in a *suisha gaeshi*, simultaneously moving forward with a right *neko ashi*.

24–Standing in a right reverse *neko ashi* stance, execute a right forward *neko ashi* to the north and thrust the *bo* with a right *oi zuki* to the throat.

25–Move backward to the south with a right *neko ashi* and adopt a right vertical defensive position.

26–Twirl the *bo* in front of your body with a *fusha gaeshi* and rotate your head, and then body, 180° counterclockwise to face south. Cross your right leg behind the left, using *kosa ashi*, and deliver a right *yoko mawashi uchi* with the *bo*.

27–Standing in a right *neko ashi* stance, hide the *bo* behind your left arm. Then repeat steps 1 through 26 in mirror image.

28–After completion, adopt a left vertical defensive position. Move your right leg behind the left using *kosa ashi*. Rotate your body to face the north and deliver a *bo yoko mawashi uchi oroshi*.

29–Bring your right foot forward, close to the left in a *shizen hontai*, and hide the *bo* behind your right arm.

30–Assume *zanshin*.

Then execute the standard salutation forms with the *bo* behind your right arm, pointing downward.

25

29

Sai bo no kumite

Bo: Offensive

Enter the *shiaijo* from the west side, go to your position and bow with a *keirei* to *shomen*, holding the *bo* behind your right arm, pointing downward. Face your opponent and bow with a *kenko ritsurei*.

1–Step forward with your left leg and assume a left *zenkutsu* stance. (Fig. 1)

2–Jump to the SE with your right foot and cross your left leg behind it, using *kosa ashi*. Raise the *bo* and grasp it with your left hand below the right, reversing the grip of your right hand. Execute a *jodan yoko mawashi uchi*, to the jugular vein, twisting your right hand extended on the *bo* counterclockwise and tightening the *bo* under your left armpit. (Figs. 2–3)

4–Jump to the NW with your left leg and cross your right leg behind it, using *kosa ashi*. Pull the *bo* down, changing your grip, and execute a left *gedan yoko mawashi uchi*, attacking the legs. (Figs. 4–5)

6–Move to the east with a left forward *oi ashi* and twirl the *bo* on your left side, attacking the top of the head with a *suisha gaeshi* while standing in a left *zenkutsu* stance. (Figs. 6–8)

9–Cross your left leg in front of the right. Move to the SW and bring your right leg behind the left using *hiraki ashi*, to avoid your opponent's attack to the left knee. (Figs. 9–11)

11–Move with a left backward *neko ashi* to the NW, holding the *bo* vertically with your hands stretched apart. (Fig. 12)

13–In this position execute a *jodan uke* and then drive the *bo* vertically into the ground, holding it with your left arm outstretched in front of your left foot, to ward off the thrust of the *sai*. (Figs. 13–14)

14–Move with a left forward *neko ashi* to the east and, with the *bo*, execute a left *jodan uchi* to the top of the head. (Fig. 15)

16–Move backward to the west with a left *neko ashi* and assume a *chudan kamae* (offensive guard), pointing the *bo* at your opponent's eyes. (Fig. 16)

17–Move with a left forward *neko ashi* to the east and use the *bo* to execute a left *jodan oi zuki* to the throat. (Figs. 17–18)

sai: Defensive

Enter the *shiajio* from the east side. Go to your position and bow with a *keirei* to *shomen*, holding both *sais* in your right hand. Face your opponent with a *sai* in each hand and bow with a *kenko ritsurei*.

1–Slide your right leg backward in a left *neko ashi* stance, your right hand hidden behind your body and the left *sai* in an upward vertical defensive position at eye level. (Fig. 1)

3–Jump to the north with your right leg and cross your left leg behind it, *sais* pointed forward. Execute a *jodan morote uchi uke nagashi* with both *sais*, standing in a right *zenkutsu* stance. (Figs. 2–3)

5–Jump to the SE on your left leg and cross your right leg behind it, using *kosa ashi*. Execute a *gedan morote uchi uke nagashi*. (Figs. 4–5)

7–Jump to the NE with your right leg crossing behind the left and swing both *sais* counterclockwise above your head to deliver a *jodan morote uchi oroshi*, standing in a right *sotobiraki jigotai* stance. Twirl both *sais* inward. (Figs. 6–8)

8–Move forward, using *okuri ashi*, to the NW and deliver a right *sokuto yoko geri oroshi* to your opponent's knee. Pull your right foot back to your left knee and put it down in front of your body. Twirl both *sais* inward. (Figs. 9–11)

10–Step forward to the NW with your right leg and execute a *jodan gyaku uchi* to the face with the right *sai*. (Fig. 12)

12–Follow with a left *hineri zuki* to the solar plexus, with the left *sai* pointed forward and the right *sai* pointed forward in front of your face in a *chudan kamae*. (Figs. 13–14)

15–Execute a right backward *neko ashi* to the east and adopt a *morote chudan juji kamae*, standing in a right *neko ashi* stance. (Figs. 15–16)

18–Execute a right backward *neko ashi* to the NE and with the right *sai* deliver a *uchi gedan barai*, deflecting the *bo*. (Figs. 17–18)

Bo: **Offensive**

20–Move with a left backward *neko ashi* to the west and turn the *bo* around and behind your hips. Cross your left leg behind the right, using *kosa ashi*, at the same time inverting your hands on the *bo*, your right hand coming in front of the left. (Figs. 19–21)

22–Execute a right forward *neko ashi* and follow with a left *jodan oi zuki*, using the *bo* to attack the throat. (Figs. 22–23)

25–Avoid the *sai* attack with a right backward *neko ashi*. (Figs. 24–25)

27–Move to the SE with your left leg, using *kosa ashi*. Slide your right leg to the east and twirl the *bo* above your head to deliver a *jodan yoko mawashi uchi* to your opponent's temple. (Figs. 26–27)

29–Move east, crossing your left leg behind the right, using *kosa ashi*. Shift your right leg forward to the NW, and twirl the *bo* above your head to deliver a *jodan yoko mawashi uchi* to the temple or jugular vein of your opponent. (Figs 28–29)

32–Jump south with your left leg and shift your right leg behind, using *hiraki ashi*. Deliver a *sukui uchi* from the lower left to the upper right, standing in a left *zenkutsu* stance. (Figs. 30–33)

34–Keeping the *bo* across your chest, step to the NE with your left lg and execute a right *hineri geri* with the heel to the groin. Pull your right leg back in front of the left. (Figs. 34–35)

37–Slide your left leg backward to the SW and then duck, putting your left knee on the ground in a *kata hiza* stance. Raise the *bo* horizontally above your head, both arms stretched out in front of your body. (Figs. 36–37)

38–From this poition, execute a *yoko mawashi uchi oroshi*. Then stand up and cross your left leg behind the right (*kosa ashi*). (Fig. 38)

39–Execute a right *sokuto yoko geri* to the knee of your opponent. Pull your right leg back to your left knee before putting it down in front of your body (Figs. 39–41).

Sai: Defensive

19–Move with a left forward *oi ashi* to the west and deliver a left *jodan uchi* to the top of your opponent's head. (Figs. 19–20)

21–Move east with a left backward *neko ashi* and in a left *neko ashi* stance, adopt a *chudan juji kamae*. (Fig. 21)

23–Move to the SE with a left backward *neko ashi* and execute a *uchi gedan barai* with the left *sai* to deflect the *bo*. (Figs. 22–23)

24–Move west with a right forward *oi ashi* and deliver a *jodan uchi* with the right *sai* to the top of your opponent's head. (Figs. 24–25)

26–Move east with a right backward *neko ashi* and in a right *neko ashi* stance, adopt a *jodan juji kamae*. (Fig. 26).

28–Move with a right backward *neko ashi* to the NE and circle both *sais* counterclockwise above your head to deliver a *jodan morote mawashi uchi*. (Fig. 27)

30–Slide your right leg to the SW and cross your left leg behind it facing east. Then swing both *sais* above your head to deliver a *jodan morote mawashi uchi* and then twirl both *sais* inward. (Figs. 28–29)

31–Execute an *oi geri* with the heel of your right foot to the groin of your opponent and pull your leg back in front of your body. (Figs. 30–31)

33–Jump to the SE with your left leg and bring your right leg behind it. Deliver a *gedan morote uchi uke nagashi*. (Figs. 32–33)

35–Twirl both *sais* downward in a low left *zenkutsu* stance, then twirl them inward before jumping to the NE with your right leg and crossing the left behind it with *kosa ashi*. Twirling the left *sai* downward, execute a *gyaku soto gedan barai*. (Figs. 34–35)

36–Swing both *sais* above your head and deliver a *jodan morote uchi oroshi* to the top of your opponent's head. Then twirl both *sais* inward. (Figs. 36–37)

40–Jump to the SE with your left leg and cross your right leg behind it, using *kosa ashi*. Then twirl the left *sai* forward to execute a *gedan uchi sukui uke*. (Figs. 38–40)

Bo: Offensive

42–Jump to the NW with your right leg, bending your body forward. Rotate your body 180° counterclockwise to face SE. (Fig. 42)

43–Move your right leg forward with an *oi ashi* to the SE and execute a right *jodan uchi oroshi* with the *bo*, to the top of the head. (Figs. 43–44)

46–Move with a right backward *neko ashi* to the SW and execute a right *jodan uchi uke*. (Figs. 45–47)

48–Move with a right backward *neko ashi* to the NW and dodge, in a low *sotobiraki jigotai* stance. Then reverse the grip of your right hand on the *bo* and slide it down to the closest end of the *bo*. (Figs. 48–49)

49–Step forward to the SE with an *oi ashi*. Reverse the grip of your left hand and sweep the *bo* in a large circular motion parallel to the ground; 'kuruma gaeshi' (*gedan yoko mawashiuchi* to the legs). (Figs. 50–52)

52–Execute a right *yoko ukemi* (side break-fall). (Figs. 53–54)

55–Sit up with your right knee bent and then adopt a left *kata hiza* stance (right knee on the ground), pointing the *bo* at your opponent's eyes. (Fig. 55)

56–Stand up and execute a left backward *neko ashi* (to the west). (Fig. 56)

57–Cross your left leg behind the right and twirl the *bo*, with your right hand, in front of your body (*fusha gaeshi*). Adopt a right *neko ashi* stance with a defensive guard, the *bo* being held vertically with the right hand at hip level and the left hand at shoulder level.

58–Assume *zanshin*.

Pull your right leg back in a *shizen hontai* and twirl the *bo* behind your right arm.

Bow with a *kenko ritsurei* to your opponent, facing east.

Bow with a *keirei* to *shomen*.

Sai: Defensive

41–Step west with a right *oi ashi*, raising your right knee high. Twirl the right *sai* forward to execute a *jodan uchi oroshi* to the top of your opponent's head. (Figs. 41–42)

44–Move west with a right forward *neko ashi* and, standing in a right *zenkutsu* stance, execute a *jodan morote juji uke*. (Figs. 43–44)

45–Catch the *bo* between the two *sais* and pull it down on your left side, pivoting on your right foot and bringing your left leg behind the right in a counterclockwise circular motion to the west. Then execute a *gyaku uchi* with the left *sai*. (Figs. 45–47)

47–Move with a right forward *oi ashi* to the west and deliver a *jodan uchi oroshi* with the right *sai*. The twirl both *sais* inward. (Figs. 48–50)

50–Jump high in the air to avoid the attack to your legs. (Fig. 51)

51–Throw your opponent with a right *ashi barai* behind his left knee. (Figs. 52–53)

53–Twirl the right *sai* downward and execute a *jodan uchi oroshi* to the face of your fallen opponent from a left *kata hiza* stance (your right knee on the ground), then stand up. (Fig. 54)

54–Slide your left leg to the east, facing west in a right *zenkutsu* stance with both *sais* in a *chudan kamae*.(Fig. 55).

57–Pull your right leg back towards the east behind your left leg and, standing in a left *neko ashi* stance, swing both *sais* counterclockwise on your right side. Adopt a *chudan morote juji kamae*. (Fig. 56)

58–Assume *zanshin*.

Then execute the standard salutation forms, both sais pointing inward. The *sais* are held in the right hand to bow with a *keirei* to *shomen*.

The Kenkokan School of Karatedo

Aims of the School

The true values of budo are losing ground nowadays because in karatedo too much emphasis is being put either on form alone, or on competition. The aims of the Kenkokan school are to foster a strong technical knowledge of both *karate ho* and *buki ho* and at the same time to instill in each student a strong character and will, power, courtesy and courage, and a drive for self-perfection. These goals are summarized by the slogans of the school: *"Spiritual development of the individuality in mind and body," "Effective use of creation for all,"* and *"The fist the creator of life,"* which encapsulate the concern of the Shorinjiryu Kenkokan school for personal development both mental and physical, according to one's own personality and needs.

Organization of the school

The headquarters, So Hombu Dojo, of the Shorinjiryu Kenkokan Karatedo school are located at: 20 Kikui-cho, Shinjuku-ku, Tokyo 162, Japan Tel. 03–3203–5765 Fax. 0473–81–4140. Branches have been established in the U.S.A., Canada, Australia, New Zealand, Russia, Algeria, Switzerland, Spain, India, South Africa, Mali, and Venezuela. Addresses of these branches can be obtained from the So Hombu Dojo in Tokyo.

Rules and Regulations of the School

Regular practices are held from 4 P.M. to 10 P.M. every day throughout the year except on Sundays and national holidays. Instruction is given by karate professors and high-ranking instructors. Special classes and private instruction can also be arranged. Grading examinations are held every two months. Black-belt examinations take place twice a year in April and November.

Tournaments and special events:

Monthly competitions are held at the Hombu Dojo, an annual open championship tournament is organized and held in Japan or other countries. Two special training camps are held in winter and summer. Twice a year (spring and fall), a *kohaku shiai* (red-and-white team competition) is organized. All students also participate in an annual exhibition.

Dojo Kun: Kenkokan School Principles

I. Maintain propriety, etiquette, dignity, and grace.
II. Gain self-understanding by tasting the true meaning of combat.
III. Search for the pure principles of being: truth, justice, and beauty.
IV. Exercise positive personality, that is to say—confidence, courage, and determination.
V. Always seek to develop the character further, aiming towards perfection and complete harmony with creation.

Acknowledgments

I would like to sincerely thank the President and staff of the Charles E. Tuttle Publishing Company, who kindly decided to assist in bringing this book back into print.

Acknowledgments are also due to Mr. Iwao Yoshizaki, President, and Mr. Toshihiro Kawahara, Director, of Japan Publications, Inc., for granting me permission to reprint this book.

The first edition of this book was published in 1976. Since then, Karatedo's popularity has been expanding rapidly, especially since I invented Supersafe protective equipment and developed the Koshiki competition system. Supersafe has revolutionized karatedo training and competition as it allows practitioners to truly test their techniques without the risk of serious injury. Furthermore, the Koshiki Karatedo competition system has broken the barrier that separated the different martial arts and has brought their practicioners together to compete and train with one another safely and realistically. This is one of the most suitable methods for introducing the martial arts into the school system, and ultimately the Olympic Games.

We are now witnessing a great number of people beginning to practice Shorinjiryu Kenkokan Karatedo and implementing the Koshiki competitive system in many countries around the world. As such I felt it was necessary to reprint and update this book.

I would like to express my gratitude to the following individuals for their time, efforts, and support: Shihan Toru Yoshizawa, Kengo 5th Dan, Renshi 6th Dan in Koshiki, 1984 World Champion and four-time silver medalist in the All Japan Koshiki Karatedo Championships; Shihan Takechia Miyazaki, Kengo 5th Dan, Renshi 6th Dan in Koshiki, 1983 World Champion and silver medalist in the 1985 All Japan Koshiki Karatedo Championships; Hiroshi Hisataka, Renshi 6th Dan in Koshiki, who is currently World Champion in Kumite and Kata and who has won three other gold and two silver World Championship medals and was the All Japan Champion in 1985; Isamu Horiuchi, Gyoshi, 2nd Dan, who participated in the All Japan Championships three times; and the members of the Shorinjiryu Kenkokan Karatedo of North America and Japan. The preceding individuals were kind enough to perform for the photographs in the updated preset sparring sequences in this new edition.

I would like to extend my deepest appreciation to Mr. Alain Hourde-Baight, Kengo 5th Dan, who asssisted in the preparation and writing of the original text. Without his help this text might never have become a reality. I would also like to acknowledge Mr. Ian McKenzie, Yushi, 1st Dan, who translated and proofread this new edition, and acted as a translator at the 1st Karatedo Summit, which was held in Tokyo in 1994.

Lastly my sincere thanks go out to Mr. Tolly Wisenberg and Professor Ikko Fukunaga, whose fine photography captured the correct movement of the techniques and the spirit of the art.

And finally it is with warmest appreciation that I say *arigato* (thank you) to all the people from foreign countries who have supported my teaching and practiced with open acceptance, trust, perserverance, dedication, sincerity, and . . . friendship.

MASAYUKI KUKAN HISATAKA, Kenmei, 9th Dan
Tokyo, Japan

Glossary of Karatedo Terms

age   upward
age zuki   upward punch
ago   chin
anza   sitting form (lotus position)
ashi barai   foot sweep
ashi   foot or leg
ashi sabaki   footwork
ashi sukui age   upward leg scooping
ashi tori   leg hold
ate waza   hitting techniques
awase   together

barai   sweep
bassai   fortress; name of kata
bisen   bridge of the nose
bito   head of the nose
bo   a long stick used as a weapon
bogu   protective equipment
bogyo   defensive
Bodhidharma   founder of Zen Buddhism in China
budo   martial arts; "the way of the samurai"
buki ho   the practice of weapons; "the way of weapons"
bushido   code of honor of the samurai

chikara kurabe   early Japanese fighting form
ch'üan fa   the way of the fist
chudan   middle level
chui   warning

da ashi   a snake crawling step
dachi   stance
dan   black-belt degree
de ashi barai   front foot sweep
do   way, body
do basami   body scissors
dojo   practice hall
dojo kun   school principle

eki kin gyo   physical part of Zen; I-chi-ching
empi   elbow
eri tori   collar grabbing

fukushiki   multiple combinations
fumikomi ashi   stamping step
fusemi   forward fall
fusha gaeshi   windmill 'bo' motion (see bo)
fushito   outside of thigh

ganka   chest
gankyu   eyeballs
gedan   lower level
gedan barai   downward leg sweep
genko   closed hand, fist (seiken)
geri (or keri)   kick
go   hard, the name of the Chinese form of checkers, five
gohon   five ways or five techniques
gohon kumite   five-technique kumite (fighting form)
goshin jutsu   self-defense techniques
Gojuryu   style of karate; "hard and soft style"
gyaku ken   reverse fist

gyaku uchi   reverse strike
gyaku waza   armlock techniques

hadaka jime   strangle hold (bare-hand choke)
haishu   back of the hand
haito   ridge of the hand
hajime   begin
haku (shiro)   white
hanmi   half-face front
han da ken   four-finger knuckles
han kaiten   half turn
hangetsu hoko   half-moon step
hansoku   disqualification
hantei   decision
hantei kachi   winner by decision
happiken   name of a kata; "to use the elbow like a monkey in eight directions"
hara   stomach
harai waza   sweeping techniques
hasami   scissors
hasso kamae   a versatile posture
hato mune   sternum
heian   name of a kata; "peaceful mind"
heijoshin   placid state of mind (ability to maintain one's calm)
heiko dachi   parallel foot stance
heisoku dachi   foot together stance
hichu   neck's notch (neck cavity)
hidari   left
hijitsume (hiji)   (elbow) back side of the elbow
hikitate geiko   form of training
hineri hanmi   rotation of the trunk
hineri zuki   twist punch
hiraki ashi   open leg stance
hiraki mi   open leg rotation
hirate   inside of the hand
hitai   forehead
hiza   knee
hiza basami   leg scissors
hiza ke age   upward knee kick
hiza otoshi ate   downward knee kick
hiza sukui·hineri   twisting knee scooping
hiza tsubomi   back side of the knee
hojo undo   complementary exercises
hoko   walking form

inazuma   side of the stomach
ippon   one point
ippon ken   forefinger knuckle
ippon shobu   one point match

jikan   time
jinchu   upper lip
jiyu   free, freedom
jo sokutei   ball of the foot
jodan   upper level
jogai   outside of the contest area, out of bounds
jogaku   upper part of the jaw
joseki   the seat of honor
joshi waza   arm techniques
jujitsu   a Japanese martial art, original form of judo
juji uke   cross block
junbi undo   preparatory exercises

ka fuku bu   lower abdomen
kagaku   lower part of the jaw

kagi zuki	hook punch	kote gaeshi	outward wrist twist
kagi geri	hook kick	kotobu	back of the head
kaiten geri	wheel kick	ko uchi gari	minor inner reaping
kakari geiko	a form of training	kumi ai jutsu	the name of an early form of fighting
kama	reaping hook used as a weapon	kumite	encounter; fighting form
kamae	guard	kumi uchi	a grapple, a scuffle
kamae kata	fighting stance	kung-fu	a Chinese martial art
kamaete	ready, prepare to begin	kurubushi	ankle
kansetsu waza	armlock techniques; reversal of a hand hold	kuruma gaeshi	swing in large circle motion parallel to the ground
kappo	unique life-preserving techniques primarily utilized in injuries incurred in martial art practice	kusari gama	a sickle attached to a chain used as a weapon
kara (空)	empty, air	kuzushi	opening; opportunity to attack
kara (唐)	Japanese term for T'ang dynasty (A.D. 618–970)	kyu	non black-belt rank, below yudansha
karatedo gi	the uniform of karatedo	maai	distance, space
karate ho	the way of empty handed fighting	mae	front
kari waza	reaping techniques	mae kaga mi	leaning forward
ka sokutei	heel of the foot	mae sori mi	leaning backward
kashi waza	leg techniques	makiwara	a wooden post covered with straw, punching or kicking board
kassatsu	spine	mate	stop
kasumi	temples	mawari ashi	crossed leg rotation
kata	shoulder; a form of practice performed alone, form	mawari mi	turning form
kata ashi tori	one leg throw	mawashi geri	roundhouse kick
kata hiza dachi	one-knee stance	migi	right
kawashi waza	dodging techniques	mikazuki geri	crescent kick
ke age	snap kick , upward kick	mizo ochi	solar plexus
keichu	back of the neck	mokuso	concentration, meditation
keido myaku	jugular vein	morote	double; both hands
keirei	ceremonial bow	morote soe uke	supported two-fist block
kekomi	thrusting kick	mudansha	non-black-belt students
kemari	a Chinese game of kicking ball	musubi dachi	attention stance
kempo	Chinese fighting techniques, the way of fist	nagashi uke	sweeping block
ken	fist	nage waza	throwing techniques
kendo	the Japanese martial art of fencing	Naha te	fighting form from Naha (Okinawa)
kenko (or genko)	fist	naihanchin dachi	horseman stance
Kenkokan	the main school of karatedo	naka daka ken	middle finger knuckle
kentsui	hammer fist	neko ashi	cat step
keoroshi	downward kick	nekozeken	back hand of the wrist (cat back)
keri	kick	nidan	second degree black belt, two level
kesa	a monk's habit uniform	nidan zuki	two level fist punch
ki	inner energy; spirit (harnessed strength of mind which takes on a biological form)	nihon	two points, two techniques
		nijushiho	twenty-four techniques, steps, movements name of a kata
katsu	reanimation techniques (first aid)	niseishi	twenty-four techniques; the ancient name of nijushiho
kiai	manifestation of the ki (simultaneous union of spirit and expression of physical strength)	nodo botoke	Adam's apple
		nodo jime	Adam's apple choke
kibi	spine tip	nukite	spear-hand
kime waza	scoring techniques, finishing techniques	nunchaku	flail used as a weapon
kin jime	groin choke	obi	belt
kinate	lower abdomen protections	oi mawashi geri	front leg roundhouse kick
kin teki	testicles	oi zuki	lunge punch
Kodokan	the main school of judo in Japan	Okinawa te	fighting form from Okinawa
kogeki	offensive	okuri ashi barai	sliding foot sweep
ko haku	red and white	okuri eri jime	collar choke, assist lapel strangle
koho daisharin	backward cartwheel	oroshi	downward, take down
koho kaiten	backward role	osoto gari	major outer reaping
kokei	tibia	osoto otoshi	major outer drop
koken	ridge of the hand	otoshi	dropping
kokutsu dachi	backward stance	otoshi mi	knees bent, ducking motion
kosa ashi dachi	crossed leg stance	ouchi gari	major inner reaping
koshi	hip		
ko soto gari	minor outer reaping	pinan	ancient name of heian kata
kote	forearm		

randori	fight, free fighting kumite		tate ken	fundamental fist, vertical fist
rei	salutation, bow		te	hand, technique
renshu shiai	training for competition, practice competition		tegatana	knife-hand, karate chop
			tento	top of the head
ristu Zen	standing meditation		tettsui	iron hammer
ruidai	stage (ring) where fights were held during T'ang dynasty		tobi	jumping or flying
			tobi geri	jump kick
ruidai-o	winner (King) of fight on stage		tobi mi	jumping motion
ryo ashi tori	tackling both legs		tokushu geiko	special practice, training clinic
ryo kado	both sides of a corner		tome waza	stopping techniques
			tonfa	millstone handle used as a weapon
ryojikou kabotoke	mastoid, also both sides of the cavity below the ears		tori	holding, attacker
			tsuki	punching
ryu	school, style		tsukuri kuzushi	opportunity to attack
			tsumasaki	the tip of a toe
sagi ashi dachi	one leg stance		uchi	striking, also inside
sai	three-bladed weapon		uchikomi geiko	a form of training for offensive technique practiced with partner
saiten	point score			
samurai	Japanese warrior		uchimata jigotai dachi	defensive closed leg stance
sanchin	three phases, name of a kata			
sanchin dachi	defensive closed foot stance		ude	forearm
san kaku tobi	triangle jumping step, attack		ude gaeshi	arm twist
satori	highest mental state of Zen Buddhism; a state of grace achieved via sudden illumination		ude garami	arm wrap
			uke	blocking, defender
			ukemi	break-fall
seiri undo	supplementary exercises		uraken	back fist
senjutsu	strategy		ushiro	rear or back
shiai	competition, fighting contest		ushiro hiki otoshi	backward drop
shiaijo	place of competition, fighting area			
shihan	name or title of high ranking instructor (above 6th dan)		ushiro kakato	back side of the heel
			ushiro mawashi geri	back roundhouse kick
shinan	name or title of highest instructor			
shitsuto	knee cap		ushiro oi geri	front leg back kick
shizen hontai dachi	natural stance, fundamental stance		uwagi	jacket, upper part of the uniform
shochu geiko	summer training camp		waki gatame	armpit armlock
shomen	the place of honor, the front		washi jime	eagle choke
Shorin ji	name of a temple		waza	technique
Shorin ryu	name of an Okinawan form of karate		waza ari	half point
Shorinji ryu	style or school of Shorin ji fighting techniques (Shaolin)		yako	inguinal region
			yakusoku	pre-arranged, a promise
shotei	heel of the palm		yang	positive principle
shubaku	a Chinese game of kicking		yin	negative principle
shuko	back of the hand (haishu)		yoko	side, sideways
shuto	knife hand (karate chop)		yoko furimi	leaning sideways
sokko	instep of the foot		yoko geri	side kick
sokumen	side of face		yoko ken	horizontal fist
sokutei	sole of the foot		yoko tobi geri	side jump kick
Sonshi	name of a great warlord		yudansha	black-belt holder
sotobiraki jigotai dachi	defensive open foot stance		zanshin	state of perfect execution, perfect completion
suisha gaeshi	water wheel			
sukui uke	scooping block		zarei	sitting bow
sumo	ancient Chinese fighting form, Japanese wrestling		zazen	sitting meditation
			Zen	a sect of Buddhism stressing self-realization through simplicity; a form of contemplative religion aimed at creating a state of grace by sudden illumination, satori
sute geiko	one of the special training methods			
tachi kata	postures			
tea kwan do	Korean martial art			
tai chi ch'uan	a Chinese fighting form		zen kaiten	full turn
tai otoshi	body drop		zenkutsu	foreward
tani otoshi	valley drop		zenpo dai sharin	foreward cartwheel
tai sabaki	body motion		zenpo kaiten	foreward role
tameshi wari	breaking test		zenshin	preparatory state of concentration
tanden	lower abdomen		zokko	continue
tanshiki	single form or single technique			
tatami	straw mat			

INDEX